Edwardus Ward.
Ætat Sua 54 1714

(From a painting and mezzotirt by T. Johnson)

THE LONDON SPY

THE VANITIES AND VICES OF THE TOWN EXPOSED TO VIEW

BY

NED WARD

EDITED WITH NOTES

BY

ARTHUR L. HAYWARD

WITH EIGHT FULL-PAGE ILLUSTRATIONS

CASSELL AND COMPANY, LTD
London, Toronto, Melbourne and Sydney

First Published 1927

Printed in Great Britain

CONTENTS

v

CONTENTS

LIST OF ILLUSTRATIONS

FOREWORD

NED WARD, whose *London Spy* is now, for the first time, published in a form suitable for general reading, was the lively host of the King's Head Tavern, next door to Gray's Inn, and the author of over seventy pieces of humour and satire. Most of these have long since sunk into well-merited oblivion, and he is now chiefly known for *The London Spy*, which has furnished material, mostly unacknowledged, for every writer on the social life of the early eighteenth century.

In his time, however, Ward was best known for the violent political views he loved to express. Like most of his trade he was a staunch High Churchman and an uncompromising Tory, and he launched such a bitter attack on the Whigs in his *Hudibras Redivivus* (1705) that he was stood in the pillory at Charing Cross and at the Royal Exchange, where he was pelted with rotten eggs and abused by the crowd with the utmost zest and enjoyment.

Apart from his political sallies, Ward lived quietly enough at his inn in Fulwood's Rents, holding a little court in his bar where ' with his wit, humour and good liquor, he afforded his guests a pleasurable entertainment, especially the High Church party.' He had come into contact with many men of letters in his time, and as the years passed he loved to regale an admiring audience with stories of the good things he said to them and they to him. He died in 1731.

The London Spy appeared in monthly parts, beginning in November, 1698, and was published in volume form in 1703. There is something amusingly ingenuous about Ward's assumption of the part of a scholarly recluse, for what little learning he had was a mere veneer and no man loved less to be alone than he. From first to last he was a man of the streets, who wandered the streets and found in the streets an epitome of life. His first visit in the *Spy* is to a tavern, and until his farewell in Chancery Lane he takes his reader through one crowded scene after another until practically the whole of late Stuart London has been surveyed.

There is a tavern atmosphere throughout the book ; it is mainly the seamy side of London life that is exposed to view. Most men are knaves and most women harlots; and he has little good to say of anyone unless it be of the mighty in the land, of whom he writes with somewhat cringing loyalty.

The London Spy has not been in general circulation because of the grossness of the language in which it was written. But although this adds a certain meretricious point to the style, it has no intrinsic value and the book loses nothing by expurgation. At the same time it should be remembered that the Stuart women read little; like most of his contemporaries, Ward wrote exclusively for men, and for men who did not suffer from squeamishness. In modern values, he merely expressed himself with the directness of the four-ale bar rather than with the evasion and circumlocution of the teashop.

A. L. H.

THE LONDON SPY

CHAPTER ONE

Introduction—The Spy entertained at a Tavern—Description of a
Coffee-house—The East India Company—Songs at a Tavern

AFTER a tedious confinement to a country hut, where I
dwelt like Diogenes in his tub, or an owl in a hollow
tree, taking as much delight in my books as an
alchemist does in his bellows, I grew tired with seven years'
search after knowledge, and began to reckon with myself for
my time and examine what a Solomon my diligent enquiry
into the uncertain guesses of our forefathers had made me.
But I soon fell to the opinion of Socrates, and found myself
as much the wiser as if, like the looby Hercules, I had spent
my hours at a distaff. It was no little vexation to a man of
my genius to find my brains loaded to no purpose with as
many *tringum trangums* as are lodged in the whimsical noddle
of an old astrologer, and yet could make twice ten no more
than a junior soph. or a chalk accountant.

These reflections put me into as great a passion with myself
as a beau when he befouls his clothes or makes a false bow
in saluting his mistress. So I resolved to be no longer like a
tinker's ass, carrying a load of the frenzical notions and musty
conceits of a parcel of dreaming prophets, fabulous poets and
doting philosophers, but shifted them off one by one, with a
fig for St. Austin and his doctrines, a puff for Virgil and his
elegancy, and a rap for Descartes and his philosophy. By this
means I eased my brains of those troublesome crotchets which

had raised me to the excellence of being half fool and half madman by ſtudying the weighty difference betwixt upside-down and topsy-turvy.

Having broken loose from the scholar's gaol, my ſtudy, and utterly abandoned the conversation of all my old calf-skin companions, I found an itching inclination in myself to visit London. But to shun the censure of my sober country friends I projeċted, for their satisfaċtion and my own diversion, the following journal intended to expose the vanities and vices of the town as they should, by any accident, occur to my knowledge, so that the innocent might see by refleċtion what I should gain by observation and intelligence, and not by praċtice or experience.

With this design I made my journey, and the second day entered our metropolis. I had not passed far through Aldgate,[1] like a ball through a port of a billiard-table, but by good fortune I met an old schoolfellow who, I found, had laid down the gown and taken up the sword, being tricked up in as much gaiety as a dancing-maſter upon a ball day, or a young sheriff at a country assizes.

After we had dispatched our compliments to each other, and I had awkwardly returned in country scrapes his *à la mode* bows and cringes, he needs muſt prevail with me to join him at a tavern hard by and dine with some gentlemen of his acquaintance. Being an utter ſtranger to the town, I very readily embraced the opportunity. He entered the tavern firſt, like a young squire attended with his father's chaplain, for a black coat and band are as great signs of a parson or pedagogue as a blue frock is of a butcher or a tallow-chandler. Besides, by often handling, my hat had been tugged into such a canonical flap that I looked like a young deacon who had laid by his crape with a view to rebaptizing his soul in claret, without the danger of being seen ſtaggering in his faith.

[1] This City Gate was demolished in 1760, when the street was widened.

As we came near the bar a thing started up, all ribbons, lace and feathers, and made such a noise with her bell and her tongue that had half a dozen paper-mills been at work within three yards of her, they'd have signified no more to her clamorous voice than so many lutes to a drum, or ladies' sighs to a peal of ordnance. This alarmed two or three nimble-heeled fellows aloft, who shot themselves downstairs with as much celerity as a mountebank's Mercury upon a rope from the top of a church steeple, every one charged with a mouthful of 'Coming ! Coming !'

This clatter at our appearance so surprised me that I looked as silly as a bumpkin translated from the plough-tail to the play-house when it rains fire in the *Tempest*, or when Don John's at dinner with the subterranean assembly of terrible hobgoblins. He that got the start and first approached us, desired us to walk up, telling my companion that his friends were above. Then, with a hop, stride and jump, he ascended the stairhead before us, and from thence conducted us to a spacious room where about a dozen of my school-fellow's acquaintance were ready to receive us. Upon our entrance they all started up, and screwed themselves into so many antic postures that had I not seen them first erect, I should have queried with myself whether I was fallen into the company of men or monkeys.

This fit of wriggling was almost over before I rightly understood the meaning on't, and found at last that they were only showing one another how many sorts of apes' gestures and fops' cringes had been invented since the French dancing-masters undertook to teach our English gentry to make scaramouches of themselves, and how to entertain their poor friends and pacify their needy creditors with compliments and *congées*.

When everyone, with abundance of pains, had shown his breeding by contending about a quarter of an hour who should sit down first, we proceeded to a whet of old Hock, to sharpen our appetites to our approaching dinner. I confess, as to my own part, my stomach was keen already as a miserly livery-man's, who has fasted three days to prepare himself for a Lord Mayor's feast.

The honest cook gave no leisure to tire our appetites by a tedious waiting, for in a little time the cloth was laid, and our first course, which consisted of two calves' heads and a couple of geese, was ushered up by the *dominus factotum* in great ceremony, to the table. I could not but laugh to think with what judgement the caterer had provided so lucky an entertainment for so suitable a company.

After the victuals were well cooled in compliments as to who should begin first, we all fell to; and, i'faith, I found by their eating they were no ways affronted at their fare, for in less time than an old woman could crack a nut we had not left enough to dine the bar-boy. The conclusion of our dinner was a stately Cheshire cheese, of a groaning size, of which we devoured more in three minutes than a million of maggots could have done in three weeks.

After cheese comes nothing; all we desired was a clear stage and no favour. Accordingly, everything was whipped away in a trice, by so cleanly a conveyance that no juggler could have conjured away his balls with more dexterity. All our empty plates and dishes were, in an instant, changed into full quarts of purple nectar and unsullied glasses. Then a bumper to the Queen led the van of our good wishes, another to the Church Established, a third was left to the whim of the toaster, till at last their slippery engines of verbosity coined nonsense with such a facile fluency that a parcel of alley-gossips at a christening, after the sack had gone round twice, could not with their tattling be a greater plague to a fumbling godfather than these men's lame jests and impertinent conun-drums were to a man of my temper.

Oaths were plentiful as weeds in an almshouse garden, and in triumph they flew about from one to t'other like squibs

and crackers in Cheapside, when the Cuckolds-all-in-a-row[1]
march in splendour through the City. But thanks to good
fortune, in a little time my friend redeemed me out of this
purgatory, for, perceiving my uneasiness, he made an apology
for our going, and so we took our leave. I offered to pay
my proportion, but the whole body of the society ſtood up
nemine contradicente and bid me heartily welcome to so small
a collation, with a thousand thanks to me for my good company, though I had sat all the time as silent as a Quaker
unmoved by the Spirit at a humdrum meeting.

As soon as we got clear of our flatterers I began to ask
my friend what sort of generous gentlemen those were who
had so kindly treated us. He smiled at my enquiry, and told
me I could scarce guess by what measures they buoyed up
such a seeming grandeur.

'Did you take notice,' said he, ' of the gentleman in blue
coat, red ſtockings, silver-hilted sword, and edged hat, who
sat at the upper end of the table? He was a sword-hilt maker
by trade, but proved so very ingenious at his tools that he
hath acquired the art of cutting medals and ſtamps, and is
mighty great with moſt of the bankers and topping gold-
smiths about Town. He keeps his brace of geldings, and a
great many brace of worse cattle, living at the rate of a thousand pounds a year, and passes, to those that know him not,
for a gentleman of good account in the North of England;
and his bills will pass as current in Lombard Street as the
beſt merchant's in the City.

'There was a handsome young fellow who sat next him,
with a full periwig on, and a whole piece of muslin about his
neck, who ſtank as ſtrong of orange-flower water as a Spaniard
does of garlic. The other day he was but a wine-cooper's
'prentice, but a brisk young dame in the City, who was forced
by her father to marry an old merchant for the sake of his

---

[1] A contemptuous name for the Train-bands, which were recruited from
citizens, a class conventionally supposed to be much deceived by their wives.

riches, maintains him in the condition you see, for keeping
her company when she is lonely. He is grown so prodigal
that he won't wash his hands in anything but juice of oranges
and Hungary-water¹; dines every day at the tavern; goes to
the play-house every night; ſtirs nowhere without a coach;
has his fencing-maſter, dancing-maſter, singing-maſter,
French-maſter; and is as complete a City beau (notwithſtand-
ing he was bred to the adze and driver) as you shall see in
Lombard Street church on a Sunday, or in Drapers' Gardens²
an hour before dinner-time.

'If you observed, there was a demure spark in a diminutive cravat and fox-coloured wig, with a hat as broad as
an umbrella, whose level brims revealed that it was carefully
preserved in that order by a hat-case and smoothing-iron.
You might see by his garb that he seems greatly to affeẟ
antiquity, though the coat he has on has not been made above
this two months; yet he would have it in the ancient mode,
with little buttons, round cuffs, narrow skirts, and pockets
within two inches of the bottom, as the moſt proper fashion
for his business. And for all 'tis so scanty, he makes it serve
him for a cloak with which to cover abundance of shame and
a great deal of knavery. He's an incomparable herald, and
will give you the exaẟ genealogy of moſt good families in
England to which he has the art of making himself akin when
he sees it convenient. To be short with you, he is one of those
genteel beggars we call *cadators*; he goes a circuit round
England once a year, and under pretence of being a decayed
gentleman gets both money and entertainment at every good
house he comes to. If he has opportunity to convey away a

¹ This was a distilled water prepared from the tips of flowers of rosemary
and other aromatic herbs.
² Drapers' Gardens were in Throgmorton Street. They had once been the
gardens of Thomas Cromwell's house, but on his attainder were bought by the
Drapers' Company. The gardens extended as far as London Wall and were a
fashionable resort, having an extensive view over the intervening country to the
Highgate Hills.

silver beaker, or a spoon or two, he holds no long dispute with his conscience about the honesty of the matter. Then he comes up to Town and enjoys the benefit of his rural labours.

'Another you must take particular notice of; he plucked out a pair of pocket pistols, and laid them in the window. He had a great scar across his forehead, a twisted wig, and laced hat on, and the company called him Captain. He's a man of considerable reputation amongst birds of the same feather, who I have heard say this much in his praise, that he is as resolute a fellow as ever cocked pistol upon the road. And indeed, I do believe he fears no man in the world but the hangman, and dreads no death but choking.

' He's generous as a prince; treats anybody that will keep him company; loves his friend as dearly as the ivy loves the oak, and will never leave him till he has hugged him to his ruin. He has drawn in twenty of his associates to be hanged, but always had wit and money enough to save his own neck from the halter. He has good friends at Newgate, who give him now and then a squeeze when he is full of juice, but promise him, as long as he's industrious in his profession and will but now and then show them a few sparks of his generosity, they will always stand between him and danger. This he takes as a verbal policy of insurance from the gallows till he grows poor through idleness, and then (he has cunning enough to know) he may be hanged through poverty.

' He's acquainted with the ostlers about Bishopsgate Street and Smithfield, and gains from them intelligence of what booties go out that are worth attempting. He pretends to be a disbanded officer, and reflects very feelingly upon the hard usage " we poor gentlemen meet with, who have hazarded our lives and fortunes for the honour of our prince, the defence of the country, and safety of religion; after all to be broke for the dangers and difficulties we have run through. At this rate, Zounds, who the devil would be a soldier ? " At such sort of cant he is excellent.

B

'He that sat near him, in the plate-buttoned suit and white beaver hat, is a kind of amphibious rascal, a compound of two sorts of villainy! He always keeps at his beck three or four handsome young wenches, well equipped and in good lodgings, who are all modesty without and nothing but lewdness within; who can seem as innocent as doves and be as wicked as devils; whose education, from their cradles, under some skilful matron of iniquity, has made them pleasant companions, taking love-mates, expert jilts, incorrigible sinners, and good managers of a bad design. Under a deceitful countenance they are so case-hardened in impudence that they never were sorry for anything but that they were too young to walk the streets when they were old enough to endeavour it.

'These are his tools, who, by their beauty, youth and airiness, insinuate themselves into the affections of young merchants, shopkeepers' apprentices and others whose juvenile fury carries them too often into the ruinous embraces of these treacherous strumpets. When, with their wanton gestures, they seem most obliging to their admirers, their mercenary thoughts are projecting something to their injury, like a Water Lane[1] Protestant who, when seeming most devout at church, yet is picking the pocket of some over-penitent Christian who is so zealous at his prayers that he neglects to watch and whilst he has God in his heart has the devil fumbling about his breeches.

'He accounts his wenches rare cattle if they calve once in a year, for there's never a child they have but is worth two or three hundred pounds to him, as well as the advantage he makes by their prying into the affairs and secrets of whom they can manage. And when their practice has rendered them unfit for his purpose, he ransacks their wardrobes, strips them

---

[1] This was the old name for Whitefriars Street, Fleet Street. It belonged to the unsavoury quarter of Alsatia, and Water Lane is here used as a synonym for rogue.

of their plumes, and discards them, so that they are forced to fly to some common bawdy-house for refuge, and walk the streets for subsistence. Thus they sin on, in public shame and misery, till the gallows or an hospital at last brings them to repentance.

' The other part of this man's life is tricking people out of their money by false dice and cards. He handles these with such dexterity and preaches the parson with such a fraudulent deception of the sight, that he will drain the pockets of a large company in six minutes as clean as the Royal Oak Lottery[1] shall in six hours. He is often to be seen with a country cloth-coat on, all over dirt or dust according to the weather, as if he had come a fifty-mile journey, though he's only travelled from Salisbury Court to Smithfield, where he keeps the market as constantly as a Town wench does Bartholomew Fair, or an old one the Sacrament. In his rusty garb he looks like an honest grazier. He is constant to no sort of dress, but changes his clothes as often as a whimsical woman does her mind, and, statesman-like, always suits his apparel to his project. Being a rare tongue-pad he can out-flatter a poet, out-huff a bully, out-wrangle a lawyer, out-cant a Puritan, out-cringe a beau, out-face truth, and out-lie the Devil.

' The rest you saw were men who have not cunning enough to project a piece of roguery themselves, but, like a well-meaning brother, will lend a shoulder to the villainy. The former are your rare sycamore rogues, who flourish finely for a season, and the other are the caterpillars that hang upon 'em.'

' But pray, old acquaintance,' said I, ' what is your employment in the world, that you are so well acquainted with its scandalous society ? '

' Why, I'll tell you,' said he. ' I studied a little physic at the

---

[1] This was the only lottery declared legal by the Act of 1698. It was ostensibly for the benefit of the Royal Fishing Company but really a means of enriching the patentees who managed it. Thousands bought shares in it and lost their all to a parcel of unscrupulous rogues.

University, and I have gained some small knowledge of
surgery since I came to Town, and the narrowness of my
fortune obliges me to make use of this. I have had most of
these dark engineers you saw as my patients; for they are
seldom free from some ailment or thumps, cuts and bruises,
and part to their surgeon with pounds as freely as fools did
with their pence to the Wheel of Fortune Lottery.[1] Come,'
continued my friend, ' let us step into this coffee-house. As
you are a stranger to the Town it will afford you diversion.'

Accordingly, in we went, where a parcel of muddling muck-
worms were as busy as so many rats in an old cheese-loft;
some going, some coming, some scribbling, some talking,
some drinking, others jangling, and the whole room stinking
of tobacco like a Dutch barge or a boatswain's cabin. The
walls were hung with gilt frames, containing an abundance of
rarities, viz., Nectar and Ambrosia, May Dew, Golden Elixirs,
Popular Pills, Liquid Snuff, Beautifying Waters, Dentifrices,
Drops, Lozenges, all as infallible as the Pope. *Where* (as the
famous Saffold[2] has it) *everyone above the rest, Deservedly has
gained the name of best*; good in all cases, curing all distempers; every medicine pretends to be nothing less than
universality. Indeed, had not my friend told me 'twas a coffee-
house I should have took it for Quack's Hall, or the parlour
of some eminent mountebank.

When we had each stuck in our mouths a pipe of sotweed,
we began to look about us.

' Do you observe,' says my friend, ' yon old sophister,
with an Indian pipe between his meagre jaws, who sits staring
at the candle with as much steadfastness as a country visitor at

[1] This lottery was got up in 1699 with a capital prize of £1000. Shares
in it were a penny each, and only one share was to win the whole prize.

[2] This was an egregious quack who, in 1674, received a licence from the
Bishop of London to practise as a physician. He had a shop in Blackfriars,
whence he issued a number of advertisements written in the crudest doggerel,
puffing his various empirical wares. Falling ill in 1691 he tried to cure himself
with his own pills, but died from their effect. He was succeeded by the notorious
quack astrologer Dr. Case.

Bow Steeple, or a child at a raree-show? That's a strange, whimsy-headed humorist. Observe his posture! He has as many maggots in his noddle as there are mice in an old barn. He has a wonderful projecting head, and has lately contrived one of the prettiest pocket-engines for the speedy blanching of hazel-nuts and filbert kernels that ever was invented; he'll crack and skin two for a squirrel's one, and in a few years, by a little alteration, will improve it to the use of walnuts. I assure you, he's a member of the Royal Society; puts great faith in the Philosophers' Stone; and believes he shall one day be as rich as Crœsus, though he has almost beggared himself in the search on't.

' He tried a notable experiment the other day, in setting fire to a large haystack he had in the country, and ordered the ashes to be brought to Town, from which he proposed to prepare a medicine, called *Sal Graminis*, which should infallibly cure all distempers in horses, and be the rarest medicine for cows, sheep, or oxen, and all creatures that feed upon grass. But sending his hay up in the wrong season the ashes got wet in their journey and quite lost their virtue, so that he was forced to sell them to a West Country bargeman in order to dung land. Yet 'tis thought by the wise that he might have sold it in the hay to ten times the advantage.

' He has abundance of whims in him, very remarkable. He lives over against a church, so that when he dies he may not have far to travel upon four men's shoulders. As soon as the clock strikes nine, if he gets not his shoes off before it has done striking, in order for bed, he is immediately seized with such a violent fit of gout that he roars like a Tower lion at a woman pregnant with male child.[1] If he is not up just as the clock strikes five in the morning, he thinks himself bed-ridden. If his victuals be not brought to the table whilst the clock goes twelve, he eats nothing all that day; his stomach is always the meridian height the same time the sun is. He's

[1] See note, page 225.

a wonderful antiquary, and has a closet of curiosities that out-vies Gresham College.[1] He tells you that he has a tooth-pick of Epicurus, which he always uses after eating; it is made of the claws of an American humming-bird, and is to be used like a rake, and will pick four teeth at once. He has Diogenes' lantern, which he carried about Athens at noonday to seek for an honest man. He says he has some of Heraclitus's tears, which dropped from him in a hard winter and are frozen into crystal; they are set in a locket, and every time anybody looks upon it they cannot forbear weeping. Also a tenpenny nail drawn out of the Ark, and though it's iron, toss it into a tub of water and 'twill swim like a feather. He pretends to have one of Judas's thirty pence, and every time he looks upon't he is ready to hang himself. A mighty collection of these sort of trinkets he tells the world he's master of, and some give credit to his ridiculous romance.

'Look at that spark who has just come. Four years ago his reputation was but slender, and in so little time he has had three wives, all good fortunes, and now he is looked upon to be worth ten thousand pounds.'

''Tis to be observed,' said I, ' that money is thrown into the mouths of Fortune's minions, and some men must grow rich if the lucky accidents that Chance can give will make them so.'

My friend, in reply, observed that he believed there was some foul play practised, because, said he, it is a thing so common in this city for a man to grow rich by plurality of wives, and send them so methodically to the grave one after another, as if he had a trick of translating them into another world a little before their time. ' I must confess,' said he, ' I know an apothecary who, if a man will trust him with the care of his family, once in a twelvemonth's time will certainly take an opportunity to do him such a piece of service if he gives him but the least notice of his slender affections towards his helpmate. I have often heard him say that women are

[1] See page 49.

always the best patients, especially if they die under his hands, for then, says he, let me make never so unreasonable a bill, it's never disputed but generously satisfied, with as good a will as a married man will pay the tax for the birth of the first child,[1] or an extravagant heir the charges of his father's funeral.

'See the little blade in the cloak, talking with a parson. He's a bookseller in this City, and has got an estate by starving authors. I'll warrant you, the priest has been conjuring his brains together to raise some wonderful work to the Church's glory and his own fame; he has been providing a *Scourge for the Pope's Jacket*, or a *Cudgel for Antichrist*,[2] or else a mess of good Protestant porridge to scald the mouth of an unbeliever, or some such business.

'But as to the bookseller, I tell you he's as honest a man as ever betrayed his trust, or built his own welfare upon another's ruin. He was appointed trustee for a young gentlewoman, and had the charge of an estate of between two or three hundred pounds *per annum*. He very carefully secured this to himself by marrying her to his 'prentice and obliging him, upon that consideration, to buy his stock; whereby he has become well paid for a great deal of waste paper. So he is crept into the estate, and they are got into his books for it. There is abundance of such sort of plain-dealing practised among our worthy citizens, for you must know they do not always tell the truth in their shops, or get their estates by honesty.'

Being choked with the steam that arose from their soot-coloured ninny-broth [coffee], and the suffocating fumes of their nasty puffing-engines, my friend and I paid for our

[1] By an Act of 1694 a tax was imposed on births, burials, bachelors and widowers, to raise money for carrying on the war with France. A duke paid £30 at the birth of his eldest son and £25 for each other child; a knight paid £5 for his eldest and £1 for subsequent children; the majority of commoners paid two shillings for each child.

[2] A hit at the controversial pamphlets which, at that time, every sect and school of thought was hurling at its opponents.

Mahometan gruel and away we came. Passing along Leaden-hall Street I saw some ships painted upon the outside of a great wall, which occasioned me to enquire of my school-fellow what place it was. He told me 'twas the house belonging to the East India Company,[1] which are a corporation of men with long heads and deep purses, who had purchased with their money that which nobody ought to sell, and to get money had dealt in those commodities which it's a pity anybody should buy. They are very rich in England and very poor in the Indies; were a schedule of their effects scored on one side and their Indian debts scored on the other, it is believed more bad debts would arise upon the reverse than are due to tradesmen from all the persons of quality in Town, or perhaps than were ever found owing to either Army or Navy; which they have neither will to pay, nor power to satisfy, to the great honour of Christianity in that heathenish country.

There are two companies now, and it's hoped by many honest traders and merchants in the City that they may luckily prove the breaking of each other. Both have sent ships to the Indies, and 'tis thought they will give one another a warm salutation by the way, and maintain the truth of the old proverb that two of a trade can never agree.

'Pray take notice,' says my friend, 'of that gentleman that is stepping into his coach; I will tell you a pretty story of him. There was a poor woman, not far from this place, who sold earthenware. Lately she had the good fortune to have a rich relation die and leave her forty thousand pounds. On hearing this, he, though a man of considerable wealth, thought it a bait worth snapping at. In order to do this he became one

[1] The old East India Company, founded in 1600, had its offices in Leaden-hall Street and the painted ships mentioned in the text were probably the principal charge in their coat of arms, 3 ships under sail, proper. In 1702 this old company and its rival, mentioned later, which had been established in 1698 were united under one charter and became the Honourable East India Company of famous memory.

of her earliest suitors, but she soon gave him a repulse, and told him Man was an earthen vessel too brittle for her to deal in, and she had heard he had a great many flaws in his fortune which she would not be at the expense of mending; and since she had never received any testimonials of his affection before the happy change in her condition, she had reason to believe his desire tender to her money and not her person, therefore she would not be made a lady at so great an expense. She added that she hoped he would give himself no further trouble, assuring him that as her mind was steadfast so would his pains be fruitless. Upon this he feigned a melancholy humour, and sighing like a man at his wife's funeral, told her his passion for her was so great that unless she gave him a more satisfactory answer he would drown himself in the Tower Ditch. To this she replied, smiling, " Perhaps, sir, you propose that to yourself which is not in your power to do. You know not but Heaven has decreed for you a drier destiny! " Upon this he rose in a great passion, crying, " Z——ds, madam, do you think I'll hang myself ? " and so departed.

' Now,' says my schoolfellow, ' we'll spend the evening over a cheerful glass. Here's a tavern, hard by, where a parcel of pleasant companions of my acquaintance use; we'll see what diversion we can find in their society.' Accordingly we stepped in, and in the kitchen found half a dozen of my friend's associates, in the height of their jollity, as merry as so many Cantabrigians at Stir-bitch Fair,[1] or cobblers at a Crispin's feast.[2] After a friendly salutation, free from all foppish ceremony, down we sat, and when a glass or two had given

[1] Stir-bitch or Stourbridge Fair was held in a field near ' bawdy ' Barnwell. a mile or so from Cambridge, and lasted for 14 days from September the 18th, In his *Step to Stir-Bitch Fair* Ward tells of it as a place ' where vice, merchandize, and amusement draw the Cambridge youth, London traders, Lynn whores and abundance of ubiquitarian strollers, all contributing something to either the pleasure or profit of one another.' There was a Pie Powder Court and a Proctors' Court, and the fair was one of the wildest, for amusement, in the country.

[2] October the 25th is the feast of St. Crispin, the patron saint of shoemakers and cobblers, who formerly made great festival on that day.

fresh motion to our drowsy spirits, and we had abandoned all those careful thoughts which make man's life uneasy, wit begot wit, and wine a thirsty appetite to each succeeding glass; then open were our hearts and unconfined our fancies. My friend and I contributed our mites to the treasure of our felicity. Song and catches crowned the night, and each man in his turn elevated his voice to fill our harmony with the more variety. Amongst the rest, we had one song against music which, because of its being the first essay in this nature, I have thought it worth inserting:

A SONG AGAINST MUSIC

Music's a crotchet the sober think vain;
  The fiddle's a wooden projection;
Tunes are but flirts of a whimsical brain,
  Which the bottle brings best to perfection.
Musicians are half-witted, merry and mad;
  The same are all those that admire 'em;
They're fools if they play, unless they're well paid;
  And the others are blockheads to hire 'em.

Chorus

The organ's but humming,
Theorbo but thrumming,
The viol and the voice
Is but jingle and noise,
The bagpipe and fiddle
Go tweedle and diddle,
The hautboy and flute,
Is but toot-atoot-toot.
Your scales and your cleffs, keys, moods and dull rules,
Are fit to please none but madmen and fools.

The novelty of this whimsy gave diversion to the whole company except one, who was by nature a poet; but having Fortune to his nurse, careless of her charge, she dropped him from her lap, bruised the noddle of the tender babe and made his fancy rickety, numbed his faculties, and so eclipsed his genius that he dwindled into a musician.

Angry at hearing his profession disparaged, he resolved immediate revenge upon the author, called for pen and ink, and went to work with as much eagerness and inveteracy as a parson when he writes an order to his attorney to sue a parishioner for neglected tithes. After some intervals of deliberation, the following crotchet started from his brain, like Æsop's mouse from the mountain, to the great laughter of the whole company:

A SONG BY A MUSICIAN AGAINST POETRY

Poetry's fabulous, loose and prophane,
    For truth you must never depend on't;
'Tis the juvenile froth of a frenzical brain,
    Hung with jingling tags at the end on't.
Poets are poor, full of whimsy and flight,
    For amorous fops to delight in,
They're fools if they write, lest they get money by't,
    And they're blockheads that pay 'em for writing.

Chorus

Their soft panegyric,
Is praise beyond merit;
Their lampoon and satire
Is spite and ill-nature;
Their plays and romances
Are fables and fancies;
Their drolls and their quips
Are mere froth on fools' lips
Their figures and similes only are fit
To please the dull fool that gives money for wit.

This raised among the society such an evil spirit of poetry, that it began to have as much power over us as the Devil has over a gang of Lapland witches. We now were all so highly inspired we could scarce speak without rhyme and measure, and among others, the following verses were lugged out of a pocket-library, written upon the following occasion,

as the author insinuated to the company. Being blest with
the conversation of some young ladies, one whose wit and
beauty was aspiring above the rest knowing he had some little
fancy in poetry, told him she took it very unkindly of him
that he never thought her worthy of his muse's notice. To
this he replied that he was at all times ready to oblige so fair
a lady, adding, if she would be pleased to lend him a pen and
ink, he would take a copy of her perfections while she was
there ready to sit for her picture. These she instantly fetched
and very nimbly placed upon the table, with a pleasing expectancy of being flattered. Upon this he obliged her with these
following lines:

> Madam, how great and good your virtues are,
> I can't well tell, or truly do I care;
> Nor can that wit which you from plays have stole,
> Admired be by any but a fool,
> Who may, perhaps, through his weak judgement own
> That you have sense, 'cause he himself has none.
> Believe, I no such wrong opinion hold,
> I can discern false metal from true gold.
> Your ill-timed jests, so sharp in your conceit,
> Are spoiled for want of judgement to repeat;
> Like an unskilful play'r, who lames each line,
> Which by the poet read, or spoke, is fine.
> If you have wit which you can boast your own,
> Let it in some return to this be shown,
> Or I, proud lady fair, shall justly think you've none.

This he presented to the lady, who, upon the first glance,
blushed in her disappointment, then ran into her closet, fired
with indignation and revenge. She soon showed the pregnancy
of her wit by the speediness of her answer, which I have also
given you:

> Two lively figures in one piece you've shown,
> A true-bred poet, and an ill-bred clown;
> Virtues not understood by you, I boast,
> Such that in our weak sex are valued most;

As truth, good nature, manner, though not wit,
Graces that never crowned a poet yet.
To rail at a weak woman is a strain
Does little merit in its wit contain;
It may be like a scribbler, but unlike a man.
A self opinion from your lines I'll raise,
And fancy you discovered in my face
Virtues beyond your reach, and so above your praise;
As envious beggars spitefully disdain,
And rail at blessings which they can't obtain.
Though I'm abused, yet I'll good-humoured be,
And beg for once you'd take advice of me,
Much rather let your wit in silence rest,
Than lose a friend, or mistress, for a jest;
Mix manners and good nature with your parts,
And you'll deserve more thanks, and win more hearts.

This being the product of a female genius was much admired by our whole assembly of poetasters, who are always so favourable to the fair sex as to seem as much opiniated of what they write as a fond father is of the witty sayings of his own progeny; it being as natural for a young poet to dote upon a woman as 'tis for a hound to love horse-flesh. And I must confess, whenever we rail at 'em, it is more for their virtues than vices; for the latter we are as busy to seduce them to as the rest of our neighbours, and are never very angry with them but for denying us what they impart to others, or when by their prudence they secure that treasure to themselves at which we want to be nibbling. A pretty woman is but a piece of Heaven's poetry, wherein as many changes are to be seen as in Ovid's Metamorphoses, and whenever she is attempted to be read out by earthly sons of Apollo, she is found a crabbed piece, and the measure of her verse too long for human scanning.

Another in the company being willing to contribute toward our mirth and pastime, communicated to the board this poem in manuscript, written by a fellow in Bedlam, who ran mad through ambition and fancied himself a king; but not being contented with the government of his sublunary dominions, he was ambitious (as you will find by his lunatic raptures) of conquering larger territories above the moon, or somewhere whither his frenzy led him. Therefore as the poetical pill-maker[1] says of his learned works, *Read, try, judge, and speak as you find.*

THE MADMAN'S FLIGHT

Could I the sceptre of the heavens sway,
And make Dame Nature my commands obey,
The ocean I'd unbound and quench the fiery day.
Fearing no thunder could from Jove be hurled,
I'd then in darkness ravage through the world;
Till met by devils in amazing throngs,
Armed with huge scorpions and infernal thongs;
Shrieking like souls oppressed, I'd bid 'em come;
And stare so fierce I'd brazen out my doom.
Knowing my soul is too divine an air
For fiends or devils to torment or tear.
I'd forwards press and to repulse their aim
Would drive those hellish tribes from whence they came;
Then mount to Heaven and kindle up the sun,
To see what mischiefs I on earth had done;
Behold, like cruel tyrant, with delight
The crimson ills that ſtained the sable night.
My power, like theirs, I'd build on others' fate,
And glory in black deeds that made me great.
When I through all these purple crimes had run,
That could be, by unbounded greatness, done,
Then the bright chariot of the sun I'd seize,
And drive it where my God-like soul should please.
The moon would I compel to be my guide;
Thus splendidly through Heaven would I ride,
There huff, and ſtrut and kick the gods aside.
In my career, my fury to expose,
I'd caſt down ſtars upon the heads of those,
That either Fate or choice had made my foes,

[1] This was Dr. Saffold, already mentioned.

Then the proud demons of the air to scare,
The clouds in sundry pieces would I tear,
And puff 'em up like bubbles in the air.
I'd jostle clouds, heaven's harmony confound,
And fix those orbs that now dance nimbly round.
If any bold Olympian sent'nel dare
Question my office, or my business there
Or if against me offer to rebel,
I'd grasp his hair and strike him down to Hell.
Thus by degrees would I the gods unthrone,
Till Heaven should at last become my own,
Then to demolish earth's infernal crew,
I'd damn this old world and create a new.

This frantic piece of bombast pleased wonderfully. No profane jest to an atheist, or bawdy story to an old bachelor, could have been more acceptable. One commended the loftiness of his fancy, another the aptness of the language; a third, the smoothness of the verse; so that the madman had like to have run away with the bays from us all had not in the company been an author in print, who, if he would have worn as much bays as the common vogue of the people had given him a title to, his head would have appeared as fine as a country casement in the midst of the Christmas holidays.

By this time the spirits of the reviving juice had rather overpowered than enlivened the noblest of our faculties, and my friend and I thought it high time to take our leave; which, after the payment of our clubs we did accordingly, agreeing to give ourselves the pleasure of two or three hours' ramble in the streets.

Having spent the time at the tavern till about ten o'clock, with mirth and satisfaction, we were now desirous of prying into the dark intrigues of the Town, to experience what pastime the night accidents, the whims and frolics of staggering bravadoes, and strolling strumpets might afford us. An account of which we will give you in our next.

CHAPTER TWO

Head-dressers' shops—The Widow's Coffee-house and the Ladies
therein—A Foundling—The Constable Appears—Billingsgate

ACCORDING to the wisdom of our forefathers, we had
carefully taken the old gentleman by the forelock;
for though we thought it ten o'clock when we left
the blessings of dear Hymen's palace, yet it proved but the
misers' bedtime, the modest hour of nine being just pro-
claimed by Time's oracle from every steeple. The joyful
alarm of Bow Bell called the weary apprentices from their
work to unhitch their folded shutters and button up their
shops till the next morning.

The streets were all adorned with dazzling lights[1] whose
bright reflections so glittered in my eyes that I could see
nothing but themselves and thus walked amazed, like a
wandering soul in its pilgrimage to Heaven when it passes
through the spangled regions.

My ears were so serenaded on every side with the music
of sundry passing-bells, the rattling of coaches, and the
melancholy ditties of *Hot Baked Wardens and Pippins !*[2] that
had I as many eyes as Argus and as many ears as Fame, they

[1] Speaking of the street-lamps of London, in his *Travels in England* (1697),
Misson says: ' Instead of lanterns they set up in the streets of London lamps
which, by means of a very thick convex glass, throw out great rays of light
which illuminate the path for people that go on foot, tolerably well. They begin
to light up these lamps at Michaelmas, and continue them till Lady Day; they
burn from six in the evening till midnight, and from every third day after the
full moon to the sixth day after the new moon.' These lamps were set at every
tenth house. This street illumination was introduced in 1685 by Edward
Heming who obtained letters patent conveying to him the exclusive rights of
lighting up London.

[2] Warden pears were in great demand in the London streets.

Foreign Brokers and Merchants in the Courtyard of the Royal Exchange.

(*From a print in the Crace Collection*)

would have been all confounded, for nothing could I see but light, and nothing hear but noise.

As we stumbled along my friend bid me notice a shop wherein sat three or four very provoking damsels, with as much velvet on their backs as would have made a burying-pall for a country parish, or a holiday coat for a physician, being glorified at bottom with gold fringes, so that I thought at first they might be parsons' daughters who had borrowed their fathers' pulpit clothes to use as scarves to go a visiting in. Each has as many patches as are spots in a leopard's skin or freckles in the face of a Scotsman.

I asked my friend what he took them for; he answered, they were a kind of first-rate love-bird by their rigging, of about a guinea purchase. I further queried what reason had he to believe them to be this; he replied, because they were sitting in a head-dresser's shop which, said he, is as seldom to be found without a harlot as a bookseller's shop in St. Paul's Churchyard without a parson.

'Come,' says my friend, 'we'll call here hard-by, at the widow's coffee-house and drink a dish or two. I have some female patients that use the house who are a little in my debt, and if the luck has lately thrown a cully in their way, they may chance to be able to make me satisfaction.'

Accordingly we blundered through the dark entry of an ancient fabric, groping our way like subterranean labourers in the caverns of a coal pit, till we found the stairs, which were raised as perpendicular as a tiler's ladder, so that had I not had the use of a rope which was nailed along the wall, as a clue to guide me, I could have climbed a country maypole, or crawled up the buttock-shrouds of one of Her Majesty's first-rate men-of-war with less danger and difficulty.

At last an old weather-beaten Cerberus came to the stairs' head with a candle. She saluted us with ' Lord, gentlemen, why did you not call to be lighted up ? I protest, I thought there had been a candle on the stairs; but my careless baggage

c

is so lazy, she minds nothing that she should do. She's but lately come out of the country, and stands staring about like a bumpkin in Paul's Church, or a libertine in a conventicle.' With this sort of talk she ushered us into the coffee-room, where, at the corner of a long table next her elbow chair, lay a large Bible open, with her spectacles upon one of St. Paul's epistles; next to it was a quartern pot, two or three stone bottles, a roll of plaster, and a pipe of tobacco; there was a handful of fire in a rusty grate, with a pint coffee-pot before it, and a green earthen pot in the chimney-corner. Over the mantel-tree were two bastard china dishes, a patch-box, and a syringe. On a little shelf among phials and gally-pots, were half a dozen long bottles of *Rosa Solis*, with an advertisement of a rare whitewash for the face nailed on one side, and a brief account of the excellencies of Doctor John C——se's[1] *pills for the speedy cure of violent pains without loss of time or hindrance of Business* on the other; a grenadier's bayonet, musket and cartouche-box were behind the door; a head-dresser's block, and a quart pot (as terrible as Death's head and an hour-glass) stood frightfully in the window; also an old-fashioned clock in a crazy case, but as silent as a corpse in a coffin, stood bolt upright like a stiff-necked constable, more for ornament than use. Next this hung the reverend print of the Seven Golden Candlesticks, and against that a commode[2], adorned with a scarlet topknot; under it an abstract of the Acts of Parliament against drinking, swearing, and all

[1] Dr. John Case (fl. 1686–1700) was a notorious quack and astrologer, who succeeded Saffold in his business. Over his door was announced:

> Within this place
> Lives Doctor Case.

According to Addison (*Tatler*, No. 240) this jingle brought the doctor more money than Dryden ever made by all his works put together. Round Dr. Case's pill-boxes was inscribed:

> Here's fourteen pills for thirteen pence
> Enough in any man's own conscience.

[2] This was a form of head-dress very fashionable with ladies of the 17th century.

manner of profaneness. The floor was broken like that of an old stable, the windows were mended with brown paper, and the bare walls were full of dust and cobwebs.

After I had walked about and taken a view of this antiquated haunt, I set myself down; but of a sudden I felt such a trembling in the fabric that the windows jarred, the fire-irons jingled, in short all things in the room seemed to be in motion and kept time with a tinkling noise like the bells in a Morris dance; so that had I not been furnished with some reasons to suspect the contrary, I should have been under the frightful apprehensions of an earthquake. But in a little time the violent pulsation that had given an ague to the whole house was over, and all things were again reconciled to their former rest. Immediately after came downstairs from a loftier apartment reserved for private use, a couple of airy youths who by their cropped hair, stone buckles in their shoes, broad gold hatbands, and no swords, I took to be merchants' sons, or the apprentices of topping tradesmen. They stayed not above a minute in the coffee-room, but, magpie-like, asked what o'clock, then made their bows after the newest fashion and so departed.

My friend by this time (knowing the entertainment of the house) had called for a bottle of cock-ale,[1] of which I tasted a glass but could not conceive it to be anything but a mixture of small beer and treacle.

' If this be cock-ale,' said I, ' even let coxcombs drink it. Prithee, give me a glass of brandy, or something that will dart like lightning into my spirits.'

With that the reverend doctress of debauchery (after she had approved my choice with a cheerful smile) signified her sympathizing appetite in these words, ' Sir, you are of my mind: I think there's nothing like a dram of true Nantz[2] or some such comfortable cordial. Of the former, indeed, I have

---

[1] This was ale in which a cock and other ingredients had been boiled.

[2] A kind of brandy imported from Nantes. The war with France made it difficult to obtain.

none, by reason of its scarcity, but I have an excellent distillation of my own preparing, which some call Aqua Veneris. It will restore an old man of threescore to the juvenility of thirty, or make a girl of fourteen, with drinking but one glass, as fond as an old maid of twenty-four. 'Twill make a parson dance, a Puritan lust after the flesh, and a married man as fond of his wife as if they were newly wed. I sell it to most citizens' wives in Town, who are seldom without it in their closets, to oblige their husbands or gallants; for though I say it that should not, it's the best cordial to strengthen a weak appetite in the world. Here, Priscilla, bring the gentleman a quartern!'

As a cup of corroboration was moving round, who should bolt downstairs from the fools' paradise above but a couple of mortal angels as nimble as squirrels, with looks as sharp and eyes as piercing as a tiger's. They saluted my friend with 'Your servant, Doctor!' He returned their compliment and desired their company, which they as readily granted.

By help of paint, powder and patches, they were of a waxwork complexion, and thus dressed: their under-petticoats were white dimity, embroidered like a turkey-work chair, or a fool's doublet, with red, green, blue and yellow; their pin-up coats of Scotch plaid, adorned with bugle lace; and their gowns of printed calico. But their heads were dressed up to the best advantage, like a vintner's bar-keeper or a church-warden's daughter upon an Easter Sunday. These girls, I suppose, devil-like, would play at small game rather than stand out, and sooner condescend to the acceptance of a shilling than want employment.

By the time we had sipped our nipperkin of Aqua Mirabilis, our airy ladies grew so very mercurial that they could no longer contain their feigned modesty, but launched out into their accustomed liveliness, and showed us as many whimsical vagaries and diverting pranks as a young monkey with a mouse at his tail.

This rather encouraged my friend to a further freedom, for he took the boldness upon him of asking one if trade had been so good of late that she could pay the arrears due upon her laſt illness. To this she replied, 'Confound you! I owe you nothing. Did I not agree with you, when firſt we dealt together, to pay you one cure under another? Therefore the laſt is not due till I should be ill again. Pray, Mr. Eplaſtrum, don't you come that upon me, neither; for I am sure I have paid you hitherto as generously as any patient of my quality that ever you gave a pill or a bolus to; and have done you and your profession as much service as any girl of my funćtion that trades between Aldgate and Temple Bar. You know, I once let you have money to redeem your plaſter-box, when I owed you not a groat, and I have had nothing in return for my kindness, as I know on.'

This impudence so silenced my friend that he looked as tame as a shopman with his wife, and was as dumb as a ſtatue, and he was glad to appease her fury by calling for another quartern. Before we had drunk it, who should grovel upſtairs but a seemingly sober citizen in cloak and band, about the age of sixty. Upon the entrance of the grave doer of wickedness, our ladies withdrew themselves from our company, and retired like modeſt virgins to their secret work-room of iniquity, and left the old sinner to warm his grey hairs with a dram of invigorating cordial, whilſt we, paying our reckoning, were lighted downſtairs and left the old satyr (to the shame of his age) a prey to the two ſtrumpets.

Each jack-a-lanthorn [watchman] was now croaking about the ſtreets the hour of eleven. The brawny topers of the City now began to forsake the tavern, and ſtagger to their own houses. Auguſta [London] appeared in her mourning-weeds, and the glittering lamps which a few hours before sparkled like diamonds fixed as ornaments to her sable dress, were now dwindling to a glimmering snuff, and burnt as dim as torches at a prince's funeral. Harlots in the ſtreets

were grown a scarce commodity, for the danger of the
Compter had drove them home to their own poor sinful
habitations where nothing dwells but shame, poverty and
misery, the devil and themselves.

We were at a stand which way to move. At last my
companion proposed Billingsgate, where, he told me, we need
not question to find abundance of diversion amongst the
various humours of the maritime nobility. Besides, when our
faculties should grow tired with our pastime, and Nature
should require rest, we could there have the convenience of
a bed to repose our weary limbs.

We had not proceeded far towards our intended harbour,
when, at the door of an eminent shop-keeper in Gracechurch
Street, we heard, as we thought, the amorous squallings of
some cats, summoning, with their untunable voices, the neighbouring mouse-hunters to their merry meeting. By the help
of a watchman's lanthorn, who met us in the passage, we
discovered a hand-basket, from whence we conceived proceeded this ingrateful discord.

' Hey day,' says the watchman, ' what in the name of stars
have we got here?' He opens the wicker hammock, and
finds a little lump of mortality crying out to the whole parish
to lend him their assistance, with this inscription, written in
a fair hand, pinned upon his breast:

> I was got by an honest poor man
>   Who sails in Her Majesty's service,
> My mother is called Mistress Nan,
>   The name of my father is Jervice.
>
> Have mercy upon me, I pray,
>   And carry me out of the weather,
> For all that my mother can say,
>   The Parish must be my father.

The unusualness of a posy upon so unwelcome a present
made us as merry as a young comedian over a lame jest,

or a constable at a bellman's verse.[1] The watchman coughed up a phthisical hem, as a signal to his associates of some mischance, which was conveyed from one to t'other till it alarmed the leader of the Hour-grunters, who soon came up, attended with his guard and saddled his nose with a pair of glazed horns, to read the superscription, and see to whom the squalling packet was directed.

But when he found the infant lay drivelling upon a whole slabbering-bib of verses, ' Alack, alack,' says Father Midnight, ' I'll warrant 'tis some poor poet's brat. Prithee, take it up, and let's carry it to the watch-house fire. Who knows but, by the grace of Providence, the babe may come to be a second Ben Jonson? Prithee, Jeffery, put the lappit of thy coat over it, I'll warrant 'tis so cold it can scarce feel whether it be a boy or a girl.' Away trooped his Midnight Majesty with his feeble band of crippled parish pensioners, to their nocturnal rendezvous, all tickled with the jest, and as merry over their hopeful foundling as the Egyptian Queen over her young prophet in the rushes.

We blundered on in pursuit of our felicity, but scarce had walked the length of a horse's tether, ere we heard a noise so dreadful and surprising, that we thought the devil was riding on hunting through the City, with a pack of deep-mouthed hell-hounds, to catch a brace of tallymen for breakfast. At last bolted out from the corner of the street, with an ignis fatuus dancing before them, a parcel of strange hobgoblins covered with long frieze rugs and blankets, hooped round with leather girdles from their cruppers to their shoulders, and their noddles buttoned up into caps of martial figure, like a knight-errant at tilt and tournament with his wooden head locked in an iron helmet.

One was armed, as I thought, with a faggot-bat, and the rest with strange wooden weapons in their hands in the

---

[1] An allusion to the bellman of St. Sepulchre's who recited certain verses to condemned felons on their way to Tyburn.

shape of clyster pipes, but as long, almost, as speaking-trumpets. Of a sudden they raised them to their mouths, and made such a frightful yelling, that I thought the world had been dissolving and the terrible sound of the last trumpet to be within an inch of my ears.

Under these amazing apprehensions I asked my friend what was the meaning of this infernal outcry? ' Prithee,' says he, ' what's the matter with thee ? Why these are the City waits, who play every winter's night through the streets.'

' Lord bless me ! ' said I, ' I am very glad it's no worse. Prithee let us make haste out of the hearing of them.'

At this my friend laughed at me. ' Why, what,' says he, ' don't you love music? These are the topping tooters of the town, and have gowns, silver chains, and salaries, for playing *Lillabolaro* to my Lord Mayor's Horse through the City.'

' Marry,' said I, ' if his horse liked their music no better than I do, he would soon fling his rider for hiring such bug-bears to affront his ambleship.'

The next scene the night presented to our view was a young crew of diminutive vagabonds, who marched along in rank and file like a little army of Prester John's countrymen, as if advancing in order to attack a bird's nest. My friend was almost as great a stranger to this little gang of tatterdemalions as myself, and for our satisfaction, to be better informed, we saluted them after this manner:

' Pray what are you, for a congregation of ragged spirits ? And whither are you marching?'

' We, Master? ' replied one of them. ' We are the City Black-Guard,[1] marching to our winter quarters. Lord bless

---

[1] These were a regularly constituted force of ragamuffins who loitered around the stables and kitchens of large houses. A proclamation of the Lord Steward's office in 1683 begins: ' Whereas . . . a sort of vicious, idle and masterless boys and rogues, commonly called the Blackguard, with divers other lewd and loose fellows . . . do usually haunt and follow the Court . . . We do hereby charge all those so called . . . who have intruded themselves into his Majesty's court and stables . . . to depart upon pain of imprisonment.'

you, Masters, give us a penny or a halfpenny, amongst us, and you shall hear any of us, if you please, say the Lord's Prayer backwards; swear the compass round; give a new curse to every step in the Monument; call a harlot as many proper names as a peer has titles.'

'Yes,' said I, 'you are a parcel of hopeful sprouts.' However, we gave the poor wretches a penny, and away they trooped, with a thousand 'God Bless ye's,' as ragged as old stocking mops, and I'll warrant you as hungry as so many cat-a-mountains; yet they seemed as merry as they were poor, and as contented as they were miserable.

'What a shame it is,' said I, 'that an infamous brood of vagabonds should be trained up in villainy, ignorance, laziness, profaneness, and infidelity, from their cradles, in such a well-governed Christian city as this, where are so many grave magistrates and parish officers whose care it ought to be to prevent such growing evils. Yet to suffer such a nest of heathens to be nursed up in blasphemy and contempt of religion, under the very walls of their churches, is certainly a scandal to our laws, and a shame to those in authority; to me 'tis very strange.'

'They are poor wretches,' says my friend, 'that are dropped here by gypsies and country beggars, when they are so little they can give no account of parents or place of nativity, and the parishes not caring to bring a charge upon themselves, suffer them to beg about in the daytime, and at night sleep at doors, and in holes and corners about the streets till they are so hardened in this sort of misery that they seek no other life till their riper years (for want of being bred to labour) puts them upon all sorts of villainy. Thus, through the neglect of churchwardens, and constables, from beggary they proceed to theft and from theft to the gallows.'

As we were reflecting upon the miserable condition of these unhappy wretches, another midnight King of Clubs was going his progress round his scanty dominions attended with his whole court of myrmidons. Popping on us unawares, his well-fed majesty bid his *Guard de Corps* halt, and with a 'Hem,' clapping his painted sceptre to the ground as hard as a pavior does his rammer, he bid us stand and come before the constable. We, like prudent ramblers, obeyed the voice of authority, and with uncovered heads paid reverence to his awful presence.

He demanded, after an austere manner, who and what we were. My friend, in order to satisfy his worship's curiosity and make him something the wiser, answered his foolish examination with as much submission and respect as a proud peevish dunce in authority could expect, or a prudent man, when at the mercy of such a coxcomb, give.

He asked my friend what his profession was. He answered him, 'A surgeon.'

'A surgeon!' says our learned potentate, in derision, 'and why not a chirurgeon, I pray, sir? I could find in my heart to send you to the Compter for presuming to corrupt the King's English before me, his representative.'

''Twas my mistake, Mr. Constable,' said he. 'Pray excuse it, and be not so severe with us. We are very sober, civil persons, who have been about our business and are going quietly to our own habitation.'

'Civil and sober persons?' said he, 'how do I know that, Mr. Prattle-box? You may be drunk for aught I know, and only feign yourselves sober before my presence to escape the penalty of the Act.'

My friend put his hand in his pocket and plucked out a shilling. 'Indeed, Mr. Constable,' says he, 'we tell you nothing but the naked truth. Here is something for your watch to drink; we know it is a late hour; but hope you will detain us no longer.'

With that, Mr. Surlicuff directs himself to his right hand janizary, 'Hem! hah! Aminadab. I believe they are civil gentlemen.'

'Aye,' said he, ' Master, you need not question it; they don't look as if they had fireballs about 'em.' ' Well, gentlemen, you may pass; but pray go civilly home. Here, Colly, light the gentlemen down the hill, they may chance to stumble in the dark, and break their shins against the Monument.'

' Thank you kindly, sir,' said we, ' for your civility, we know the way very well, and shall need no watchman. Your servant, sir, good night to you.'

' I am very glad,' says my friend, ' we are out of the clutches of this inquisitive constable. This grey-headed lump of grave ignorance takes as much pride in being the most officious fool in his parish as a victualler does to be one of the jury, or a vintner to be made an ensign of the Train-bands. This is the most ill-natured blockhead that ever was centred in a circle of lanthorns, and if he had said our heads had been made of Hackney turnips, one word of contradiction would have cost us a night's lodging in the Compter, for he makes no more of committing a man than a tavern-drawer does of kissing the cook.

' The thirsty retinue that attend him are hard-mouthed fellows at an oath, and can swear as heartily that you were drunk, though you drank nothing but coffee for three days before; and that you abused the constable, though you gave him not an ill word; and swore abundance of oaths, though your communication (Quaker-like) was nothing but Yea, yea, and Nay, nay.

' The good these fellows do in the streets is to disturb people every hour with their bawling, under pretence of taking care they may sleep quietly in their beds; and call every old fool by his name seven times a night, for fear he should rise and forget it next morning; and often, instead of preventing mischief, they make it, by carrying honest persons to the Compter who would fain walk peaceably home to their own habitations and by their sauciness provoke gentlemen to commit these follies 'tis properly their business to prevent.

In short, it is reasonable enough to believe they play more rogues' tricks than ever they detect, and occasion more disturbance in the streets than ever they hinder.'

By this time we were come to Billingsgate, and in a narrow lane, as dark as a burying vault, which stank of stale sprats and dirt, we groped about like a couple of thieves in a coal hole, to find the entrance of that nocturnal theatre in whose delightful scenes we proposed to terminate the night's felicity. At last we stumbled upon the threshold of a gloomy cavern where, at a distance, we saw lights burning like candles in a haunted cave where ghosts and goblins keep their midnight revels.

We no sooner entered, but we heard such a number of female tongues so promiscuously engaged in a mess of tittle-tattle, that had a waterman knocked down his wife with a stretcher, and been tried for the fact by a Parliament of fish-women, they could not have exercised their nimble instruments with more impatience.

We turned ourselves into the smoky boozing-den amongst them, where, round the fire, sat a tattered assembly of fat motherly flat-caps, with their fish-baskets hanging upon their heads instead of riding hoods, with every one her nipperkin of warm ale and brandy, and as many rings upon their thumbs as belongs to a set of bed curtains; everyone as slender in the waist as a Dutch skipper in the buttocks, and together, looking like a litter of squab elephants. Their noses were as sharp as the gnomon of a dial, and looked as blue as if they had been frost-nipped. Their cheeks were as plump as an infant's buttocks, but as crimson as the face of a nobleman's butler who has lived forty years in the family, and plainly proved by the depth of their colour, that brandy is a nobler dye than claret. Their tongues were as loud as the Temple horn, that calls the cuckold-makers[1] to their commons, and

[1] The lawyers of the Temple had a reputation for gallantry among the City wives.

every word they spoke was at least in the pitch of a double gamut. Their chief clamour was against high head-dresses and patches, and they said it would have been a very good law if Queen Mary had effected her design, and brought the proud minxes of the Town to have worn high-crowned hats instead of top-knots.

Then one, looking over her shoulder and spying me behind her, accosts me after this manner: 'God save you, honest master, will you pledge me?' 'Aye, dame,' said I, 'with all my heart.' 'Why then,' says she, 'here's a health to me and confusion on those that owe me money.'

'Lord help my poor masters!' said another. 'They look as if they had disobliged their wives or their landladies, and they would not rise and let them in to-night.'

'Come, come away,' says my friend, 'let's seek another apartment. These saucy-tongued old cats will tease us to death.'

These unhappy words one of them overheard, and starting up like a fury thus gave her lungs a-breathing:

'You white-livered son of a Fleet Street tailor. Who is it that you call cat?'

Away slunk my friend and I into another room and left them to spend their malignant spirits by themselves, and were as thankful to Providence we escaped so imminent a danger, as if delivered from the rage of so many wild cats. And, indeed, if their talons were as sharp as their tongues, they need not fear a combat with all the beasts of America.

We were now tumbled into a company composed of all sorts of rakes. One, in a long wig and muff, looked as fretful as a broken gamester, biting his nails as if he were ready to curse aloud, *Confound the dice.* Another was as full as if his grey mare was the better horse, and had denied him entrance for keeping late hours; the next, as brisk and lively as if just come of age and had got his means in his own hands, bought his time of his master and feared no colours, but thinking the day too short for his fortune had resolved the night should make amends in lengthening out his pleasures.

In a corner sat a couple of brawny watermen, one eating broiled red herring, and the other bread and cheese and onions.

Then, in blunders a drunken tar, as great in his thoughts as an Admiral, and calls to the boy in the bar after this manner: 'You freshwater lubber, why don't you hand me a candle, and induct me to my cabin, that I may belay myself?' As the boy lights him upstairs, he stumbles and curses. 'The devil d—n the rattlings of these wooden shrouds, for I have broke my shins against 'em; I had rather run up to the cross-trees of the main-topmast in a storm than six rounds of these confounded land ladders, after the drinking of a can of flip or a bowl of punch.'

Next came a spruce blade, with a pretended wife and asking what time the boats went off to Gravesend, they told him about four in the morning. 'Alas,' says he, 'that will be too long to sit. Can't my wife and I have a bed here?' 'Yes, yes, sir, if you like,' replied the pious beldam, 'we have several couple above in bed, that wait for the tide as well as you, sir.'

After these, in bolted two seamen with a little crooked fiddler before them, short pipes in their mouths, oaken truncheons in their hands, thrum caps upon their heads, and canvas trunks upon their rumps. We had the good luck for these to stagger into our company, and their unpolished behaviour, apish gestures, and maritime nonsense, added no small pleasure to the night, but gave us hopes of as much mirth as a London apprentice finds at a Bartholomew Fair puppet-show, or a country squire among a gang of strolling comedians.

These two subjects of the pickled god Neptune, having washed off their brine with a plentiful dose of fresh-water ale, began to be as brisk as a Town rake that has shaken off his poverty, or a Court libertine his old mistress. In their frolics they happened to espy a hook driven into the mantel beam, which they immediately converted into a very comical use, for laying violent hands on my little Lord Fiddler by the hind slit of his breeches they hung him upon the tenter. In this condition, pendant like a play-house machine or a brazen cherub over a church branch, he hung sprawling, begging with humble submission to be set safe upon *terra firma*. At last, by wriggling, he broke the string of his breeches, and down came our broiled scraper into the ashes.

This put the whole company into such an extravagant fit of laughter that had we seen a bailiff baited or a fellow break his neck at football it could not have been a greater jest to the spectators. But as soon as the angry homunculus had gathered himself up he gave the two Tritons such an untunable lesson upon his ill-tuned organ, that the whining of a dog, or the winding of a cat-call could not have disobliged our ears with less grateful harmony. When he had thus given vent to his ungovernable indignation he cocked the arm of his humped shoulder on his hip, and away rolled the runlet of gall, turning his back upon the company.

The tarpaulins now began to talk to each other of travels and of the sundry remarkable accidents which had happened in their voyages. One swore they once found it so excessive hot going to Guinea that they used no fire to boil the kettle, but dressed all their beef above deck in the sunshine and could bake, boil, fry or stew as well as in an Admiral's cook-room.

Says the other: ' I never was in so hot a climate as that; but I have been so many degrees to the norrard, where it has been so cold it has frozen our words in our mouths, so that we could not hear one another speak till we came into a warmer latitude to thaw 'em; and then all our discourse broke out together like a clap of thunder, that there was never such a confusion of tongues ever heard at Babel.'

Says his companion: ' That's very strange, but I have known stranger things to be true. I once was sitting upon my chest,

between decks, mending an old canvas jacket. We had found
by our observations that day we were within a few minutes
of being under the tropic of Cancer; and on a sudden it began
to lower, and the larboard watch handed in our sails, for fear
of a tornado or a squall. At last a beam of lightning darted
through an open port, melted one of the guns, went through
a pair of buckskin breeches I had on, and burned the lappets
of a blue shirt to tinder. It hissed as it came, like a rattle-
snake, but did my body no manner of damage.'

As our saltwater wits were thus romancing, who should
stagger into our company but an old acquaintance of my
friend's, who (as understood by his talk) was a kind of mongrel
match-maker. He made more a-roaring than half a dozen
drunken porters, and was as full of freaks as a madman at a
full of the moon. He guzzled and rattled, smoked and stared
like a fury; and every time he spoke 'twas with so much
earnestness that I thought his eyes would have flown out of
his head in pursuit of his words. All he talked was loud
nonsense, and the heat of his brain setting fire to his tongue,
made everything he said so wonderfully hot that the ears of
all people that heard him, glowed. At last he plucked out a
catalogue of what fortunes he had at his disposal, viz.:

A mercer's daughter on Cornhill, about seventeen, who was
unluckily kissed by her father's 'prentice; which being spread
among the neighbourhood, he is willing to give her two
hundred pounds advance above an equality, to salve up the
flaw, to any honest young shopkeeper that will wink at a fault
to better his condition.

An old maid that has lived 30 years in an alderman's family
who, with her wages, lady's old clothes, and money got for
private service, is worth about three hundred pounds, and
thinks herself qualified for keeping a victualler's bar. She is
willing to bestow herself upon any honest freeman, if clear in
the world, though not worth a groat.

A young buxom widow, on the back-side of the 'Change,

was married five years but never had a child, is still in her mourning, wonderfully pretty and tolerably honest. She is willing to dispose of herself to a brisk, lively man, within or without the year; is in a good shop, well customed and needs no money.

About half a hundred Exchange girls, some tall, some short, some black, some fair, some handsome, some housewifely, some homely, some virtuous, and will make very good wives for those who have more money than wit and more faith than jealousy.

A vintner's daughter, bred at the dancing-school, becomes a bar well, steps a minuet finely, plays sweetly upon the virginals, makes a very graceful figure and is as proud as she is handsome; will have a great many quart pots, old pewter, linen, and other household stuff in her portion, but whoever marries her must ride her with a curb, or she may prove unlucky, to the bane of her rider.

When he had thus diverted us with his catalogue of Job's comforters, which he asserted were for sale and at his disposal, my friend began to put me in mind of the considerable business we had upon 'Change, at Gresham College, Bedlam, and other places on the morrow. This occasioned us to think of bed, though with as much indifference as a new-married woman does her prayers. For the pleasures of the night were so engaging and every various hour such a wakeful piece of drollery, that a mountebank and his jack-pudding[1] or a set of morris dancers could not give more content to a crowd of country spectators than the lively action of what is here only repeated did afford us.

But to qualify ourselves the better for our task we thought it necessary to take some rest. So, accordingly, we were conducted to a room which stunk as bad as a ship between decks, when the tars are in their hammocks. But the seasonableness of the hour forced us to be content. And so good night to ye.

---

[1] A merry-andrew.

D

CHAPTER THREE

London Bridge—The Cuſtoms House—The Monument—Gresham
College—The Museum there—A Visit to Bedlam—The Royal
Exchange—The People described

WHEN we had cooled the fever of our brains with
a plentiful dose of that reviving cordial, sleep,
and our wakeful faculties had shaken off Morpheus's leaden plummets from our drowsy eye-lids, after a
few slug-a-bed yawns and lazy ſtretches we found it was high
time to make our resurrection. Accordingly, we ſtarted from
sluggard's paradise, the bed, and collected our scattered
garments.

After much rubbing, scrubbing, washing and combing
we made ourselves tolerable figures to appear by daylight,
and descended from our snoring kennel, which was so finely
perfumed by the fuſty jackets of its tarpaulin gueſts that it
smelt as odoriferously grateful as a Suffolk cheese toaſted over
a flaming pitch-barrel. The ceiling was beautified like a
soldier's garret, or a Compter chamber, with smutty sketches
done by unskilful hands with candle-flame and charcoal. The
bed, 'tis true, was feathers, but moſt of them were large
enough to make pens or tooth-picks. There was also an
earthen vessel, as big as a three-gallon ſteen, glazed o'er
with green, which looked as fine as any Temple mug or
country pudding-pan.

Having turned our backs on these cubicular conveniences
we crept, being cold, to a new-kindled smoky fire, where we
fortified our appetites with a pennyworth of burnt bread
softened in a mug of ale, improved with slices of Cheshire.

This we gobbled up (being hasty to be gone) with as much expedition as a citizen's wife does an Islington cheesecake[1] when treated by her husband. We then satisfied our tun-bellied host and left the infernal mansion to the sinful sons of darkness, there to practise their iniquities.

We turned down to Thames Side, where the frightful roaring of the bridge waterfalls[2] so astonished my eyes and terrified my ears that like the inhabitants near the Cataract of the Nile, I could hear no voice softer than a speaking trumpet, or the audible organ of a scolding fish-woman. After I had feasted my intellect with this surprising novelty, we turned towards Billingsgate, where a parcel of fellows came running upon us in a great fury, crying out as I thought, ' Scholars, Scholars, will you have any hoars?' 'Lord bless me,' said I to my friend, ' what a wicked place is this, that a man in a black coat cannot go about his business without being asked in public such an abominable question?' My friend laughed heartily at my ignorance, telling me they were watermen who distinguished themselves by the titles of *Oars* and *Scullers*, which made me blush at my error, like a bashful lass that has dropped her garter, or a modest man who cripples his jest by hesitation.

After we had loosed ourselves, with much difficulty, from the unparalleled insolency of Charon's progeny, we turned from a crowd of thumb-ringed flat-caps, from the age of seven to

[1] Islington cream and cakes were famous throughout the 17th and 18th centuries, and it was a favourite recreation of London citizens to take their wives and sweethearts out to the village for a stroll among the fields, a fresh syllabub, and a little duck-hunting among the ponds.

[2] Old London Bridge, which stood some 100 feet below the present bridge, consisted of 19 stone arches and a wooden drawbridge. The massive piers were further protected by projecting starlings which broke the rush of water on the bridge. Some of the arches were too narrow for boats of any kind to pass through, the widest was only 36 feet, and this considerable dam to the force of the river caused such a rapid under the bridge that the water raced and roared through in a cataract. Shooting the bridge was a feat which sometimes brought even experienced watermen to grief. At flood-tide the passage was impossible, and at ebb-tide it was exceedingly dangerous.

seventy, who sat snarling and grunting at one another over their sprats and whitings, like a pack of domestic dogs over the cook-maid's kindness, or a parcel of hungry sows at a trough of hogwash.

Having quitted the stink of sprats and the untunable clamour of the wrangling society, we passed round the dock, where some salt-water slaves, according to their well-bred custom, were pelting names at one another. One, unhappily being acquainted how to touch the other in his tenderest part, galled his impatient adversary with the provoking name of cuckold, which intolerable indignity so fermented the choler of the little snail-catcher, that he resolved to shew himself a champion in defence of his wife's virtue, and leaping into the other's boat, there, like a true-bred cock, made a vigorous assault upon his enemy on his own dunghill.

But a disaster attended the poor combatants, for in their scuffle they fell overboard. The tide being half spent the water was not high enough to cool their courage, for they maintained an amphibious fight and battled like ducks and drakes, in two elements at once, till the cuckold had bravely subdued his antagonist, and made his poor victim (half drowned and half knocked o' the head) publicly acknowledge the unspotted reputation of the victor's duchess, who, at the end of the fray, having received intelligence of her lord and master's engagement, came down to the dock-side crowned with an oyster basket, and there, with an audible voice, set up a passionate justification of her own honesty, to the great diversion of the whole auditory. Her Leviathan shape was a good testimony of her virtues, for had our first she-parent been but half so homely, the devil would have been damned nine times deeper into the infernal abyss, before he would have robbed her of her innocency.

From thence we passed to a stately fabric before which a parcel of robust mortals were as busy as so many ants; some running about in circular jimcracks, like turnspits labouring

in their jack-wheels; others as deeply engaged in hooping
casks as if they were taking all imaginable care that every tub
should stand upon its own bottom. Many scales were at work
and such abundance of eagle-eyed vermin hovering about 'em,
that I thought at first Justice might have resided there. But
my friend told me No; these were her agents.

'Prithee, friend,' said I, 'what is that grizzly bacchanalian,
with a pen twisted in his hair, whose face looks as if it cost
as much in dyeing as would set up a topping vintner?'

Says my friend, 'He's one of the cormorants called a land-
waiter. His business is to take care that nobody cheats the
Queen but himself. With honesty his post is worth a hundred
a year; but with the help of an open hand and a close mouth
he can (without burden to his conscience) make it worth
thrice the money.'

'What is he in the long wig with a fox-skin muff upon
his button, and his pocket-book in his hand?'

'Why he,' replied my school-fellow, 'is a beau, 'prentice to
some topping merchant. He is taking the weight of his
master's goods, to see that he is not wronged in the Customs.
He is very careful nobody cheats him abroad, and his master
is forced to be just as watchful that Mr. Finikin does not
injure him at home; for a flattering companion, or a jilting
mistress will at any time make him dip his fingers in the
cash, to treat them with a new play, or solace them with a
bottle.

'Pray,' says my friend, 'take notice of that gentleman in the
camlet-cloak; he will tell you from his own experience that
any man may grow rich from humility and industry, and that
'tis nothing but pride and laziness that begets poverty and
misfortune. When he first came to town, he had but threepence in the world, which he prudently laid out in a new broom
that might sweep clean. This he very dexterously applied,
with his utmost labour, to the dirty wharf, without anybody's
bidding; but he had sense enough to know that it belonged

to somebody, who would at least give him thanks, if not recompense his trouble. The master of the wharf happening to espy him at his task, gave him some small encouragement to continue his cleanliness, which he practised daily till he had gained his end and curried favour with the merchant so that he is now become a man of great estate and considerable authority. But if any poor man ask him for an alms, he tells him there are riches buried in the dirt, and good fortune in a broom, and if he will sweep as he was forced to do, he may come in time to be Lord Mayor of London. To this a cross old mumper once replied, "If you had not got more by knavery and usury than ever you did by your honesty and industry, you might have been apprenticed to your broom till this time, and never have been made a freeman." '

I enquired of my friend what they called this busy spot. He told me 'twas the Custom House, and in that stately edifice the Commissioners sat, about whom I asked some questions, but found my friend too shy to give me satisfaction, saying,' If I tell you the truth, I'm a fool to myself: if I tell you false, I am unjust to my friend, and make you become a liar to the world. I shall therefore, instead of what you expect, give you proverbial caution, viz., they are a parcel of edged tools, with whom there is no jesting, and he that attempts to eat fire to please a crowd, if he find cause to complain he has burnt his mouth, maketh himself but a laughing stock.'

By the advice of my companion we turned back till we came to a place called Pig Hill, which resembling the steep descent down which the Devil drove his hogs, I suppose it is for that honoured with the aforesaid title. There they are always in a condition to turn the stomach of a Jew, or poison a Scotchman; and can satisfy an epicure's appetite, or save a lady's longing, with pig or pork at any hour of the day, or any day in the year. The cooks, according to report, keep many spaniel bitches as wet nurses for the due suckling of their sow babies; this adds, they say, such a sweetness to their flesh, that they eat as fine as any puppy dog. And all such persons as are admirers of this luxurious food may have it there ready dressed the whole winter without the danger of fly sauce, which is more than in summer I'm able to promise you. All the elements contribute to their cooking of every squeaker they dress. He is first scalded in water, then dried in the air, and half-baked in the sun; then afterwards he is roasted by the fire, then dissected by a choleric executioner, and his quarters disposed of to hungry citizens.

As we walked up the hill, as lazily as an Artillery captain[1] before his company upon a Lord Mayor's day, or a Paul's labourer up a ladder with a hod of mortar, we peeped in at a gateway where we saw three or four well dressed blades with hawks' countenances, attended by half a dozen ragamuffinly fellows, shewing poverty in their rags and despair in their faces, mixed with a parcel of young wild striplings like run-away 'prentices. I could not forbear enquiring of my friend about this ill-favoured multitude.

'That house,' says my friend, 'which they are entering, is an office where servants for the plantations bind themselves to be miserable as long as they live, without a special Providence prevents it.[2] Those fine fellows, who look like footmen upon a holiday, are kidnappers, who walk the 'Change and other parts of the town, in order to seduce people who want employment and young fools crossed in love to go beyond seas. For every wretch they trapan into this misery they get

[1] The Honourable Artillery Company is the oldest military body in England. It has occupied its present drill-ground since 1642. St. Paul's was at this time being rebuilt after its destruction by fire, and the labourers were taking their time at it. See page 79.

[2] Those who wished to emigrate to the American plantations and had not the means of paying passage money, engaged themselves with a ship's master or an office-keeper to allow themselves to be sold for a term of years in return for their passage money. This term was usually four years. On arrival these poor wretches were sent to their purchasers and lived as slaves until the sum for which they had contracted was worked off. They were shipped mostly to Virginia, Maryland and Pennsylvania, and in the first two plantations were driven to work on the tobacco fields with the negroes.

so much a head from masters of ships, and merchants who go over. Those young rakes and tatterdemalions you see so lovingly herded are drawn, by their fair promises, to sell themselves into slavery, and the kidnappers are the rogues that run away with the money.

'Now,' said my friend, 'I'll show you a towering edifice, erected through the wisdom and honesty of the City as a very high memorandum of its being laid low, either by a judgement from Heaven for the sins of the people, or by the treachery of the Papists, according to the inscription of the Monument, which I suppose knows as little of the matter as I do.

'You'll be mightily pleased with the loftiness of this slender column, for its very height was the first thing that ever occasioned wry necks in England by the people staring at the top on't. To the glory of the City, and the everlasting reputation of the worthy projectors of this high and mighty Babel, it was built more ostentatiously than honestly by the poor orphans' money. Many of them have since begged their bread, and the City has here given them a stone. Look ye now, ye may see it; pray view and give me your opinion.'

'What! Is it of no use but only to gaze at?'

'Yes, yes,' says my friend. 'Astrologers often go to the top on't, when they have a mind to see Mars and Venus in conjunction, though the chief use of it is for the improvement of vintners' boys and wine-drawers, who come every week to learn the tavern trip by running up to the balcony and down again, which fixes them in a nimble step, and in a month's practice makes them rare light-heeled emissaries. Do you observe the carving, which contains the King's and his brother's picture? They were cut out by an eminent artist,[1] and are looked upon by a great many impartial judges to be a couple of extraordinary good figures. Pray what think you? I know you have some judgement in proportion.'

[1] Caius Gabriel Cibber, a Dutchman and father of Colley, the dramatist.

' Why truly,' said I, ' they are the only grace and ornament of the whole building. But 'tis a thousand pities the stones formed into so noble order, should be so basely purchased, to the ruin of so many thousand fatherless and widows. But I suppose it was politically done, to fix the King's effigy as a testimonial of loyalty.

'As you say, this edifice, as well as some others, was projected as a memorandum of the Fire, or an ornament in the City, but it gave those corrupted magistrates that had the power in their hands, the opportunity of putting two thousand pound in their own pockets whilst they paid one towards the building. I must confess all I think that can be spoke in praise of it is that 'tis a monument to the City's shame, the orphans' grief, the Protestants' pride and the Papists' scandal; and only serves as a high-crowned hat, to cover the head of the old fellow that shows it.'[1]

When my friend had obliged me with a full prospect of our metropolitan maypole, we turned up Gracechurch Street, in order to go to Gresham College. There we met a fellow in a gown, with a piece of prodigality called a mace upon his shoulders; another like one of Justice's sumpter-horses, laden with scales, weights and measures and a third armed with a pick-axe. These advanced attended by a troop of loiterers in gowns who hobbled after, with as much formality as a parcel of gossips going to a christening at the parish church. By and by they pitched down a triangular device and of a sudden began to be all as busy as so many sheriff's men at an execution. I enquired of my friend how these mortals were dignified or distinguished, and what was the weighty affair they were engaged in?

He told me these were a part of the worthy members of the

[1] The Monument was erected, 1671–77, about 200 feet from the baker's house, in Pudding Lane, where the Great Fire broke out. Wren's idea was to have a colossal brass-gilt statue of Charles II on the top, but the king decided on the existing vase of flames. It was at one time used by astronomers for observations, but its vibration made it unsuitable for that purpose.

Quest, whose business was to inspect weights and measures, taking care that every shopkeeper's yard be of the standard length, whilst the wife (sitting behind the counter) laughs in her sleeve all the time they were measuring. They give warning for the mending of pavements, and removing all nuisances, under the penalty of a fine. Their meeting is generally at a hall, except they have a Quest House, from whence they go to church to pray and return back to be drunk. They detect very few people in their faults, for they honestly take care not to injure their neighbours, but inform them when they shall walk their rounds, so that they may remove their false weights and measures out of the way.

The inhabitants of every precinct are obliged to give 'em their company at dinner; where he that does not behave himself generously, and purchase his security at the expense of ten shillings, shall be surely returned upon the Jury the next panel. They have an old custom of brewing spiced ale, and he that does not take care to send his wife a jug full, runs the hazard, by his negligence, of raising an evil spirit in his family that no conjurer can lay in a fortnight. They have as many offices amongst 'em as are in a nobleman's family, viz., Foreman, Controller, Treasurer, Steward, Butler, etc. They have a groat a house from each inhabitant, besides their fines, with which they feast their stomachs with luxurious excesses.

From thence we passed, without anything remarkable, till we came to Wiseacres' Hall, more commonly called Gresham College,[1] which we entered as gravely as a couple of sanctified harlots into B———'s Meeting House.[2] We stepped through

---

[1] Gresham College was at this time between Broad Street and Bishopsgate Street.

[2] Daniel Burgess (1645–1713) was a well-known Nonconformist who for nearly thirty years ministered at a meeting-house in Brydges Street, Covent Garden. His broad humour and occasionally indecorous drollery in the pulpit attracted crowds who wished rather to laugh than pray. In the reign of William III he announced that the people of God, descended from Jacob, were called 'Israelites' because God did not choose that His people should be called 'Jacobites.' He is frequently mentioned by Swift and others of the time.

a little brick court, and then came into a spacious quadrangle, where, in a melancholy cloister, we saw a philosopher walking, ruminating, as I suppose upon his entities, essences and occult qualities, or else upon the Philosophers' Stone, looking as if he very much wanted it. His steps he measured out with such exactness and deliberation, that I believe, had the right number failed to bring him to the end of the cloister, he would have been in a great passion with his legs. During his perambulation his eyes were fixed upon the pavement, from whence I conjecture he could see as far into a mill-stone as another. He seemed to scorn gloves as much as Diogenes did his dish, crossing his arms over his breast, and warming his hands under his armpits; his lips quaked as if he'd ague in his mouth, which tremulous motion, I conceived, was occasioned by his soliloquies, to which we left him.

My friend conducted me up a pair of stairs to the laboratory keeper's apartment,[1] and desired him to oblige us with a sight of the rarities. He very courteously granted us the liberty, opening his warehouse of Egyptian mummies, old musty skeletons, and other antiquated trumpery. The first thing he thought most worthy of our notice was the Magnet, with which he showed some notable experiments. It made a paper of steel filings pick themselves up one upon the back of the others, so that they stood pointing like the bristles of a hedge-hog, and gave such life and merriment to a parcel of needles, that they danced the Hay,[2] by the motion of the stone, as if the devil were in them.

The next thing presented to our view was a parcel of shell-flies almost as big as lobsters, armed with beaks as big as

---

[1] The Royal Society met at Gresham College every Wednesday about 3 p.m. Their museum and laboratory were one of the sights of London and contained some curious exhibits, including ' human rarities ' such as ' the entire skin of a Moor, tanned with the hair on,' ' a piece of bone voided with his urine by Sir William Throgmorton,' ' a tooth taken out of the womb of a woman, half an inch long.'

[2] The Hay was an old country dance in a ring.

those of jackdaws. Then he commended to our observation that wonderful curiosity the Unicorn's Horn; made, as I suppose, by an ingenious turner, of the tusks of an elephant; it is of an excellent virtue, and by report of these that know nothing of the matter, will expel poison beyond the mounte-banks' Orvietan.[1] Then he carried us to another part of the room, where was an aviary of dead birds, collected from the extreme parts of Europe, Asia, Africa, and America, amongst which were an East India owl, a West India bat, and a Bird of Paradise, the last being beautified with a variety of colours, having no discernible body but all feathers; when alive it feeds upon nothing but air, and though 'tis as big as a parrot, 'tis as light as a cobweb. It is reported by the sage philosophers of this society that a feather of this fowl, carried about you, is an infallible security against all evil temptation; for which reason they have pretty well plucked it, to carry home presents of it to their wives and daughters.

Then he ushered us among sundry sorts of serpents, as the Noy, Pelonga, Rattle Snake, Alligator, Crocodile, etc., so that, looking round me, I thought myself hemmed in amongst a legion of devils. When we had taken a survey of these monsters, we turned towards the skeletons of men, women and monkeys, birds, beasts and fishes; abortives put up in pickle, and abundance of other memorandums of mortality. They looked as ghostly as the picture of Michael Angelo's *Resurrection ;* as if they had collected their scattered bones into their original order, and were about to march in search after the rest of their appurtenances.

When we had taken this view of the wonders of the world, we crossed the hand of our raree-show interpreter with a piece of silver, who, like the crooked orator to the Abbey tombs, made a notable harangue upon every bauble in this store-house.

---

[1] Orvietan, or Venice Treacle, was an electuary supposed to be a counter-poison or antidote.

Glutted with the sight of those musty relics and philosophical toys, we determined to steer our course towards Bedlam. Midway between both, my friend bid me take notice of a man who was scuffling along in as much haste as a scrivener to make a will, or a poor quack to a rich patient.

'That man,' says he, 'that walks like a Mercury, as if he had wings to his heels, is a topping virtuoso, and a Member of the Royal Society. He is, by his profession, a labourer to the physician, but has made himself, by a curious inspection into the mysteries of universality, a Jack-of-all-trades, and is thought by the learned to be as knowing as he that has peeped seven years into a pitch-barrel. He's a wonderful artist at cleaning of a foul stomach, or sweeping of a gut. He publishes a weekly paper for the improvement of trade and husbandry, wherein, for the benefit of the public, he has inserted the most choice receipts for the making of pancakes, fritters, puddings, dumplings, also to make porridge, that were ever extant.

'He likewise, through his wisdom and generosity, has taught the world, at the expense of half a crown, to sweeten a dozen of old glass bottles, which you may buy now for two shillings, also how, at thirty shillings charge, we may improve an acre of land to be worth twenty. Amongst the rest he is a joiner of sexes; whatever match he makes, he seldom fails of his double reward, that is, to get money on one side, and curses on the other, for he is a man of such conscience and consideration that he generally takes care to couple those who are worth money to such as want it.'

Thus we prattled away our time till we came in sight of a noble pile of building,[1] which diverted us from our former discourse, and gave my friend the occasion of asking me my thoughts on this magnificent edifice. I told him, I conceived

---

[1] Bethlehem Hospital was then in Moorfields, on the site now occupied by Liverpool Street. The magnificent building here described was erected in 1676 at a cost of £17,000. It was one of the show-places of London where, for twopence, anyone might wander in and gaze at the poor distracted wretches behind their bars and bait them with foolish and cruel questions.

it to be the Lord Mayor's Palace, for I could not imagine so stately a structure could be designed for any quality inferior. He smiled at my innocent conjecture, and informed me this was Bedlam, an hospital for mad folks.

' In truth,' said I, ' I think they were mad that built so costly a College for such a crack-brain society,' adding, it was a pity so fine a building should not be possessed by such as had a sense of their happiness. It was a mad age when this was raised, and no doubt the chief of the City were in a great danger of losing their senses, so contrived it the more noble for their own reception, or they would never have flung away so much money to so foolish a purpose.

' You must consider,' says my friend, ' this stands upon the same foundation as the Monument, and the fortunes of a great many poor wretches lie buried in this ostentatious piece of vanity; and this, like the other, is but a monument of the City's shame and dishonour, instead of its glory. Come let us take a walk in, and view its inside.'

Accordingly we were admitted through an iron gate, within which sat a brawny Cerberus of an indigo colour, leaning upon a money-box. We turned in through another iron barricade, where we heard such a rattling of chains, drumming of doors, ranting, holloaing, singing and rattling, that I could think of nothing but Don Quevado's[1] vision, where the damned broke loose, and put Hell in an uproar.

The first whimsy-headed wretch of this lunatic family that we observed, was a merry fellow in a straw cap, who was saying to himself that he had an army of eagles at his command. Then clapping his hand upon his head he swore by his crown of moonshine that he would battle all the stars in the skies but he would have some claret. In this interim came a gentleman with a red face to stare at him. ' No wonder,' said his Aerial Majesty, ' that claret is so scarce, look there's

[1] This refers to one of the satires of Francisco Gomez de Quevado, a Spanish writer of the mid-17th century.

a rogue carries more in his nose than I, that am Prince of the Air, have had in my belly for a twelvemonth.'

'If you are the Prince of the Air,' said I, 'why don't you command the Man in the Moon to give you some?' To which he replied, 'The Man in the Moon's a sorry rascal; I sent to him for a dozen bottles but t'other day, and he swore by his bush, his cellar had been dry this six months. But I'll be even with the rogue. I expect a cloud laden with claret to be sent me by the Sun every day, and if a spoonful of lees would save him from choking, the old drunkard should not have a drop.'

We then moved on till we found another remarkable figure worth our observing, who was peeping through his wicket, eating bread and cheese, and talking all the while like a carrier at his supper, chewing his words with his victuals. All that he spoke was in praise of bread and cheese. Bread was good with cheese, and cheese was good with bread, and bread and cheese was good together, and abundance of such stuff, to which my friend and others stood listening.

The next unhappy object amongst this scatter-brained fraternity was a scholar of St. John's College, in Cambridge, who was possessed with melancholy, but was very inoffensive, and had the liberty of the gallery. He was a very musical man, which is thought to be one great occasion of his distemper. My friend walked up to him, and introduced some talk, to divert himself with a few of his frenzical extravagancies.

Another lunatic who had liberty of ranging the house caught hold of my school-fellow's arm, and expressed himself after this manner: 'Dost thou know, friend, what thou art doing? Why, thou art talking to a madman, a fiddling fellow, who has so many crotchets in his head that he cracked his brains about his bass and trebles.' 'Prithee,' says my companion, 'what was the occasion of thy distemper?' To which he answered, 'I am under the confinement for the noble sin of drinking; and if thou hast not a care it will bring thee into the same condition.'

We peeped into another room where a fellow was as hard at work as if he'd been treading mortar.

'What is it, friend,' said I, 'thou art taking all this pains about?'

He answered me thus, still continuing in action: 'I am trampling down conscience under my feet, lest he should rise up and fly in my face. Have a care he does not fright thee, for he looks like the devil and is as fierce as a lion, but that I keep him muzzled. Therefore get thee gone, or I will set him upon thee.' Then he fell a-clapping his hands, and cried, 'Halloo, halloo, halloo, halloo, halloo,' and thus we left him raving.

Another was holding forth with as much vehemence against Kingly government, as a brother of Commonwealth doctrine rails against plurality of livings. I told him he deserved to be hanged for talking of treason. 'Now,' says he, 'you're a fool; we madmen have as much privilege of speaking our minds, within these walls, as an ignorant dictator, when he spews out his nonsense to a whole parish. Prithee come and live here, and you may talk what you will, and nobody will call you in question for it. Truth is persecuted everywhere abroad, and flies hither for sanctuary. I can use her as I please and that's more than you dare do. I can tell great men such bold truths as they don't love to hear, without the danger of a whipping post, and that you can't do. For if ever you see a madman hanged for speaking of truth, or a lawyer whipped for lying, I'll be bound to prove my wig a wheel-barrow.'

We then walked into the women's apartment to see what whimsical vagaries their wandering fancies would move them to entertain us withal.

One poor object that happened under our observation was a meagre, old, grey-headed wretch, who looked as wild as an angry cat, and all her tone was, 'The wind is—blow,

The Beau's Disaster.
A street scene near Temple Bar, with the crowd baiting a man who gave himself airs.
(From a print in the Crace Collection)

devil, blow; the wind is—blow, devil blow.' A seaman who was staring at her, and listening to what she said, must needs be inquisitive how the wind sat, and asking her, ' Where is the wind, mother?' She hastily replied, ' The wind is at my stern. Blow, fool, blow.' She was so pleased she had sold him a bargain, that she fell into an extravagant fit of laughter in which he left her.

Having well tired ourselves with the frantic humours and rambling ejaculations of the mad folks, we took a turn to make some few remarks upon the looseness of the spectators, amongst whom we observed abundance of intriguing. Mistresses, we found, were to be had of all ranks, qualities, colours, prices and sizes, from the velvet scarf to the Scotch plaid petticoat. Commodities of all sorts went off, for there wanted not a suitable Jack to every Jill. Every fresh comer was soon engaged in an amour; though they came in single they went out by pairs; 'tis a new Whetstone's Park[1] now the old one's ploughed up, where a sportsman at any hour in the day may meet with game for his purpose; 'tis as great a conveniency to London, as the Long Cellar to Amsterdam, where any stranger may purchase a purge at a small expense. All that I can say of Bedlam, is this, 'tis an almshouse for madmen, a showing room for harlots, a sure market for lechers, a dry walk for loiterers.

We needed no clock to give the hour of the day. Our stomachs, as true as those of the 'Change, went One, and after redeeming our liberties from this prison, at the expense of twopence, we were led by our appetites into a cook's shop. And when we had refreshed Nature with a necessary supply of

---

[1] Whetstone's Park, between Holborn and Lincoln's Inn, was notorious for its great immorality. It was attacked by London 'prentices in 1682 and soon afterwards was turned into stables and low tenements. ' After I had gone a little way in a great broad street I turned into a tavern hard by a place they call a Park; and just as one Park is all trees, that park is all houses. I asked if they had any deer in it, and they told me not half so many as they used to have; but that if I had a mind to a doe, they would put a doe to me.' Crowne's *Country Wit.* (1675).

E

what she most coveted, we marched towards the Royal
Exchange, to which traders were trotting in as much haste
as lawyers at Westminster, or butchers to Smithfield.

The pillars at the entrance of the portico[1] were adorned
with sundry memorandums of old age and infirmity, who
stood here and there selling cures for your corns, glass
eyes for the blind, ivory teeth for broken mouths, and
spectacles for the weak-sighted. The passage to the gate
was lined with hawkers, gardeners, mandrake-sellers and
porters.

After we had crowded a little way amongst this miscellaneous
multitude, we came to a pippin-monger's stall, surmounted
with a chemist's shop where drops, elixirs, cordials and
balsams had justly the pre-eminence of apples, chestnuts,
pears and oranges, the former being ranked in as much order
upon shelves, as the works of the Holy Fathers in a bishop's
library; and the latter being marshalled with as much exactness as an army ready to engage.

We then proceeded and went on to the 'Change. Advertisements hung as thick round the pillars of each walk as bells
about the legs of a morris dancer, and an incessant buzz, like
the murmurs of the distant ocean, made a diapason to our talk,
like a drone to a bagpipe. The wainscoat was adorned with
Quack's bills, instead of pictures; never an empiric in the
town but had his name in a lacquered frame, containing a
fair invitation for a fool and his money to be soon parted;
so that he that wanted physic, or a wet-nurse for a child, might
be furnished at a minute's warning.

After we had squeezed ourselves through a crowd of Italians,
we fell into a throng of strait-laced monsters in fur, and

---

[1] The Royal Exchange stood on the N. side of Cornhill. The original
building was destroyed in the Great Fire and the second Exchange was built
in 1669. It was surrounded by shops, and the actual courtyard itself was divided
into Walks—Italian Walk, Clothiers' Walk, Barbadoes Walk, etc., where the
various merchants met. Above were some 160 shops occupied, for the most
part, by milliners and such-like.

thrum-caps, with huge logger-heads, effeminate waists, and buttocks like a Flanders mare, with slovenly mien and swinish looks, whose upper lips were gracefully adorned with brown whiskers. These, with their gloves under their arms, and their hands in their pockets, were grunting to each other like hogs at their pease. My friend told me these were the Dutchmen, the water rats of Europe, who love nobody but themselves, and fatten upon the spoils, and build their own welfare upon the ruin of their neighbours.

We had no sooner jostled through this cluster of commonwealth's men, but we were got amongst a parcel of lank-haired formalists, in flat crowned hats and short cloaks, walking with as much state and gravity as a snail o'er a leaf of a cabbage, with a box of tobacco-snuff in one hand, and the other employed in charging their nostrils from whence it drops into their mustachoes, which are always as full of snuff as a beau's wig is full of powder. Every sentence they spoke was graced with a shrug of the shoulders, and every step they took was performed with as much leisure as a cock strides. These, my friend told me, were Spaniards. Says he, 'you may know them by their smell, for they stink as strong of garlic as a bologna sausage.'

These were confusedly jumbled among people of sundry nations such as our neighbouring antics the French, who talk more with their heads and hands than with their tongues; who commonly speak first, and think afterwards; step a minute as they walk, and sit as gracefully on an Exchange bench, as if in a great saddle; their bodies always dance to their tongues, and they are so great lovers of action that they were ready to wound every pillar with their canes, as they passed by, either in tierce, écarté, or sacoon.

There, likewise, were the Lord's vagabonds, the Jews, who were so accursed for their infidelity that they are generally the richest people in all nations where they dwell. They, like the Spaniards, were great consumers of snuff. These, said my friend, are the hawks of mankind, the spies of the universe, subtle knaves, and great merchants.

Here were also a few amber-necklace sellers, as my friend called them; men with fur caps, long gowns, and grave countenances seeming wise in their carriage, retaining something of the old Grecian grandeur in their comely deportment. Among them was one very handsome young fellow, which my companion bid me take particular notice of, for, said he, that spark in the red gown was very familiar with some of our sweet-lipped ladies of the City. He was very much admired and courted by several topping benefactresses at this end of the town and received their favours, till the fool, proud of his happiness, must needs boast of their kindness to the disreputation of his humble servants; so they all discarded him with such hatred and contempt that he is now become the scorn and ridicule of every woman in the City.

'Pray,' said I, 'what tall sober-looking gentleman is that in the long black wig and formal hat that stands as level in the brim as a pot-lid? He seems to be wonderfully reverenced by a great many much finer than himself.'

'That man,' said my friend, 'is the greatest merchant we have in England, and those fellows that keep astern, and now and then come upon his quarter with their top-sails lowered, are commanders of ships, who are soliciting for employment. He that plies so close, they call Honour and Glory, who lately bore a command in the Service. He was originally a poor fisherman, but did a very notable exploit, that recommended him to a commission. But either for want of discretion or honesty, he is turned out, and I suppose rather than return to his nets, he is willing to enter into the merchant service.'

In the next walk we went into were some swordsmen with twisted wigs, and laced hats, with broad faces, and flattish noses, saluting one another commonly by the title of Captain. But they looked as if they had been a long while out of commission, for most of them were out of repair, some like gentlemen without estates, and others like footmen out of places, many of them picking their teeth, often plucking out large tobacco boxes to cram a wad in their mouths, as if most of their food was minced meat.

The other sort were a kind of lean, carrionly creatures, with reddish hair and freckly faces, very much given to scratching and shrugging, as if they held lousiness no shame, and the itch no scandal; stooping a little in the shoulders, as if their backs had been used to a pedlar's pack. Amongst them was a poor parson, who came to the wrong place to look for a benefice. These, I found, were a compound of Scotch and Irish, who looked as if they rather came to seek for business, than dispatch any.

We came to the back gate of the 'Change. On the east side of this sat a parcel of women, some looking like jilts who wanted cullies, and others like servants who wanted places.

We passed by them, and squeezed amongst costers and English traders, who were as busy in outwitting one another as if plain-dealing was a crime and cozenage a virtue.

'Take notice,' says my companion, 'of that camel-backed spark. He is dignified with the title of My Lord and has as many maggots in his head as there are holes in a cullender. Though the rickets have crushed him into that lump of deformity, he has the happiness, or curse, I know not which, of having a very handsome woman for his wife, whose glances have tempted such custom to her shop that he can afford to spend three or four hundred pounds a year in a tavern without doing himself any harm. She very generously allows him to do this out of her gettings, some censorious people are apt to imagine as a gratuity for his toleration for her liberty of conscience. She is never without a shop-full of admirers, whom she poisons with her eyes, and bubbles as she pleases. Give her her due, she's as beautiful as an angel, but as subtle as the devil; as courteous as a courtesan, but sharp as a needle;

very free, but very jiltish, very inviting, yet some say very virtuous.

'Now,' says my friend, 'we are got amongst the Plantation traders. This may be called Kidnappers' Walk, for a great many of these Jamaicans and Barbadians, with their kitchen-stuff countenances, are looking as sharp for servants, as a gang of pick-pockets for a booty.'

'Pray,' said I, 'what is the meaning of this inscription in golden capitals over the passage, *My Lord Mayor's Court ?*'

My friend replied that that was the nest of City cormorants who, by scraping a little out of many men's estates, raise great ones to themselves, by which means they teach fools wit, and bring litigious knaves to repentance.

Within that entry is an office of intelligence pretending to help servants to places and masters to servants. They have a knack of bubbling silly wenches out of their money, who loiter hereabouts upon the expectancy of work, till they are picked up by the Plantation kidnappers, and spirited away into a state of misery and harlotry.

'Now,' says my friend, 'let us walk on the middle of the 'Change and view the Statue. This,' says he, 'is the figure of King Charles II, and those are stock-jobbers, who are hovering about him, and are, by report, a pack of as great knaves as ever he had in his dominions. The rest are a mixed multitude of all nations, and not worth describing. Now I'll conduct you upstairs, where we'll first take a view of the fair ladies, and so adjourn to the tavern and refresh ourselves with a bottle.'

So we went up, where women sat in their pinafores, begging of custom with such amorous looks, and after so affable a manner, that I could not but fancy they had as much mind to dispose of themselves as the commodities they dealt in. My ears, on both sides, were so baited with 'Fine Linen, sir, Gloves and Ribbons, sir,' that I had a milliner's and a sempstress's shop in my head for a week together,

CHAPTER FOUR

A Quakers' Tavern—The Angel, Fenchurch Street—A Meddlesome Constable—The Poultry Compter—The Guildhall—Cheapside

BEING now well tired with the day's fatigue, our thirsty veins and drooping spirits called for the assistance of a cordial flask. In order to gratify our craving appetites with this refreshment, we stood a while debating what tavern we should choose. My friend recollected a little sanctified Aminadab in Finch Lane, whose purple nectar had acquired a singular repetition among the staggering zealots of the sober fraternity.[1]

When we had entered our land of promise, which overflowed with riches more healthful than either milk or honey, we found all things were as silent as the mourning attendance at a rich man's funeral; no ringing of bar-bell, bawling of drawers, or rattling of pot-lids, but a general hush ordered to be kept through the whole family.

In the entry we met two or three blushing Saints, who had been holding forth so long over the glass, that had it not been for their flapping umbrellas,[2] puritanical coats, and diminutive cravats, shaped like the rose of a parson's hat-band, I should have taken them by their scarlet faces to be good Christians. They passed by us as upright and as stiff as so many figures in a raree-show; as if a touch of the hat had been committing a sacrilege, or ceremonious nod a rank idolatry.

A drunken-looking drawer showed us the kitchen, which

---

[1] There was a Quakers' meeting-house in White Hart Court, Gracechurch Street, near by where George Fox preached a few days before his death. Aminadab was a nickname commonly applied to Quakers.
[2] Not the umbrella as we know it, but a kind of loose cloak.

we told him we were desirous of being in for the sake of
warmth. Several slouching disciples sat hovering over their
half-pints, like so many coy gossips over their quarterns of
brandy, as if they were afraid anybody should see 'em. They
cast as many froward looks upon us, who were wearing
swords, as so many misers would be apt to do upon a couple
of sponging acquaintances, staring as if they took us for some
of the wild Irish,[1] that should have cut their throats in the
beginning of the Revolution.

However, we bid ourselves welcome into their company,
and like true Protestant topers, scorning the hypocrisy of
tippling by half-pints, as if we drank rather to wash away our
sins than our sorrows, appeared bare-faced and calling for a
quart at once, soon discovered our religion by our drinking;
whilst they, like true Puritans, were unwilling to be caught
over more than half a pint, though they'll drink twenty of
these at a sitting.

We had not sat long, observing the humours of the drowsy
saints about us, but several amongst them began to look as
cheerful, as if they had drowned the terrible apprehensions
of futurity and thought no more of damnation. The drawer
was now constantly employed in replenishing their scanty
measures; for once warmed they began to drink so fast that
'twas the business of one servant to keep them going.

---

[1] The dread of an Irish rising, culminating in the ' Irish Night,' December
12–13, 1688, was long remembered in London with a shudder. James II had
fled; Jeffreys had been caught; wild rioting had taken place during the last few
days. Citizens were just going to bed when ' it was said that the Irish whom
Faversham had let loose were marching on London and massacring every man,
woman and child on the road. At one in the morning the drums of the militia
beat to arms. Everywhere terrified women were weeping and wringing their
hands, while their fathers and husbands were equipping themselves for fight.
. . . Candles were blazing at all windows. The public places were as bright as
noonday. All the great avenues were barricaded. More than twenty thousand
pikes and muskets lined the streets. The late daybreak of the winter solstice
found the whole City in arms ' (Macaulay). It transpired that the whole thing
was a scare, maliciously got up, nobody knew by whom, to heighten popular
animosity against the Catholics.

By this time the subtle spirits of the noble juice had given a fresh motion to the wheels of life, insomuch that my friend muſt needs be so frolicsome as to tune his pipes, and entertain us with a song. And because the words happened to be in some measure applicable to that present junĉture, I have thought it not amiss to insert 'em.

SONG

Why should Chriſtians be reſtrained
  From the brisk enliv'ning Juice,
Heaven only has ordained
  (Thro' love to men) for human use?
Should not claret be deny'd
  To the Turks, they'd wiser grow;
Lay their Alcoran aside
  And soon believe as Chriſtians do.

Chorus

For wine and religion, like music and wine
As they're good in themselves, do to goodness incline,
And make both the spirit and flesh so divine
That our faces and graces both equally shine.
Then ſtill let the bumper round Chriſtendom pass,
For Paradise loſt may be found in a glass.

Juſt as my friend had ended his sonnet, in came the little lord of the tippling tenement, about the height of a ninepin, with his head in a hat of such capacious dimensions that his body was as much drowned under the disproportioned brims of this unconscionable caſtor, as a pigmy under the umbrage of a giant's bongrace. He was buttoned in a plain veſtment that touched no part of his body but his shoulders, his coat being so large and his carcase so little that they hung about him like a scarecrow upon a cross-ſtick in a country pease-field, his arms dangling like a mob's Taffy mounted upon a red-herring on St. David's Day, and his legs so slender that they would bid defiance to any parish ſtocks.

He waited a little while for the motion of the Spirit, and when he had composed his countenance, and put himself in a fit posture for reproof, he breaks into this following oration. ' Pray, friend, forbear this profane halloing and hooting in my house! The wicked noise thou makest among my sober friends is neither pleasing to them nor me, and since I find this wine too powerful for thy inward man, I must needs tell thee I will draw thee no more of it. I therefore desire thee to pay for what thou hast had, and depart my house, for I do not like thy ways, nor does anybody here approve of thy ranting doings.'

We were not surprised at this piece of fanatical civility, it being no more than what we expected; but the manner of his delivery rendered his words so very diverting that we could not forbear laughing him into such a passion, that the looks of the little Saint revealed as great a devil in his heart as a pious disciple of his bigness could be well possessed with. Then, according to his request, we paid our reckoning, and left him in a great ferment.

From thence, pursuant to my friend's wishes, we adjourned to the sign of the Angel in Fenchurch Street. There my friend had the good fortune to meet some of his acquaintances, with whom we joined, and made up together as pretty a tippling society as ever were drawn into a circumference round the noble centre of a punch-bowl, though our liquor was the blood of the grape, in which we found such delectable sweetness that as many thirsty pigs round a troughful of ale-grounds could not have expressed more satisfaction in their grunts than we did in our merry songs and catches.

Time taking advantage of our carelessness had pruned his wings, and fled with such celerity that the noon of night was brought upon our backs before we had measured out a sufficiency of the noble creature to our craving appetites; and as we were contending with the drowsy master for the other quart, who should come in and put an end to our controversy but a tall, meagre carrionly constable,[1] and with him his crazy crew of halbardiers, who looked together like Judas and his accomplices. When he had given us a fair sight of his painted staff of authority, which he stamped down upon the boards before him with as much threatening violence as a buffoon in a music-house, at the end of every strain, when dancing with a quarter-staff. He opened his mouth like a Baalam's ass, and thus spake:

' Look you, d'ye see, gentlemen? 'Tis an unreasonable time of night for people to be tippling. Every honest man ought to have been in bed an hour or two ago.'

' That's true,' said I, ' for nobody ought to be up so late, but constables and their watches.'

At this some of the company tittered, which gave great offence to the choleric conservator of Her Majesty's peace, who commanded us instantly to begone, or he would commit us to the Compter. A wine-cooper in the company, being well acquainted with this shred of authority, used importunate solicitations for the liberty of drinking another quart. Said he: ' Pray, Mr. Constable, don't be thus severe! 'Twas but last night you and I were drinking, at a later hour together; I therefore hope you won't deny us the privilege yourself has so lately taken.'

This bitter reflection, tossed into the mouth of a magistrate, had such an unsavoury relish that he could not swallow it, but commanded his blackguards to take us to the Poultry Compter,[2] who immediately fell on us like so many footpads. They first secured our weapons, and then led us along by the elbows, in triumph to the Rats' Castle, where we were forced to do penance till the next morning in obedience to the will of a tailor, good Lord! at whom I had flung a remnant of

---

[1] Constables for the parish or ward were drawn from the householders, who had to serve in rotation a year at a time.

[2] The Poultry Compter was one of the Sheriff's prisons and, bad as it appears from Ward's description, was by no means the worst in London.

hard words, which made the cross-legged nitcracker more particularly my enemy.

After we had passed through a spacious porch, where in a forenoon knaves may be seen in clusters as thick as pick-pockets round Tyburn at an execution, we came to a frightful gate, where, after three knocks of authority were given at the gate, a single-handed Cerberus, in a fur cap, let fall a chain from the back of a barricado. Then, with a key much bigger than St. Peter's, in which there was enough iron to have made a porridge pot, and consisted of more wards than parishes in the City, he opened the wicket of the poor man's purgatory, into which they thrust us, one upon another, like so many swine into a hog sty.

After we had taken two or three turns in a paved yard, viewing the strength and loftiness of our garrison by starlight, we began to reflect upon the mischance we had fallen under. As we were thus ruminating upon our present circumstances, we heard the laughing of many voices, mixed with the confused wranglings of a different society. We asked the under-turnkey the meaning of this noise. He told us that the prisoners on the Common Side were driving away sorrow, and making themselves merry with some of their pastimes. Upon this we made it our choice to be of their society and accordingly desired admittance amongst 'em, as a means to pass away the tedious-ness of the night with some diversion, and also that we might judge the better of confinement, and the hardships of a prison.

When we entered this apartment, under the title of the King's Ward, the mixtures of scents that arose from tobacco, dirty sheets, stinking breaths, and uncleanly carcases, poisoned our nostrils far worse than a Southwark ditch, a tanner's yard or a tallow chandler's melting room. The ill-looking vermin, with long rusty beards, were swaddled up in rags, some with their heads covered with thrum-caps and others with them thrust into the tops of old stockings. Some quitted the play they were before engaged in, and came hovering round us, like so many cannibals, with such devouring countenances as if a man had been but a morsel with 'em, crying out, ' Garnish, Garnish,'[1] like a rabble in an insurrection, crying ' Liberty, Liberty.' We were forced to submit to the doctrine of non-resistance and comply with their demands, which extended to the sum of two shillings each.

Having thus paid our initiation fees we were welcome into the King's Ward, and to all the privileges and immunities thereof. This ceremony being ended, the lousy assembly of tatterdemalions returned to their sports, and were as merry as so many beggars in a barn.

At last the whole family grew as silent as so many hogs when their bellies are full, nothing being heard but snoring, or an ingrateful sound like the untunable drone of a bag-pipe. With this sort of music were our ears entertained all night, and that my eyes might be obliged with answerable satisfaction, I thought it now the only time to look about me.

I observed men lay piled in cabins one upon another, like coffins in a burying-vault, possessing only the same allowance above ground as the dead have under, their breadth and length, that's all. Other poor curs, that wanted the conveniency of kennels, were lain upon the benches, as if they had been bred up courtiers' footmen. Others coiled underneath, like dogs, and slept as sound as Low-country soldiers. Some lay round the fire, almost covered with ashes, like potatoes roasting, head to tail like hogs upon a dunghill. Another was crept into a corner and had upturned over his head the ash-tub, and so made a night-cap of an ale-firkin, to defend his head from the coldness of the weather.

With these sort of observations we passed away the dull hours of confinement till the morning, and were all as glad to see daylight again as a man would be to see the sun, who had

---

[1] This was the name given to the fee—varying with the circumstances of the sufferer, extorted from every new-comer to a gaol by the older inmates.

tumbled by accident into a neglected coal-pit. Our fellow-sufferers now began to awake, stretch and yawn. Now I must confess, I was forced to hold my nose to the grate, and snuff hard for a little fresh air, for I was e'en choked with the unwholesome fumes that arose from their uncleanly carcases. Had the burning of old shoes, draymen's stockings, the dipping of card matches[1] and other horrors been prepared in one room, as a nosegay to torment my nostrils, it could not have proved a more effectual punishment.

At last I heard the keys begin to rattle, which, though they were indifferent music over night, were very pleasing to our ears in the morning. According to my wishes the turnkey now let us into the yard, where we drew a little new breath and breathed out into the world those pestilential fumes which our bodies had imbibed from the three fatal sisters, filth, poverty and laziness.

We now thought it necessary to fortify our stomachs with a morning's draught, and accordingly descended into the Cellar, where every captive that had either money or credit, was posting with all speed for the same purpose.

Now we were come into the conversation of the ladies, who (poor creatures) in tattered garments, and without head clothes, looked as if they were just delivered from the rude hands of an unmerciful rabble. One among the rest, who had something more than ordinary in her person to recommend her to our notice, I drank to, and begged the favour of her company, which without importunity she granted.

After a little, I took the freedom to ask her what she was in for? She hesitated a little, at last told me she was imprisoned at the suit of a tallyman in Houndsditch, for things to the value of four pounds, and that he offered to kiss it out, but she would not let him, for which reason he arrested her, and had run her up to an execution. 'But I suppose, Madam,'

---

[1] Early matches were made by dipping pieces of card into melted sulphur.

said I, ' you have heartily repented since that you refused the offer.'

' No, sir,' she replied, ' rather than I would satisfy the desire of such unmerciful rogues as either a tallyman, pawnbroker, or bailiff, I would proſtitute myself to honeſt porters in the Town; for I'd have you to know, sir, I scorn to defile my body with such vermin, such inhuman knaves, that can't be content with cheating people out of their money, but muſt cozen them out of their liberty, too. Here are but thirteen poor wretches of us on the Common Side, and twelve of 'em were brought in upon the tally account, and if Providence shew us no more mercy than our creditors, here they will keep us as examples of their cruelty, to frighten others in their books to turn either harlot or thief to get money to be punctual in their payments, which many have been forced to do to my certain knowledge, to satisfy the hungry demands of those unconscionable usurers.'

I was much pleased with the woman's talk because I thought it reasonable to believe there was abundance of truth in it.[1] For people that are too poor to pay such unreasonable extortion as cent per cent, it's a scandal to the laws and a shame to Chriſtianity that such indigent wretches should be so heavily oppressed, contrary to all charity and juſtice, to satisfy the unreasonable intereſt, or else the unmerciful revenge of such unconscionable misers.

I rose up and peeped a little to survey this subterranean boozing ken, and found it divided by many partitions. The walls were tarnished with the slime of snails, and had nothing to cover their nakedness in the coldeſt of weather but a tiffany cobweb, wherein hung spiders as big as bumble bees, that had not been moleſted with a broom since they were firſt enlivened. The tables and benches were of ſturdy oak, handed

---

[1] Ward and other contemporary writers can find no words strong enough to express their hatred of the tallyman or itinerant vendor of goods on the instalment plan.

down through many ages to posterity. Like undutiful children, we trod and spat upon the bare skin of our first parent, Earth, for 'twas floored like a barn, though it stunk like a stable.

By this time came down the constable who committed us, with a countenance as white as the head of a Romford calf, and both his sleeves armed with needles of all sorts and sizes, with here and there a remnant of basting thread and stitching silk hanging upon his coat and stockings. By virtue of his painted rolling-pin, he removed us from the plagues of Scotland, and carried us before our betters, Sir Milk and Maycril, to answer what Mr. Goosequill could allege against us.

When his Worship had set his band to rights, and dressed his countenance with abundance of gravity, he betook himself to his elbow-chair, placed within a bar to keep unmannerly transgressors at their due distance, and also to secure his corns from the careless affronts of whispering constables, who are commonly proud to be seen standing between Justice and the People.

Our business was soon dispatched. 'Twas a case so familiar to his Worship that he had it at his fingers' end; for all the charge delivered against us was tippling at an unseasonable hour, and refusing to go home according to the command of authority.

But Mr. Buckram being highly displeased at some aggravating words I had given him over-night, told his wisdom I threatened him, and said I would make him pay five pound an hour for detaining me.

' Now,' says Sir Serious, ' pray what are you, that you value your time at so precious a rate; or that you dare speak such affrighting words to the face of the Queen's representative ? '

I replied, 'An't it please your worship, I am a gauger—an Excise officer—and was out last night about the Queen's business as well as Mr. Constable; and the Queen for ought I know, has sustained two or three hundred pounds damage by my being detained from my duty, for which, as I hope to make matters appear, Mr. Constable must be answerable, for I assure him I will give a report of the matter to the Commissioners.'

This put his gravity to his Hem's and Ha's. 'I must confess, Mr. Constable,' said he, 'you did not do well to commit one of Her Majesty's officers. It was very unadvisedly done of you. Well, gentlemen, paying your fees, you may go about your business, I have nothing further to say to you.'

Had it not been for the assistance of a few brains and a little confidence, I had been bound over to the Sessions. But, I bless my stars, a lucky providence prevented the misfortune and restored us to our former liberty.

Being glad we had shaken off the yoke of confinement at so easy a rate without paying for either drunkenness, swearing or the like, which are as commonly accumulated upon transgressors under our circumstances as it is to find canvas, stay-tape and buckram in a tailor's bill. As we had been fellow-sufferers together, there was no parting without a glass, so we went to the Rose Tavern in the Poultry,[1] where the wine had justly gained a reputation according to its merit; and there in a snug room, warmed with brush and faggot, over a quart of good claret, we laughed at our night's adventure, and cursed the constable. And that all others who fall into his clutches may do the like, I have here furnished them with an Anathema proper for their purpose.

> May rats and mice consume his shreds
> His patterns and his measures,
> May nits and lice infest his bed
> And care confound his pleasures.

[1] The Rose was one of the best-known City taverns and dates back to early Tudor times. The proprietor in 1660 was one William King, whose wife was in labour when Charles II was making his triumphant progress through the City. As she expressed a wish to see him, he rose in his stirrups as he passed the tavern and kissed his hand to her as she was supported by some cronies at the window.

F

May his long bills be never paid;
And may his help-mate horn him;
May all his ills be public made
And may his watchman scorn him.

When old may he reduced be
From constable to beadle,
And live until he cannot feel
His thimble from his needle.

After we had drank a refreshing glass, my friend and I took leave of our companions, and concluded to take a turn in Guildhall, which he told me was a fine place, and my Lord Mayor's chosen dining-room upon the day of triumph. Bumpkin-like as I came out of the tavern, I could no more forbear staring at Bow steeple than an astrologer could looking at a blazing star, or a young rake at a fine woman, but I wondered the projector of such a noble pyramid should form so mean a model for the church, which compared together are just the reverse of St. Andrew's, Holborn, the one being like a woman with a beautiful face joined to a deformed body, and the other, like an old pigmy's head upon a young giant's shoulders.

'But pray,' said I, 'what is the meaning of this terrible monster upon the top, instead of a fane or weather-cock?'

'Why, that,' says my friend, 'is a brazen dragon, exalted as an emblem of the Church's persecution. The Dissenters once looked devilishly asquint at it, but now they dread it no more than More of Morehall did the Dragon of Wantley.'[1]

From thence we jostled through a parcel of busy citizens, who blundered along with as much speed towards the 'Change, as lawyers in term time towards Westminster Hall till we turned down King Street, and came to the place intended, which I entered with as great astonishment, to see the giants,

[1] An allusion to the old story of the intrepid man who clothed himself in armour studded with spikes and then bearded the famous dragon in its den, eventually kicking it in its only vulnerable place, the mouth.

as the Morocco ambassador did London, when he saw the snow fall.

I asked my friend the meaning and design of setting up those two lubberly preposterous figures, for I suppose they had some peculiar end in't.

'Truly,' says he, 'I am wholly ignorant of what they intended by 'em, unless they were set up to show the City what huge loobies their forefathers were, or else to fright stubborn apprentices into obedience. For the dread of appearing between two such monstrous loggerheads will sooner reform their manners, or mould 'em into compliance with their masters' will, than carrying 'em before my Lord Mayor, or the Chamberlain of London; for some of them are as much frighted at the names of Gog and Magog, as little children are at the terrible sound of Raw-Head and Bloody-Bones.'[1]

'Pray,' said I, 'what are yon cluster of people doing, that seem all as busy as so many fools at the Royal Oak Lottery?'

'Truly,' said my friend, 'you are something mistaken in your comparison. If you had said knaves, you had hit it, for that's the Sheriff's Court, and I must give 'em that character, for I never knew one fool among them, though they have to do with a great many. All those tongue padders, who are chattering within the Bar, are picking the pockets of those that stand without. You may know the sufferers by their pale faces; the passions of hope, fear and revenge, hath put them into such disorder, they are as easy to be distinguished by their looks in a crowd as an owl from a hawk, or a country esquire from a town sharper.

'That crowd at the end of the Hall is a Court of Conscience, whose business is to take care that a debtor of a small sum under forty shillings shall not pay money faster than he can get it. Without jesting, 'tis a very reasonable establishment for the prevention of poor people's ruin, who lie at the

---

[1] The name of a bogy with which 17th-century children were terrified.

mercy of a parcel of rascally tally men, and such-like unconscionable traders, who build their own welfare upon the
miseries and wants of others. There are several other courts
held here, besides what we now see sitting, but I think this
does the moſt good of any of 'em, except to the lawyers, and
they look upon it with as evil an eye as the Devil looked
over Lincoln.'[1]

According to my friend's proposal we next ſteered our course
towards the famous Cathedral, and as we passed along Cheapside we met with a fellow ſtark-naked from the waiſt upward,
armed with a luſty cudgel. I concluded he muſt be either a
fool or a madman, to expose his bare flesh to the sharp pinches
of so cold a season. But, however, I enquired of my friend
if he knew the meaning of his ridiculous whimsy.

He replied, he had heard he was a man of good parts and
learning, and from thence did believe he was a kind of self-
willed philosopher, who had a mind to broach some new
principles, and make people believe he firſt left off his clothes
to keep him warm, and ever since had refused to put 'em on
for fear he should catch cold by wearing 'em. But I fancy he
had made but a few proselytes. He has gone in this manner
many years till his skin is by the weather as hard as the upper
leather of a drayman's shoe. I met him the laſt snowy day
we had going into the fields to take his belly-full inſtead of
a mouthful of fresh air, as he eſteems it much better walking
than at midsummer.

By this time we were at Cheapside Conduit,[2] pallisadoed
with chimney-sweepers' brooms, and guarded with such an
infernal crew of soot-coloured funnel scourers that a countryman seeing so many black attendants waiting at a ſtone hovel,
took it to be one of Old Nick's tenements, and asked a

---

[1] A proverbial phrase alluding to a devil-shaped weathercock on Lincoln
College, Oxford. It was taken down in 1731, having lost its head in a gale.

[2] This was the little Conduit in the middle of Cheapside facing Foster Lane
and Old 'Change.

shopkeeper, why they should suffer the Devil to live in the heart of the City?

These we passed and entered into Paul's Churchyard,[1] where our eyes were surprised with such a mountainous heap of stones that I thought it must require the assistance of a whole nation for an age to remove 'em from the quarry, and pile 'em upon one another in such admirable order, and to so stupendous a height.

We turned to the right, where booksellers were as plenty as pedlars at a fair, and parsons in their shops were busily searching after the venerable conceits of our wormeaten ancestors, as if they came thither for want of brains, or in search of a library, to patch up a seasonable discourse for the following Sunday.

' Pray,' says my friend, ' take notice of that old lanthorn-jawed fellow, so thoughtfully perambulating in his warehouse of Roman saints, religious heathens, and honest social moralists. He looks as like a modern politician, as if through the whole course of his life he had studied nothing but Machiavel. In all seasons of the year you may find him walking in his shop; and he is never to be seen without his hanging coat; it is his comfortable companion at all times, and in all business. As the Satyr in the Fables could with the same breath blow hot and cold, so is his Irish mantle possessed of the like qualities, for he wears it in the winter to keep him warm, and in the summer as an umbrella to screen his withered carcase from the scorching sunbeams.

' Though he has but a small head, he has a great deal more brains than a goose, and never gave anybody that ever dealt with him occasion to call him a fool. He's so far a true-bred Englishman as to be a great enemy to the interest of France, for he rails mightily against taverns and never drinks wine, but when he's treated. He's a little too cunning to be honest, and too miserly to be generous; loves nothing more than his

[1] St. Paul's was being built. See next chapter.

money, and hates nothing so much as to part with it. Calls generosity, folly; charity, extravagance; over-reaching, wisdom; niggardliness, discretion; and unconscionable extortion, but a lawful interest. He never was known to drink strong wine but once, and then was treated by his apprentice who had found at the door a piece of money, and being upon his master's ground, he claimed the right, and after some little contest about the matter, they agreed to spend it.'

It now being about three o'clock, we concluded to go into Paul's, an account of which I shall give in my next.

CHAPTER FIVE

St. Paul's Cathedral—People seen therein—Doctors' Commons—Long
Lane—St. Bartholomew's Hospital

IN our loitering perambulation round the outside of Paul's
we came to a picture-seller's shop, where smutty prints
were staring the church in the face. I observed there was
more people gazing at these loose fancies of some lecherous
engraver than I could see reading sermons at the stalls of all
the neighbouring booksellers. Among the rest of the spectators, an old citizen had mounted his spectacles upon his
nose, and was busily peeping at the representation of the
gentleman and the milkmaid.

' Pray, father,' said I, ' what do you find in that immodest
picture worth such serious notice?'

' Why, I'll tell you, young man,' says he, ' I cannot without
wonder behold in this painting the madness and vanity of
you young fellows, with what confidence you can take a bear
by the tooth, without the dread of the danger.'

We walked a little further, and came amongst the music-
shops, in one of which were so many dancing masters, 'prentices fiddling and piping songs and minuets, that the crowd
at the door could no more forbear dancing into the shop, than
the merry stones of Thebes could refuse capering into the
walls, when conjured from confusion into order by the power
of Amphion's harmony.

Amongst 'em stood a little red-faced blade, beating time
upon his counter, as if a Bartholomew Fair concert, with the
assistance of a jack-pudding, had been ridiculing an Italian
Sonette, and was as prodigally pert in giving his instructions to

the rest as a young pedagogue tutoring a disciple in the hearing of his father. We added two to the number of fools, and stood a little, making our ears do penance to please our eyes, with the conceited motions of their heads and hands which moved to and fro with as much deliberate stiffness as the two wooden horologists at St. Dunstan's, when they strike the quarters.[1]

We left these jingle-brains to their crotchets, and went to the west end of the Cathedral, where we past by the abundance of apples, nuts, and ginger-bread, till we came into a melancholy multitude drawn into a circle, giving very serious attention to a blind ballad-singer, who was fully setting forth the wonderful usefulness of a goodly broadside, proper to be stuck up in all righteous and sober families, as a means to continue the Grace of God before their eyes and secure even the little lambs of the flock from the temptations of Satan.

After he had prepared the ears of his congregation with a tedious preamble in commendation of his divine poem, he began with an audible voice to lyric it over to a psalm tune, to the great satisfaction of the penitent assembly, who sighed and sobbed, shook their heads and cried. At last he came to the terrible words of Hell and Damnation, which he sung out with such an emphasis that he put the people a-trembling; so, liking not the harsh sound of such inharmonical bugbear words, they began to sneak off, like a libertine out of church when the parson galls old sores of conscience by pressing too hard upon his vices.

From thence we turned to the west gate of Paul's Churchyard, where we saw a parcel of stone-cutters and sawyers so

---

[1] The clock of old St. Dunstan's church, Fleet Street, had a large gilt dial overhanging the street, and above it two figures of savages, life-size, each holding a club in its right hand, with which it struck the quarters on a suspended bell, at the same time moving its head. Crowds always gathered to watch the giants, and the place was a fruitful field for pickpockets. The clock and its giants were removed, in 1830, to the house in Regent's Park where the St. Dunstan's Home for Blinded Soldiers is now established.

very hard at work that I protest, notwithstanding the vehemency of their labour and the temperateness of the season, instead of using their handkerchiefs to wipe the sweat off their faces, they were most of them blowing their nails.[1]

' Bless me! ' said I to my friend, ' sure this church stands in a colder climate than the rest of the nation, or else those fellows are of a strange constitution, to seem ready to freeze at such warm exercise.'

' You must remember,' said my friend, ' this is work carried on at a national charge, and ought not to be hastened on in a hurry, for the greatest reputation it will gain when it's finished will be that it was so many years building.'

From thence we moved up a long wooden bridge, that led to the west portion of the church, where we intermixed with such a train of promiscuous rabble that I fancied we looked like the beasts driving into the Ark, in order to replenish a new succeeding world.

The first part that I observed of this pile were the pillars that sustained the covering of the porch. ' I cannot but conceive,' said I, ' that logs of such vast strength and magnitude are much too big for the weight of so small a body it supports.' In answer to which, my friend repeated me this following fable.

There was a little carpenter, and he hewed a mighty strong stool out of whole timber to sit and smoke a pipe on at his door. A passenger coming by, seeing such a disproportion between the man and his seat, took occasion to ask why he had made such a huge clumsy stool for such a pigmy of a man. He replied, he liked it himself, and cared not whether anybody else did or not; adding, he intended it to serve the children's children of his grand-children. And besides, the

---

[1] The rebuilding of St. Paul's, after the Great Fire, was begun in 1675, and the choir was opened for Divine Service in 1697. The last stone of the lantern in the cupola was laid in 1710. The slowness of the St. Paul's labourers became proverbial.

stronger it is, said he, if anybody finds fault, the better able it is to bear their reflection.

From thence we entered the body of the church, the spaciousness of which we could not discern for the largeness of the pillars. 'What think you now?' says my friend. 'Pray how do you like the inside?'

'I'll tell you,' said I. 'I must needs answer you as a gentleman did another, who was a great admirer of a very gay lady, and asked his companion whether he did not think her a woman of extraordinary beauty? He answered, truly, he could not tell, she might be so for aught he knew, for he could see but very little of her face for patches. "Poh, poh," says the other, "you must not quarrel at that, she designs them as ornaments." To which his friend replied, since she had made them so large, fewer might have served her turn, or if she must wear so many, she might have cut 'em less. And so I think by the pillars.'

We went a little further, where we observed ten men in a corner, very busy about two men's work, taking as much care that everyone should have his due proportion of the labour as so many thieves, in making an exact division of their booty. The wonderful piece of difficulty the whole number had to perform, was to drag along a stone of about three hundredweight, in a carriage, in order to be hoisted upon the mouldings of the cupola; but they were so fearful of dispatching this facile undertaking with too much expedition that they were longer in hauling it half the length of the church, than a couple of lusty porters, I am certain, would have been in carrying it all the way to Paddington, without resting with their burden.

From thence we approached the North side of the choir, which had been very much defaced by the late fire,[1]

---

[1] On February 27, 1698–9, a fire broke out in a small room adjoining the organ gallery. It threatened to be serious but was put out before much damage had been done.

occasioned by the carelessness of a plumber, who had been mending some defective pipes of the organs.

Afternoon prayers being ready to begin, we passed into the choir, which was adorned with all those graceful ornaments that could anyways add a becoming beauty and venerable decency to so magnificent a structure.

When prayers were over, which, indeed, were performed with that harmonious reverence, and exhilarating order, sufficient to reclaim the worst of men from following the untunable discord of sin, and bring them over to the enlivening harmony of grace and goodness, we returned into the body of the church, happily intermixed with a crowd of good Christians who had concluded, with us, their afternoon's devotion.

We now took notice of the vast distance of the pillars, from whence they turn the cupola, on which, they say, is a spire to be erected, three hundred foot in height, whose towering pinnacle will stand with such stupendous loftiness above Bow Steeple dragon, or the Monument's flaming urn, that it will appear to the rest of the holy temples like a cedar of Lebanon among so many shrubs, or a Goliath looking over the shoulders of so many Davids.

As we were gazing with great satisfaction at the wondrous effects of human industry, raising our thoughts by degrees to the marvellous works of Omnipotence, from those of his creatures, we observed an old country fellow leaning upon his stick, and staring with great amazement up toward Heaven, through the circle from whence the arch is to be turned. Seeing him fixed in such a ruminating posture, I was desirous of knowing his serious thoughts, and in order to discover them I asked him his opinion of this noble building, and how he liked the church?

' Church! ' replied he, ' 'tis no more like a church than I am, Ads-heart! It's more by half like a goose-pie I have seen at my landlord's, and this embroidered hole in the middle of the top is like the place in the upper-crust, where they put in the butter.'

I could not forbear laughing at the oddness of his notion, and hoping to hear something further from him that might give us a little diversion, we continued his company. 'Prithee,' said I, 'honest country-man, since thou dost not believe it to be a church what place dost thou take it to be?'

'Why,' says he, 'I'll warrant you now, thou think'st me to be an arrant fool, but thou art mistaken; for my father was a trooper to Oliver Cromwell, and I have heard him say many a time, he has set up his horse here, and you think that the Lord will ever dwell in a house that the Roundheads converted to the use of a stable?'

'That was done,' said I, 'by a parcel of rebellious people, who had got the upper hand of the government, and cared not what murders, sacrilege, treason, and mischief they committed. But it was a church before it was converted to that heathenish use, and so it is now.'

'Why then,' says Roger, 'I think, in good truth, the Cavaliers are as much to blame in making a church of a stable, as the Roundheads were in making a stable of a church, and there's a Roland for your Oliver, and so good-bye to you.'

Away he trudged, the true offspring of schismatical and rebellious ancestors, expressing in his looks no little malice and contempt towards the magnificence of the building, which they have been always ready to deface, when they have had any opportunity.

We now begin to stifle our sober and more elevated thoughts and contemplation, and form in ourselves a suitable temper to a different undertaking, which was to observe some disconsolate figures which were wandering in the church, like mice in an empty barn, as if their melancholy cogitations had tempted them foolishly to look for what they were assured they should not find. Some of them were as pale as if troubled with the hypocondria, and fancied themselves to be walking in some subterranean cavern, far remote from that transitory world in which they had once been sinners. These had their eyes cast down as if they had great regard to their foot-steps, and were under some melancholy apprehension of slipping into that bottomless pit from whence there is no redemption.

Others walking with their arms crossed directed their eyes altogether upward, as if they were so deeply fallen in love with the beauty of the building that their senses were ravished with each masterly stroke of the skilful artificers. Amongst the rest, was here and there a lady, who looked as wild and wanton as if she thought more on a gallant than she did on her devo-tions, and would rather sing a song than say her prayers, or see a play than hear a sermon.

The next we remarked were penurious citizens, consist-ing in number of about half a dozen, who I suppose had taken sanctuary in the church to talk treason with safety, or because it was cheaper walking there, than sitting in a coffee-house. Their heads, tongues, hands and eyes were all eagerly in motion, shewing they were extraordinary intent upon some wonderful projection. At last I conjectured from words which I overheard, that they were some of the shallow-brained cullies who were drawn in by the Land Bank,[1] and were fumbling out a method of licking themselves whole, by cheating other people. These, I thought, like the money-changers, ought to have been whipped out of the Temple.

There was nothing offered worth our further observation,

[1] This was a wild scheme of finance got up in 1696 to assist the Government in the financial straits brought about by the Continental war. The intention was to advance money on the security of the land, and the sum to be raised by subscription was expected to be £2,600,000, one-quarter of which was to be paid up by August 1. But the public was nervous of the scheme, and by the appointed date only £2,100 had been subscribed. The Land Bank thereupon broke, and all who had anything to do with it were ruined.

except a parcel of wenches fit for husbands, playing at hoop and hide among the pillars. This revelling of girls I thought was very indecent, and ought to be carefully prevented, left the new church be polluted far worse than the old one, and inftead of a ftable, be defiled with beafts worse than horses.

From thence we made our egress on the South side, and quitting the consecrated bounds of this holy leviathan, crossed a dirty kennel to take a view of a parcel of cleanly beau 'prentices, who were walking in their mafters' shops with their periwigs juft combed out of buckle, well drugged with the barber's powdering puff. The extravagant use of this made them appear so parti-coloured that their upper parts looked like millers. Their coats, from the waift downwards hung in as many folds as a waterman's doublet, to show they had more cloth in the skirts of one tunica, than any of their anceftors wore in a whole suit. But this much may be said in excuse of 'em, they might the better afford it, because they were woollen-drapers.

By this time we were come to an arch, where we turned in. On the left many scutcheons were hung out, as if funerals were more in fashion at this end of the town than any part I had yet seen. I asked my friend the meaning of all these gaudy hieroglyphics being hung out in so private a thorough-fare.

'You are miftaken,' says he, 'this is a place of great business, for moft persons who travel in dead men's shoes are necessi-tated to come this way, and ask leave of those who never knew one of their family, whether they shall enjoy that which nobody has any right to but themselves. That shop where you see so many good colours flung away upon paper, like so much gold upon ginger-bread, belongs to a heraldic painter, who, indeed, to give him his due, is as honeft a man as ever guided pencil and has taken as much pains, at his own expense, to detect a knave, and prevent the public's being cheated, as ever his neighbour did to subdue a stubborn conscience, and make it pliable to his own and the Nation's interest.

' That place,' says he, ' on the left hand is a spiritual Purgatory[1] to torment fornicators and adulterers, where they bring many sinners to penance, but very few to repentance, and often excommunicate people out of the church for not going thither.'

' That, methinks,' said I, ' is like forcing a man to forbear such victuals which he cannot endure to eat, or debarring him of such company which he always hated to keep.'

' This liberty of conscience,' says my friend, ' has been a devilish thorn in their sides, for in the joyful days of Church persecution, they used to have two or three brace of Dissenters for breakfast, but now the office is dwindled into such a vacancy of business, that their neighbouring vintner despairs of ever being made an alderman, for the Whitehorse Ale House has run away with most of his customers.'

' Pray,' said I, ' whither does that passage lead where those country fellows stand gaping and staring about?'

' That,' replied he, ' is also Doctors' Commons, and they are come to Town about the probate of some last dying will and testament, administration, caveat, or some such business. It's a wonder none of the spiritual cormorants have seized them yet, for they are generally as quick-sighted as hawks, and love as dearly to prey upon a country curmudgeon, as a hound does upon horse flesh.'

We adjourned from thence back into Paul's Churchyard, and turned westward into a famous street, wherein a noble postern was presented to our view. The stateliness of its appearance made me enquire of my friend what they called this edifice; to what purpose it was built, and to what use converted. He told me it was called Ludgate[2] and was raised both as an

[1] This was Doctors' Commons, where ecclesiastical cases were tried, probate granted, etc.

[2] The old gate adjoined St. Martin's church on the south side. It was demolished in 1760.

ornament and security to the City. Through a charitable compassion to unfortunate citizens, it was made a commodious prison for freemen, furnished with such conveniences, and so plentifully supplied with provisions by the gifts of good people, and other certain allowances, that many live better in it than ever they did out on't, and are so fallen in love with their confinement that they would not change it for liberty.

After we had shot the arch, we turned up a street, which my companion told me was Old Bailey. We walked on till we came to a great pair of gates. It being a remarkable place, according to my usual custom I requested my friend to give me some further knowledge of the matter. He informed me it was Justice Hall,[1] where a Doomsday Court was held once a month to sentence such canary birds to a penitential psalm as will rather be choked by the product of hempseed, for living roguishly, than exert their power in lawful labour to purchase their bread honestly.

'In this narrow part of the street,' said my friend, 'where we are now passing, many such a wretch has taken his last walk, for we are going towards that famous University of Newgate where, if a man had a mind to educate a hopeful child in the daring science of paddling, the light-fingered subtlety of shoplifting, the excellent use of Jack and Crow, in the silently drawing bolts, and forcing barricadoes, with the knack of sweet'ning, or the most ingenious dexterity of picking pockets, let him but enter him in this college on the Common Side, and confine him close to his study but for three months, and if he does not come out qualified to take any degree of villainy he must be the most honest dunce that ever had the advantage of such eminent tutors.'

From thence my friend led me through a place called Giltspur Street, and brought me to a spacious level, which he told me was distinguished by the name of Smithfield Rounds, which

---

[1] This fine building was destroyed by the Gordon Rioters in 1780.

entertained our nostrils with such a savoury scent of roast meat, and surprised my ears with the jingling noise of so many jacks, that I stared about me like a country bumpkin. Seeing such a busy number of cooks at work, I thought myself in the kitchen of the universe, and wondered where the gluttons could live who were to devour such vast quantities of sundry sorts of food, which run so merrily round before large fires, in every greasy mansion. We soon delivered our squeamish stomachs from the surfeiting fumes that arose from their rotten roasted pork, which made the rounds stink like a Hampshire farmer's yard, when singeing bacon.

From thence we went to the rails, where country carters stood armed with their long whips to keep their teams in a due decorum. These were drawn up in the most sightly order imaginable, with their heads dressed up to as much advantage as an Inns of Court sempstress, or a mistress of a boarding school. Some had their manes frizzled up, to make 'em high withered, others had their manes plaited, as if they had been ridden by the nightmare. Amongst these cattle, here and there, was the conductor of a dung-cart, in his dirty surplice, wrangling about the price of a beast, like a wary purchaser; and that he might not be deceived in the goodness of the creature, he must see him stand three fair pulls at a post, to which the traces of the poor jade are tied, that he may exert his strength, and shew the clown his excellencies, for which he strokes him on the head, or claps him on the buttocks, to recompense his labours.

We went a little farther, and there we saw a parcel of ragged rapscallions, mounted upon scrubbed tits, scouring about the rounds, some trotting, some galloping, some pacing, and others tumbling. They blundered about in such confusion that I thought them like so many beggars on horse-back, riding to the Devil, or a parcel of French Protestants[1]

---

[1] On the revocation of the Edict of Nantes, 1685, French Protestants thronged to England for refuge.

G

upon the Dover Road, scrambling post-haste up to Piccadilly.

'Pray, friend,' said I, 'what are these eagle-faced fellows, in their narrow-brimmed white beavers, jacket-coats, a spur on one heel, and bended sticks in their hands, that are so busily peeping into every horse's mouth, and sauntering about the Market like wolves in a wilderness, as if they were seeking whom they should devour?'

'Those blades,' says my friend, 'are a sort of Smithfield fox called Horse-dealers, who swear every morning by the bridle, they will never suffer from any man a knavish trick, or ever do an honest one. They are a sort of English Jew, that never deal with any man but they cheat him, and have a rare faculty of swearing a man out of his senses, lying him out of his reason, and cozening him out of his money. If they have a horse to sell that is stone blind, they'll call an hundred gods to witness he can see as well as you can. If he is downright lame, they will use all the asseverations that the Devil can assist 'em with, that it's nothing but a spring halt. And if he be twenty years old, they'll swear he comes but seven next grass, if they find the buyer has not judgement enough to discover the contrary.'

'I perceive,' said I, 'this is a market for black cattle as well as horses.'

'Yes,' replied my friend, 'if we had come in the morning you would have seen the butchers as busy in handling the flanks of sheep and oxen, as the jockeys are in fumbling about the jaws of horses. But now the market is almost over; yet you may see some Welsh runts and Scotch carrion, which wait for the coming of Shoreditch butchers, who buy 'em up for the Spittlefields weavers, and the poorer sort of Huguenots, who have taken possession of that part of the town.

'Come,' said my friend, 'now we are here we'll take a turn quite round, and then we shall escape nothing worth observing.'

In order to complete our circular walk we moved on, but had

as many stinking whiffs of Oronoko tobacco blown into our nostrils as would have cured an afflicted patient of the toothache.

By this time we came to an arch, about the middle of the row, where a parcel of long-legged loobies were stuffing their lean carcases with rice milk and furmity, till it ran down the corners of their mouths back into their porringers. We passed by these devouring gang of milksops, and came to the corner of a narrow lane, where Money for Old Books was written upon some part or other of every shop, as surely as ' Money for Live Hair ' upon a barber's window. We took a short turn into it, and so came back, where we saw a couple of poor scholars with disconsolate looks, in threadbare black coats, selling their authors at a penny a pound, which their parents perhaps had purchased with the sweat of their brows. There was a parson in almost every shop searching the shelves with as much circumspection to find out a book worth purchasing, as ever cock used upon a dunghill of rubbish, when scraping after an oat worth pecking at.

Being now pretty well tired with our day's journey, we concluded to refresh ourselves with one quart of claret, before we walked any further; we were near the sign of honour's fountain, the Crown, the representation of which royal diadem I thought no vintner would presume to distinguish his house by, unless he had wine in his cellar fit to bless the lips of Princes.

To experience the truth of this notion, we stepped in and the jolly master, like kinsman of the bacchanalian family, met us in the entry with a manly respect and bid us welcome. We desired he would shew us upstairs into a room forward. Accordingly, in his own proper person, like a complaisant gentleman-usher, he conducted us into a large stately room, where, at first entrance, I discerned the master strokes of the famed Fuller's[1] pencil, the whole room being painted with

---

[1] Isaac Fuller (1606–72) was a well-known painter of portraits and decorative pieces. He did the altarpieces for Magdalen and Wadham colleges, Oxford, and embellished the interiors of many London taverns.

that commanding hand. His dead figures appeared with such
lively majesty that they begot reverence in us the spectators;
our eyes were so delighted with this noble entertainment that
every glance gave new life to our weary senses.

We now begged him to oblige us with a quart of his richest
claret, such as was fit only to be drank in the presence of such
heroes, into whose company he had done us the honour to
introduce us. He accordingly gave direction to his drawer,
who returned with a quart of such inspiring juice that we
thought ourselves translated into one of the houses of the
Heavens, and were there drinking immortal nectar, amongst
gods and goddesses.

My friend, like myself, was so wonderfully pleased at this
obliging usage, that he was very importunate with me to
scribble a few lines in commendation of our present state of
happiness, which, to gratify his desire, I performed, and have
here presented to the reader.

> Who can such blessings, when they're found, resign?
> An honest vintner, faithful to the vine;
> A spacious room, rare painting, and good wine?
>
> Such tempting charms what mortal can avoid?
> Where such perfections are at once enjoyed,
> Who can be dull, or who be ever cloy'd?
>
> If you would love, see there fair Pallas stands,
> How chaste her looks, how fine her breasts and hands!
> Her awful mien each gen'rous heart commands.
>
> If you to wit or music would aspire,
> Gaze at the Nine, that blest harmonious choir,
> They'll kindle in your thoughts new sparks of fire.
>
> If to the war-like Mars you'd be a friend,
> And learn to bravely conquer, or defend,
> See Ajax and Ulysses there contend.

If neither love nor arms your fancy suit,
Nor would you be wise, musical or stout,
Here's wine will make you truly blest without.

By this time we had tippled off our salubrious juice, and business denying us leisure to renovate our lives with t'other quart, we took our leave, with a promise to recompense his respectful usage on some better opportunity.

We had not gone above ten strides from the door, but we saw a cluster of tunbellied mortals, with malignant aspects, armed with sturdy oak of an unlawful size, looking as sharp upon every passenger, as if, cannibal like, they were just ready to devour 'em. I enquired of my friend, what he took those ill-favoured crew to be, whose bulldog countenances and preposterous bodies rendered them in appearance betwixt men and monsters?

'These fellows,' says my companion, 'which you seem to be so much amazed at, are nothing but Serjeants, who are awaiting to give some bodyguard a clap on the shoulder. This corner is their plying place, and is as seldom to be found without a rogue as Gray's Inn Walks without a town-lady, or Newgate Market without a basket-woman.'

We moved from thence, till we came to the corner of Long Lane[1] where a parcel of nimble-tongued sinners leaped out of their shops, and swarmed about me like so many bees about a honeysuckle. Some got me by the hands, some by the elbows, and others by the shoulders, and made such a noise in my ears, that I thought I had committed some egregious trespass unawares, and they had seized me as a prisoner. I began to struggle hard for my liberty, but as fast as I loosed myself from one, another took me into custody. 'Zounds!' said I, 'what's the matter? What wrong have I done you? Why do you lay such violent hands upon me?'

---

[1] Long Lane was a rag-market in the neighbourhood, where all passers-by were importuned to purchase cast-off clothing.

At last a fellow, with a voice like a speaking trumpet, came up close to my ears, and sounded forth, ' Will you buy any clothes?'

'A pox take you,' said I, 'you are ready to tear a man's clothes off his back, and then ask him whether he'll buy any. Prithee let mine alone, and they will serve me yet this six months.' But they still hustled me backwards and forwards like a pickpocket in a crowd, till at last I made loose and scampered like a rescued prisoner from a gang of bailiffs, my friend standing all the while looking on, and laughing at me.

' Pray,' said I, 'what's the meaning of these unmannerly clip-nits using passengers with this shameful incivility? Certainly 'tis a greater penance for a man to walk through this confounded wardrobe, than 'tis to run the gauntlet. But what is the reason,' said I, to my friend, ' they did not treat you after the same manner?'

' You must know,' says he, ' they can distinguish a country-man as well by his looks as you can a parson by his robes; they tease a stranger to the town, as much to make themselves sport, as to promote the sale of their goods, and if they had got you a little higher, they would have handed you quite through the lane, for it's like a gulf when you're a little way entered, the current will carry you through. The masters of those shops will give as much wages for one of those tongue-padding fellows, who stand sentinel at their doors, as an illiterate mountebank will allow to a good orator, i.e. fifty shillings, or three pounds a week. They are like the jackal to the lion, they catch the prey for their masters, and if they but get you into one of their shops, they as certainly cheat you before you come out again, as you go in with money in your pocket; for they will out-wheedle a gipsy, out-swear a common gamester, out-lie an affidavit man, and out-cozen a tallyman. They will make up new clothes, and sell them for second-hand, and get more money by 'em than the toppingest tailor in Town ever got by a young heir, when he made his clothes upon credit. They are a pack of the sharpeſt knaves about London, and are as great a grievance to the public, as the Royal Oak Lottery.'

' Why then,' said I, ' since they have served me so affrontively, and you have given me such a hopeful account of 'em I'll lend them a few of my good wishes, to revenge myself for their rudeness to me:

> May the cockroach and the moth,
> Eat such holes in their cloth,
> That the prime coſt may never return in ;
> But muſt all be laid by
> For a black, ruſty dye,
> Fit for dead monger's coachmen to mourn in.

> May their tailor's ne'er truſt,
> Nor their servants prove juſt,
> And their wives and their families vex 'em.
> May their foreheads all ache
> And their debtors all break,
> And their consciences daily perplex 'em.'

Having thus taken our farewell of those hempen-looking tormentors, we ſtrolled along till we came into a corner, where the image of a bear ſtood out upon a signpoſt,[1] perked up on his tail, with a great faggot bat in his claws. Beneath the effigies of his ugliness, a parcel of swine lay couchant in the dirt, attended with a guard of lousy ragmuffins, looking like some of the devil's drovers, smelling as frousily, together with their swine, as so many flitches of ruſty bacon in hot weather, or Bruin's bed-chamber in the bear-garden.

We jogged on from thence, to relieve our noses from their naſty jackets, and crossed over, fetlock deep in mud and filthiness, to the sheep pens, where a parcel of dirty mongrels did the drudgery of their worse-looking maſters, and reduced

[1] The Bear and Ragged Staff was a fairly common sign in London. It was the crest of the Dudleys.

each straggling innocent to his proper order and decorum. Butchers were here as busy as brokers upon 'Change; money seemed to be a plentiful commodity; for every russet-coloured clown was either paying or receiving, to the great uneasiness of such who passed by and wanted it.

We walked on till we came to the end of a little stinking lane, which my friend told me was Chick Lane, where measly pork and neck-beef stood out in wooden platters, adorned with carrots, and garnished with the leaves of marigolds ; and where carriers and drovers eat in public view, stuffing their insatiate appetites with greasy swines' flesh, till the fat drivelled down from the corners of their mouths.

Having now seen all the market could afford, we crossed the rounds, and went into a lofty cloister, which my friend told me was the Lame Hospital[1] where a parcel of wretches were hopping about by the assistance of their crutches. Women were here almost as troublesome as the Long Lane clickers, and were importunate with us to have some dealings with them.

I looked about me and could not forbear taking notice of two things, viz., the prettiness of the place, and the homeliness of the women. ' Sure,' said I, ' the noblemen never come here to choose themselves mistresses, for, I protest, I can scarce see one among them handsome enough to make a wife for a Moorfields Conjurer.' As many names were pencilled out upon the walls, as if there had been the genealogy of the twelve tribes, or a public register of all the topping cuckolds in the City. I asked my friend the meaning of this long catalogue of enquiries and worships, who told me, they were the names of the benefactors, ostentatiously set up, that every passenger might see what a number of charitable Lord Mayors and Aldermen we have had in our famous Metropolis. You may imagine by the number of names, it is largely endowed, there

---

[1] This was St. Bartholomew's, and was probably so called from the figures of two cripples on the pediment of the entrance.

being several branches belonging to the same foundation, as Kingsland Hospital, and St. Thomas's in Southwark.

'And pray,' said I, ' what are these hospitals for?'

My friend answered, for the receiving of sick and lame soldiers and seamen, and other poor wretches that can make interest, and here they keep 'em upon water gruel and milk porridge till they are dead or well, and turn 'em into this wide world, or the next, about their business.

We went from thence through a narrow entry, which led us by a parcel of diminutive shops, where some were buying gloves, some smoking tobacco and others drinking brandy, and from thence into a famous Piazza, where one was selling of toys, another turning of nut-crackers, a third, with a pair of dividers, marking out such a parcel of *tringum-trangums* to understand the right use of which is enough to puzzle the brains of an Euclid. From thence we passed into another cloister, whose rusty walls and obsolete ornaments denoted a great antiquity, where abundance of little children, in blue jackets and kite-lanthorned caps were very busy at their several recreations.

' This,' says my friend, ' was originally founded by Edward the Sixth for the education of poor children, but has been largely improved since by additional gifts, and is one of the noblest foundations in England. No youth can have the advantage of a better education than is here allowed them, they are afterwards provided for according as they're qualified, being sent either to sea, trades or the University.'

After we had taken a turn round the cloister we made our egress towards Newgate Street, in order to pay a visit to Physicians' College, and some other neighbouring places; an account of which I shall defer to my next.

CHAPTER SIX

Physicians' College—Ludgate Hill—Fleet Bridge—A Quack Doctor
—Bridewell—Women whipped there—A Visit to the Country

WE now proceeded to survey Physicians' College,[1]
which we found adorned with so lofty and large
a portico, that when we had entered it we were
no more in proportion to the spacious lanthorn o'er our heads
than a cricket to a biscuit-baker's oven.

' Pray,' said I, ' what is the cause of that great painted tub
that stands upon wheels? It looks as if it were designed as
a whimsical cottage for some maggot-brained Diogenes. I
hope there are no such fantastical humorists among this
learned society? '

' No, no,' replied my friend, ' you are much beside the
cushion; that engine is a kind of water syringe, designed to
cure such houses by injection that are under inflammation.'

' Pray,' said I, ' explain your allegory. I do not readily
understand what you mean by your syringe, etc.'

' Why, if you must have it in plain terms,' says he, ' that
which I termed so, is a device to cast water into houses that
by accident have taken fire.'

' There are a couple of fine statues, placed opposite to each
other, pray what do they represent? '

' The one,' says my friend, ' is the King's, and the other's
that worthy charitable Christian, Sir John Cutler's,[2] who, as

---

[1] The College of Physicians was a fine building erected by Wren after the
Great Fire, on the west side of Warwick Lane, Newgate Street.

[2] Sir John Cutler has been held up by Pope as a monster of avarice, but
he was a genuine benefactor to many charities, and there is some doubt as to

a means, I suppose, the better to secure his own health and long life, was so great a benefactor to this learned corporation, that when the fire in '66 had consumed their college to Amen Corner, and the ground being holden but by lease, he lent them money to purchase this foundation, and to build thereon this stately edifice. They, through the mistaken hopes they had of his generosity, received it from him as a gift, and to express their gratitude for so bountiful a donation, publicly returned him thanks for what the muddling fool never intended to give 'em, dedicating several books to him, wherein like poor poets, they expressed their unparalleled veneration of so liberal a patron.

'At last their flatteries so provoked the penurious temper of the money-loving gentleman, that he thanked them kindly for their thanks and praised them highly for their praises; but told them plainly, he feared there was a misunderstanding between them, for that he had not given them a groat, as he knew on, but only assisted them at an unhappy juncture with the loan of some money, to recover their ancient grandeur, then buried in ashes.

' This disappointment so astonished the fraternity that they looked as disconsolate one upon another as so many broken gamesters at a hazard table, hoping his worship would take it into his further consideration, and not give them so bitter a pill to purge out the grateful relish of so sweet an expectancy as they had hitherto been under. A little time after this conference had passed between 'em, the pale-faced master of the ceremonies conducted the old gentleman to the next world and his surviving relations have since demanded the money of the College, the dread of refunding which hath put some

whether his dealings with the Royal College of Physicians have not been misrepresented. When the College was being built he expressed his desire to bear part of the cost, and actually erected a magnificent theatre as well as the whole eastern side of the building. After his death, in 1699, his executors made a demand of £7000, as being the amount he had *lent*, plus interest. The claim was eventually settled by a payment of £2000 by the College.

of 'em into as loose a condition as if they had lately fed upon nothing but their own physic.'

'What privileges,' said I, 'extraordinary are granted to them in their charter, above what are held by many other physicians, who are not of their society?'

'Many,' replied my friend, 'and these in particular, viz., no person, though a graduate in physic of Oxford or Cambridge, and a man of more learning, judgement and experience than one half of their members, shall have the liberty of practising in, or within seven miles of London, without a licence under the College seal, or in any other part of England, if they have not taken some degree at one of the Universities. They can likewise fine and imprison offenders in the science of physic and all such who presume to cure a patient, after they have given 'em over, though by more excellent methods than ever were known to their ignorance.

'They have also the privilege of making bye-laws for the interest of themselves and the injury of the public, and can purchase lands in right of the corporation, if they could but find money to pay for 'em. They have authority to examine the medicines in all apothecaries' shops, to judge of the wholesomeness and goodness of many drugs and compositions they never yet understood. They are likewise exempt from troublesome offices, as jurymen, constables, etc., being no ways obliged to keep watch or ward, except with a rich patient, where they are assured of being well paid for their labour. They have also the liberty to kill as many as they please, provided they do it *Secundum Artem*, and no law shall call them to account.

'They are freed from the bearing of arms, or providing of ammunition, except pill, bolus, or potion or other things to destroy the body of sick persons they know not how to cure. Any member of the College may practise surgery, if he will but take the pains to understand it. They lately committed a more able physician than themselves without bail or main prize, for malpractice in curing a woman of a dangerous ulcer in her bladder by the use of a Cantharidid, which they affirm not fit for internal application, though the patient's life was saved by taking it; which shews they hold it a greater crime to cure, out of the common method, than it is to kill in it. And in prosecuting their antagonist for the contempt of Gallen and Hippocrates, they charged him for the doing that good which themselves wanted either will or knowledge to perform, and thus made themselves all fools in attempting to prove the other a knave, who procured his discharge at the Queen's Bench Bar, without a trial, and now sues them for false imprisonment; having also informed against 'em in the Crown Office, as common disturbers.'

From thence my friend conducted me to Bridewell, being Court day, to give me the diversion of seeing the ardour of some town ladies cooled by a cat-o'-nine tails. But in our passage thither meeting with some remarkable accidents, I think it may contribute something to the reader's satisfaction to give a rehearsal of them.

As we came down Ludgate Hill, a couple of town bullies met each other. 'D———n ye, sir,' says one, 'why did you not meet me yesterday morning, according to appointment?' 'D———n you, sir, for a coward,' replied the other. 'I was there and waited till I was wet to the skin, and you never came at me.' 'You lie, like a villain,' says t'other; 'I was there, and stayed the time of a gentleman, and draw now, and give me satisfaction like a man of honour, or I'll cut your ears off.' 'You see,' says the valiant adversary, 'I have not my fighting sword on, and hope you are a man of more honour than to take the advantage of a gentleman.' 'Then go home and fetch it,' says Don Furioso, 'like a man of mettle, and meet me within an hour in the Queen's Bench Walk in the Temple, or the next time I see you, by Jove's thunder-bolts, I will pink as many eyelet holes in your skin, as you have button-holes in your coat, and therefore have a care how you trespass upon my patience.' ' Upon the reputation of a gentleman, I will punctually meet you at your time and place,' replied the other, and so they parted.

> Bullies, like dunghill Cocks, will ſtrut and crow,
> But few or none dare ſtand a sparring blow ;
> So does the peevish mongrel take delight
> To bark and snarl, show teeth, but dare not bite ;
> Oft mischief makes, but ſtill the danger shuns.;
> If matched, he fawns, or else turns tail and runs.
> So cowards often do their swords unsheath,
> But cow'd and daunted with the fear of death
> Thus tamely shew their blades, as fearful curs their teeth.

We moved on till we came to Fleet Bridge,[1] where nuts, gingerbread, oranges and oyſters, lay piled up in movable shops that run upon wheels, attended by ill-looking fellows, some with but one eye, and others without noses. Over againſt these ſtood a parcel of trugmoldies in ſtraw hats, and flat-caps, selling socks and furmity, nightcaps and plum pudding.

Juſt as we passed by, a feud was kindling between two rival females. The one called the other a loathly quean and charged her with robbing her of her husband's love; then falling into tears, expressed herself further in these words: ' Have I lent you the money out of my pocket, the gown off my back, and even my petticoat, to be thus ungratefully rewarded? You know, Hussiff, I have given you the very bread out of my mouth, but I'll tear your eyes out.' Then with teeth and nails she made a violent assault upon her rival, who roared out for help so luſtily that the mob parted 'em, their coifs having received the greateſt damage in the fray.

Juſt as the squabble was ended and before the rabble was

---

[1] Fleet Bridge was made of stone, with sides breast-high adorned with the City arms. Round the bridge and along the sides of the river, which was navigable as far as Holborn, was a sort of unofficial market.

dispersed, who should be stumbling along upon his hide-bound prancer, but a horse-mountebank, who seeing so rare an opportunity to hold forth to a congregation already assembled, spurred up his foundered Pegasus, and halting in the middle of the crowd, plucked out a packet of universal hodge-podge, and thus began an oration to the listening herd:

' Gentlemen, you that have a mind to be mindful of preserving a sound mind in a sound body, that is, as the learned physician, Doctor Honorificicabilitudinitatibusque has it, Manus Sanaque in Cobile Sanaquorum, may here at the expense of sixpence, furnish himself with a parcel, which though 'tis but small, yet containeth mighty things of great use, and wonderful operation in the bodies of mankind, against all distempers, whether homogeneal or complicated; whether derived from your parents, got by infection, or proceeding from an ill-habit of your own body.

' In the first place, gentlemen, I here present you with a little inconsiderable pill to look at; you see not much bigger than a corn of pepper. Yet is this diminutive panpharmica so powerful in its effect, and of such excellent virtues, that if you have twenty distempers lurking in the mass of blood, it shall give you just twenty stools, and every time it operates it carries off a distemper, but if your blood's wholesome, and your body sound, it will work with you no more than the same quantity of gingerbread. I therefore call it, from its admirable qualities, Pillula Tondobula, which signifies in the Greek, the Touchstone of Nature. For by taking this pill, you will truly discover what state of health or infirmity your constitution is then under.

' In the next place, gentlemen, I present you with an excellent outward application, called a plaster, good against all green wounds, old fistulas and ulcers, pains and aches in either head, limbs or bowels, contusions, tumours of Queen's evil, sprains, fractures or dislocations, or any hurts whatsoever, received either by sword, cane or gunshot, knife, saw or hatchet,

hammer, nail or tenterhook, fire, blaſt or gunpowder, etc. It
will continue its virtues and be as useful seven years hence as
at this present moment, so that you may lend it to your neighbours in the time of diſtress or affliction, and when it has
performed forty cures 'twill be ne'er the worse, but ſtill regain
its integrity. Probatum eſt.

' The next unparalleled medicine contained in this my little
sixpenny beneficence is an admirable powder, good to fortify
the ſtomach againſt all infections, unwholesome damps,
malignant effluvias that arise from putrid bodies, and the
like. It is also a rare cordial to ſtrengthen and clear the heart
under any misfortune and will procure such an appetite, being
drank a little before dinner, that a man of an ordinary ſtomach
may eat a pound of Suffolk cheese, and twice the quantity of
rye bread, and ſtill have as good an appetite to a sirloin of
roaſt beef, as if he had not eaten a bit in a fortnight. This
moſt excellent preparation is also the moſt powerful anti-
verminous medicine ever given in England, Scotland, France
or Ireland, and if either yourselves, or your children are
troubled with that epidemical diſtemper, worms, which deſtroy
more bodies than either plague, peſtilence or famine, give or
take this, infused in a little warm ale, inſtead of wormseed
and treacle, and you will find these death's agents, that burrow
in our bodies, as rabbits in a warren, come creeping out both
ends. It is also a moſt rare dentifrice, and cleanses all foul,
and faſtens all loose teeth, to a miracle. This powder I call
my Pulvis Lubberdatus, because in my travels, I firſt gave it
amongſt the Dutch, when I was a ſtudent at Leyden, where,
gentlemen, I would have you know, I took my degrees,
although I expose myself to the world's censures by appearing thus public, for the good of my own country which at all
times, it's well known, I have been ready to serve.

' The laſt, and moſt useful medicine prepared through the
whole universe, is this my Orvietan[1] whose virtues are such,

1 See note, page 50.

The Covt Garden Morning Frolick

(From an old print)

it will, equally with the unicorn's horn, expel the rankest poison. It is absolutely necessary for all persons to carry in their pockets, for who knows how the passions of love, fear, anger, jealousy, or the like, by the subtle insinuation of Satan who is watchful of all opportunities, may prevail upon you to offer violence to your most precious lives, by taking rats-bane, mercury, arsenic, opium and the like. Why, who, I say would be without a medicine to relieve themselves under such misfortunes, which would not only hurry 'em to death, but to damnation. It is also the best sudorific, in all colds and fevers that ever can possibly be taken, working out the dis-temper by gentle perspiration, and fortifies the heart against all fainting and swooning, also the brains against all dizziness and swimming, and is, upon the word of a physician, the greatest cordial the most eminent doctor can prescribe or patients take.

'I do assure you, gentlemen, the College of Physicians offered to admit me as a member of their society, if I would have made but a discovery only to themselves of this most excellent and admirable secret. "No, hold you me there a little, gentle-men," said I, "I shall then make you as wise as myself, and should I do that, pray who would be a fool then?" Why, truly myself, for I would have you to know, gentlemen, I have more manners than to reflect upon such a learned society.'

This impudence so tickled the ears of the brainless multitude that they began with as much eagerness to untie their purses, and the corners of their handkerchiefs, and to be free of their pence, as they usually are to buy apples by the pound, or to purchase the sight of a puppet show, that it was as much as ever the doctor could do to hand out his physic fast enough. Thus they continued flinging away their money, showing there were fools of all ages, from sixty to sixteen, many of them looking as if they could scarce com-mand as much more till next Saturday night when they received

H

their wages; till at laſt, either the doctor broke the crowd of their money, or the crowd the doctor of his physic, I know not which. Then away he trotted on horseback with their pence, and left his patients to trudge away on foot with his packets.

'Pray,' says my friend, 'what think you? Is it not a shame to our English physicians to suffer such a parcel of ignorant, illiterate and impudent vagabonds to cozen poor innocent wretches out of their money, publicly in the ſtreets, when they want it themselves to purchase bread and necessaries? I can't imagine what can be urged as an excuse for the tolerating such rascals to drain the pockets of the poor by preposterous lies, jumbled into a senseless cant, to persuade the people to believe them really that, to which they are only a scandal.'

I have here given a true portraiture of such a scandalous fellow, who makes it his business to cheat the common people not only out of their money, but often out of their health, which is far more valuable.

A CHARACTER OF A QUACK

A shame to art, to learning, and to sense,
A foe to virtue, friend to impudence,
Wanting in Nature's gift, and Heaven's grace,
An object scandalous to human race;
A spurious breed by some Tom Fool begot,
Born of some common, monſtrous God-knows-what,
Into the world no woman sure could bring
So vile a birth, such an un-man like thing.
Trained from his cradle up in vice's school,
To tumble, dance the rope, and play the fool,
Thus learned, he ſtrolls with some illit'rate quack.
Till by long travels he acquires the knack,
To make the sweepings of a druggiſt's shop;
Into some unknown universal ſlop;
On which some senseless title he beſtows,
Though what is in't nor buy'r or seller knows.

Then lazy grown, he doth his booth forsake,
Quitting the rope or hoop, and so turns quack.
Thus by base means to live, does worse pursue
And gulls the poor of life and money too.

From thence we took a turn down by the Ditch Side,[1] I desiring my friend to inform me what great advantage this costly brook contributed to the town, to make it worth the expense of £74,000, which I read in a very credible author, was the charge of its making.

He told me he was wholly unacquainted with any, unless it was now and then to bring up a few chaldron of coals to two or three peddling fuel merchants, who sell them never the cheaper to the poor for such a conveniency. 'And as for those cellars you see on each side, designed for warehouses, they are rendered by their dampness so unfit for that purpose that they are wholly useless, except for lightermen to lay their sails in, or to harbour frogs, toads and other vermin. The greatest good that ever I heard it did, was to the undertaker, who is bound to acknowledge, he has found better fishing in that muddy stream than ever he did in clear water.'

We then turned into the gate of a stately edifice which my friend told me was Bridewell.[2] At my first entrance, it seemed

---

[1] After the Great Fire the Fleet Ditch was cleansed and widened so that coal barges could go up as far as Holborn. On either side wharves and warehouses were built, stout oaken palings preserving passers-by from falling into the stream at night-time. At the lowest tide the Fleet was five feet deep. The work was undertaken by Sir Thomas Fitch, who made a fortune out of the £74,000 he was paid for the job. Sea Coal Lane commemorates the coal traffic on the Ditch.

[2] The site of old Bridewell is on the western side of New Bridge Street and stretches south of Bride Lane. A large portion of the old building was destroyed in the Great Fire, but certain rebuilding took place, and it was one of the best-known houses of correction in London. Vagrants and harlots were made to beat hemp, and, if refractory, soundly thrashed on their bare backs in the presence of the governor and court. The governor sat with a hammer in his hand, and the culprit was only taken from the whipping-post when the hammer fell. The calls to *knock* when women were being beaten were loud: 'Oh, good Sir Robert, knock! Pray, good Sir Robert, knock!' became a term of reproach, hurled at any woman to denote that she had been flogged as a harlot at Bridewell. Hogarth depicts the scene of women beating hemp in Plate IV of the Harlot's Progress.

to me rather a Prince's palace than a House of Correction, till gazing round me, I saw in a large room a parcel of ill-looking mortals stripped to their shirts like haymakers, pounding a pernicious weed, which I had thought from their unlucky aspects seemed to threaten their destruction.

'These,' said I, to my friend, 'I suppose, are the offenders at work. Pray what do you think their crimes may be?'

'Truly,' said he, 'I cannot tell you; but if you have a mind to know, ask any of them their offence, and they will soon satisfy you.'

'Prithee, friend,' said I to a surly bull-necked fellow, who was thumping lazily at his wooden anvil, 'what are you confined to this labour for?'

My hempen orator, leering over his shoulder, cast at me a hanging look which so frightened me that I stepped back, for fear he should have knocked me on the head with his beetle. 'Why, if you must know, Mr. Tickle-tail,' says he, taking me, as I believe, for some country pedagogue, 'I was committed here by Justice Clodpate, for saying I had rather hear a black bird whistle *Walsingham*[1] or a peacock scream against foul weather, than a parson talk nonsense in a church, or a fool talk Latin in a coffee-house. And I'll be judged by you that are a man of judgement, whether in all I said there be one word of treason to deserve a whipping-post.'

The impudence of this canary bird so dashed me out of countenance, together with this unexpected answer, that I had nothing to say, but heartily wished myself well out of their company. As we were turning back to avoid their further sauciness another calls to me, 'Hark you, master in black, of the same colour with the devil, can you tell me how many thumps of this hammer will soften the hemp so as to make a halter fit easy, if a man should have occasion to wear one?'

---

[1] This was a very old and popular song, beginning:
> 'As I went to Walsingham, to the shrine with speed
> I met with a jolly palmer, in a pilgrim's weed.'

A third cried out, ' I hope, gentlemen, you will be so generous as to give us something to drink, for you don't know but that we may be hard at work for you.'

We were glad to escape their impudence, and so turned from the work-room to the Common Side, or place of confinement, through the frightful gates of which uncomfortable apartment a ghastly skeleton stood peeping, whose terrible aspect was so surprising that I thought some power immortal had imprisoned Death, that the world might live for ever. I could not speak to him without dread or danger, lest when his lips opened to give me an answer, he should poison the air with his contagious breath, and communicate to me the same pestilence which had brought his infected body to such a dismal anatomy.

Yet moved with pity towards so languishing an object, I began to enquire into the causes of his sad appearance, who, after a penitential look, with much difficulty raised his feeble voice a degree above silence, and told me he had been sick six weeks under that miserable confinement, and had nothing to comfort him but bread and water, with now and then the refreshment of a little small beer.

I asked him further, what offence he had committed that brought him under this unhappiness? To which he answered, he had been a great while discharged of all that was charged against him, and was detained only for his fees, which, for want of friends, being a stranger in the town, he was totally unable to raise. I asked him what his fees amounted to? He told me five groats. Bless me! thought I, such severe, nay barbarous usage, is a shame to our laws, an unhappiness to our nation, and a scandal to Christianity.

From thence we turned into another court, the buildings being magnificently noble like the former. There straight before us was another gate, which proved the women's apartment. We followed our noses and walked up to take a view of these ladies, who we found were shut up as close as nuns. But like so many slaves they were under the care and direction of an overseer, who walked about with a very flexible weapon of offence, to correct such hempen journey-women as were unhappily troubled with the spirit of idleness. They smelt as frowsily as so many goats in a Welsh gentleman's stable, and looked with as much modesty as so many Newgate Saints canonized at the Old Bailey.

They were all cheerful over their shameful drudgery, notwithstanding their miserable circumstances. Some seemed so very young that I thought it exceeding strange they should know sin well enough to bring them so early into a state of misery. Others were so old that one would think the dread of the grave, and thoughts of futurity were sufficient to reclaim 'em from all vice, had they been trained up never so wickedly. Some between both were in the meridian of their years, and were very pretty, but seemed so very lewd that, Messalina-like, they might be tired, but never satisfied.

'Pray, sir,' says one of them, 'how do you like us? You look very wistfully upon us? What do you think of us?'

'Why, truly,' said I, 'I think you have done something to deserve this punishment, or else you would not be here.'

To which she replied, 'If you'll believe me, without blushing I'll tell you the truth. I happened to live with an old scrivener, and when my mistress was out of the way, he used to tickle my lips with a pen feather; and at last she catched me, and had me before Justice Overdo, who committed me hither. where I have had more lashes on my poor back than ever I deserved since I lost my innocence.'

'Don't believe her, master,' cries another, 'she's as arrant a strumpet as ever earned her living on the streets.'

'What do you think,' replies the other, 'this harlot came hither for? I'll tell you, master,' says she, 'because I believe you have no good guess with you. 'Twas for picking a countryman of his pouch.'

I could not but wonder to hear this impudence from women,

more especially when I considered they were under such shame, misery and punishment, which one might reasonably imagine would work upon the moſt corrupt minds, and make them abominate those base pra&ices which brought 'em to this unhappiness.

Being now tired with, and amazed at the confidence and loose behaviour of these degenerate wretches, who had neither sense of grace, knowledge of virtue, fear of shame, or dread of misery, my friend re-condu&ed me back into the firſt quad-rangle, and led me up a pair of ſtairs into a spacious chamber, where the Court was sitting in great grandeur and order.

A grave gentleman whose awful looks bespoke him some honourable citizen, was mounted in the judgement seat, armed with a hammer, like a 'Change broker at Lloyd's Coffee House, and a woman under the lash was in the next room, where folding doors were opened so that the whole Court might see the punishment infli&ed. At last down went the hammer, and the scourging ceased. The honourable Court, I observed, were chiefly attended by fellows in blue coats, and women in blue aprons.

Another accusation being then delivered by a flat-cap againſt a poor wretch, who had no friend to speak in her behalf, proclamatioñ was made, viz.: 'All you who are willing E——th T——ll should have present punishment, pray hold up your hands.' This was done accordingly, and then she was ordered the civility of the house, and was forced to shew her tender back to the grave sages of the auguſt assembly, who were moved by her modeſt mien, together with the whiteness of her skin, to give her but gentle corre&ion.

Finding little knowledge to be gained from their proceedings, and less pleasure and satisfa&ion from their punishments, my friend and I thought it better to retire, and leave them to flog on till the accusers had satisfied their revenge, and the spectators their curiosity.

' Now,' says my friend, ' pray give me your thoughts of what you have seen, whether you think this sort of correction is a proper method to reform women from their vicious practices, or not.'

'Why, truly,' said I, 'if I must deliver my opinion according to my real sentiments, I only conceive it makes many harlots but that it can in no measure reclaim 'em. I think it is a shameful indecency for a woman to expose her naked body to the sight of men and boys, as if it were designed rather to feast the eyes of the spectators than to correct vice, or reform manners, therefore I think it both more modest and more reasonable they should receive their punishment in the view of women only, and by the hand of their own sex. Moreover as their bodies by nature are more tender, and their constitutions more weak, we ought to shew them more mercy, and not punish 'em with such dog-like usage, unless their crimes were capital.'

'I believe,' replied my friend, 'you are aiming to curry favour with the fair sex. This lecture to a town lady, if you had a mind to be wicked, would save you money in your pocket, though indeed, what you have urged, seems no more than reasonable. I think I have now showed you all this place affords, so we'll take our leave of it, but I hope you will give us a few lines upon it, and we'll seek some new diversion.' I could not but gratify my friend's request, and what I did to oblige him, I here present unto the reader.

ON BRIDEWELL

'Twas once the palace of a Prince,
 If we may books confide in;
But given was, by him long since,
 For vagrants to reside in.

The crumbs that from his table fell,
 Once made the poor the fatter;
But those that in its confines dwell,
 Now feed on bread and water.

No ven'son now whereon to dine,
   No frigasies nor hashes ;
No balls, no merriment, nor wine ;
   But woeful tears and lashes.

No prince of peers to make a feast,
   No kettle-drums or trumpets,
But are become a shameful nest,
   Of vagabonds and strumpets.

Where once the King and Nobles sat,
   In all their pomp and splendour,
Grave City grandeur nods its pate,
   And threatens each offender.

Unhappy thy ignoble doom,
   Where greatness once resorted,
Now hemp and labour fills each room,
   Where lords and ladies sported.

We departed from Bridewell, and willing to refresh ourselves with the smoking of one pipe, turned into a neighbouring
coffee-house. Glancing upon an old *Flying Post*,[1] we put ourselves in mind of my Dame Butterfield's invitation to her
Essex calf and bacon, with her six brass horns to accommodate
sportsmen with the delightful harmony of hunting.[2] Believing
a relation of this unusual feast might be welcome to the public,
my friend and I agreed to move with the stream, and give
ourselves a country walk to the place appointed. I am sensible
it is something of a digression, or rather a deviation from the
title, but though the feast was in the country, yet the guests
were Londoners, and therefore what we shall observe among
'em may be reasonably admitted.

Fearing old Time should slide insensibly away and cut short
our intended pastime, we smoked our pipes with the greater

[1] *The Flying Post* was a London newspaper issued three times a week.
[2] The scene of this entertainment was at Mobs Hole, in Wanstead parish.

expedition in order to proceed on our journey, which we began about eleven o'clock. And marching through Cheapside we found half the people we either met or overtook equipped for hunting, walking backwards and forwards, as I suppose, to shew one another their accoutrements. The City beaus in boots as black as jet, which shined, by much rubbing, like a stick of ebony; their heels armed with spurs so carefully preserved bright in a box of cotton that they dazzled the eyes of each beholder; their waists hooped round with Turkey leather belts, at which hung a baggonet, or short scimitar, in order to cut their mistresses' names upon the trees of the forest; in the right hand a whip, mounted against the breast, like the sceptre of a King's statue upon the 'Change; their heads adorned with twisted wigs, and crowned with edged casters, being all over in such prim and order that you could scarce distinguish them from gentlemen. Amongst 'em were many ladies of the same quality, so be-knotted with twopenny taffaty, that a man might guess by their finery, their fathers to be ribbon weavers.

We crowded along, mixed among the herd, and could not but fancy the major part of the citizens were scampering out of town to avoid the horse-plague. We moved forward without any discontinuance of our perambulation, till we came to the Globe at Mile End, where a precious mortal made us a short-hand compliment, and gave us an invitation to a sirloin of roast beef, out of which corroborating food we renewed our lives, and after strengthening our spirits with a flask of rare claret, we took leave of my honest landlord, and so proceeded.

By this time the road was full of passengers, everyone furnished with no small appetite to veal and bacon. Citizens in crowds, upon pads, hackneys and hunters, all upon the titup, as if he who rid not a gallop was to forfeit his horse. Some spurred on with speed and cheerfulness, as if they never intended to come back again. Every now and then a lady dropped from her pillion, another from her side-saddle, which though it made them blush, it made us merry. Sometimes a beau would tumble and daub his boots which to shew his neatness, he would clean with his handkerchief.

Horses, coaches, carts, waggons and tumbrils filled the road, as if the whole town had been going to encamp; all occupied by men, women and children, rich, poor, gentle and simple, having all travelling conveniences suitable to their quality. In this order did we march, like Aaron's proselytes to worship the calf, till we came to the new raised fabric called Mobs Hole, where the beast was to be eaten. The house was so surrounded by people of all sorts and sizes that there were sufficient to have eaten all the calves in Essex instead of one. We pressed hard to get into the house, which we found so full, that when I was in I thought there was but a few gasps between this place and Eternity.

Some were dancing to a bagpipe, others whistling to a bass violin, two fiddlers scraping *Lillabolaro*, my Lord Mayor's delight, upon a couple of cracked fiddles and an old Oliverian trooper was blowing upon a trumpet.

My friend and I being willing to get as far out of the noise as we could, climbed up into a garret, where we found a single lady, rectifying her dress from the abuses of the wind. I thought myself obliged in civility, to make some little use of so fair an opportunity, and accordingly welcomed her to Mobs Hall, and at last talked her into so compliant a humour that I perceived she was as willing to give us her company as we could be to ask it, until we had brought ourselves in danger of entailing trouble and expense upon ourselves, which, to tell you the truth, we thought it was prudent to avoid. So by a cooler sort of treatment than we first began with, we gave her delicious ladyship some reasons to believe that she might go a little farther and fare better. Accordingly she took her leave and squeezed downstairs, to shew her fresh looks and inviting airiness upon the terrace, where rag-tag and bob-tail were promiscuously jumbled amongst City quality, from beau to booby, and the merchant's lady to the thumb-ringed ale-wife.

Being now left by ourselves, in a room not much bigger than a hogshead, furnished with nothing but a little bedstead, and that of an uneasy height to sit on, we found, notwithstanding our tedious walk of seven long miles, we had little likelihood of a resting-place at our journey's end, but would either be forced to lie down like dogs, or lean like elephants.

When, with abundance of pains, and as much patience, we had liquored our throats with two or three slender-bodied mugs of country guzzle, we jostled down two narrow pair of stairs, and increased the numberless troop of gazing animals, who were differently disposed in divers exercises, some cramming down veal and bacon, to allay the fury of their cormorant appetites, having no table-cloth but grass, or seats but ground; others projecting better for their ease had made a table of a horse block, and blew their noses in the same napkins with which they wiped their fingers. Some were climbed into an arbour on the top of an old tree, where they sat hooping and hallowing, like so many owls, but could get nobody near 'em to bring 'em either drink or victuals.

Some ladies sat in their coaches masked, wanting, I suppose, to give some cully a ride home, that could not pay the coachmen; others were on horseback, bare-faced, conducted thither by their father's 'prentices, and many hundreds of both sexes on foot, some smoking, some drinking, others cursing and swearing, through want of that refreshment, which the more industrious spectators had very painfully procured.

From thence we went into the kitchen, in the open air, to behold their cookery, where the major part of the calf was roasting upon a wooden spit. Having lost two or three great slices off his buttocks, his ribs pared to the very bone, with holes in his shoulders, each large enough to bury a Seville orange, he looked as if a kennel of hounds had every one had a snap at him. Upon him lay the flitch of bacon of such an

Ethiopian complexion, that I should rather have guessed it the side of a Blackamoor. It looked more like a cannibal's feaſt, than a Chriſtian entertainment.

My appetite was so far from coveting a taſte, that I had a full meal at the very sight of their dainties, and I believe for the future, I shall have as great a kindness for veal and bacon as an Anabaptiſt preacher has for the Church Liturgy.

Being soon glutted with the view of this unusual piece of cookery, we departed from the kitchen, and hearing a great buſtle in the upper room of an outhouse, we went upſtairs to see what was the matter, where we found a poor fiddler, scraping over the tune of *Now Ponder Well You Parents Dear*, and a parcel of country people dancing and crying to't. The remembrance of the uncle's cruelty to the poor innocent babes, and the Robin Redbreaſts' kindness, had fixed in their very looks such signs of sorrow and compassion that their dancing seemed rather a religious worship than a merry recreation.

Having given ourselves a proſpect of all the place afforded, we returned to Stratford, where we got a coach to London.

CHAPTER SEVEN

A Coach Ride—On the River—River Wit—Dorset Theatre—
White-Friars—A Tobacco Shop—The Temple—May Fair

OUR Stratford tub, by the assistance of its carrionly
tits of different colours, outran the smoothness of
the road and entered upon London stones with as
much frightful rumbling as an empty haycart, our leathern
conveniency having no more sway than a funeral hearse[1] or
a country waggon, so that we were jumbled about like so
many peas in a child's rattle, running a great hazard of dislocation at every jolt. This we endured till we were brought
within Whitechapel Bars, where we lighted from our stubborn
caravan, with our elbows and shoulders as black and blue as
a rural Joan that has been under the pinches of an angry fairy,
our weary limbs being rather more tired than refreshed, by
the thumps and tosses of our ill-contrived engine.

' For my part,' said I, ' if this be the pleasure of riding in a
coach through London streets, may those that like it enjoy it,
for it has loosened my joints in so short a passage, that I shall
scarce recover my former strength this fortnight. I would
rather choose to cry mouse-traps for a livelihood, than be
obliged every day to be dragged about town under such
uneasiness, and if the coaches of the quality are as troublesome as this, I would not be bound to do their penance for
their estates.'

' You must consider,' says my friend, ' you have not the right

---

[1] Coaches had no other springs than the leather straps on which they were
slung ; and the London streets being paved with cobbles and ill-matched stones,
it may be imagined how uncomfortable a coach ride might prove.

knack of humouring the coach's motion, for there is as much art in sitting in a coach finely, as there is in riding the great horse, and many a younger brother has got a good fortune by his graceful lolling in his chariot, and his genteel way of ſtepping in and out, when he pays a visit to her ladyship. There are a great many such qualifications amongſt our true French-bred gentlemen, that are admired amongſt our nicer ladies nowadays, besides the smooth dancing of the minuet, the making of a love song, the neat carving up a fowl, or the thin paring of an apple.'

'Pray, friend,' said I, ' don't let us trouble ourselves how the ladies choose their husbands, or what they do with their gallants, but consider how we shall get to the other end of the town, for my pedeſtals are so crippled with our whimsical peregrination, that I totter like a foundered horse.'

My friend answered, ' You have expressed such a dislike to a coach that I know not which way to get you thither, if you cannot walk it, except you can make your supports carry you down to the Bridge, and there we may take water at the Old Swan, and land at Salisbury Court. Then we shall be properly placed to proceed further in our ramble.'

I submitted accordingly to my friend's advice and hobbled down to the waterside, where a jolly grizzle-pated Charon handed us into his wherry, whipped off his short skirted doublet, whereon was a badge to shew whose fool he was, then fixed his ſtretcher, bid us trim the boat, and away he rowed. But we had not swum a yard or two before a scoundrel crew of Lambeth gardeners attacked us with such a volley of fancy nonsense, that it made my eyes ſtare, my head ache, my tongue run, and my ears tingle.[1]

---

[1] A curious habit existed on the river of assailing the inmates of all passing boats with a torrent of abuse—River Wit, as it was called. This lasted until long after Ward's time, and even the sedate Dr. Johnson took part in it. ' It is well known that there was formerly a rude custom for those who were sailing upon the Thames to accost each other as they passed in the most abusive language they could invent; generally, however, with as much satirical humour as

One of them began with us after this manner, 'You couple of treacherous sons of Bridewell. How dare you show your ugly faces upon the River of Thames, and to fright the Queen's swans from holding their heads above water?' To which our well-fed pilot, after he had cleared his voice moſt manfully replied, 'You lousy ſtarved crew of worm-pickers and snail-catchers. You offspring of a pumpkin, who can't afford butter to your cabbage, or bacon to your sprouts. Hold your tongue, you radish-mongers, or I'll whet my needle and sew your lips together.'

This verbal engagement was no sooner over, but another squabbling crew met us, being moſt women, who, as they passed us, gave us another salutation: 'You tailors; who pawned the gentleman's cloak to buy a wedding dinner and afterwards sold his wife's clothes for money to fetch it out again? Here, Timothy, fetch your miſtress and I three hap'worth of boiled beef, see firſt they make good weight, then ſtand hard for a bit of carrot.' To which our orator, after a puff and a pull-up, being well skilled in the water dialeƈt, made this return: 'You brood of harpies and shop lifters! Have a care of your cheeks, we shall have you branded next Sessions, that the world may see your trade in your faces. You are lately come from the hemp and hammer. O, good Sir Robert, knock; pray, good Sir Robert, knock.'[1] The next boat we met was freighted with a parcel of City shop-keepers who being eager to show the acuteness of their wit, and admirable breeding, accoſted us after this manner: 'You affidavit scoundrels, pluck the ſtraw out of the heels of your shoes. You oats journeymen, who are you going to swear out of an eſtate at Weſtminſter Hall? You rogues, we shall have you in the pillory where rotten eggs are plenty. You

they were capable of producing. Johnson was once eminently successful in this species of combat. A fellow having attacked him with some coarse raillery, Johnson answered thus: "Sir, your wife, under pretence of keeping a bawdy-house, is a receiver of stolen goods."'—(Boswell).

[1] See note, page 105.

are in a safe condition, you may travel anywhere by water and never fear drowning because you are reserved for Tyburn.' Thus they ran on, till our spokesman stopped their mouths with this following homily: 'You whistling, peddling, lying, over-reaching ninny-hammers, who were forced to desire some handsome bachelor to kiss your wives and beg a holiday for you, or else you would not have dared to come out to-day. Go make haste home, that you may find the fowls at the fire. If I had as many horns on my head as you are forced to hide in your pockets, what a monster should I be? You little think what your wives are providing for you against when you come home. Don't be angry, friends, it's many an honest man's fortune.'

Said I, 'This is a rare place for a scold to exercise her faculties and to improve her talent, for I think everybody we meet is an academy of foul language. I observe 'tis as great penance for a modest man to go a mile upon the river, as 'tis for him to run the gauntlet through an alley where the good house-wives are picking oakum; bad words being as much in fashion amongst such gossips as curses at a gaming house.'

By this time we were come to our proposed landing-place, where a stately edifice (the front supported by lofty columns) was presented to our view.[1] I enquired of my friend what magnificent Don Crœsus resided in this noble and delightful mansion. He told me, nobody as he knew on, except rats and mice, and perhaps an old superannuated jack-pudding to look after it and take care that no decayed lover of the drama should get in and steal away the poet's pictures, and sell 'em to some upholsterer for Roman Emperors. I suppose there is a little else to lose, except scenes, machines or some such

---

[1] This was the Dorset Gardens Theatre which fronted the river on the east side of Salisbury Court. It was opened by the Duke's company in 1671, but ten years later was abandoned when the company amalgamated with the King's company and moved to Drury Lane. The theatre was turned over to boxing shows and other second-rate performances, and disappeared altogether about 1721.

I

gimcracks. 'For this,' says he, 'is one of the theatres, but now wholly abandoned by the players, and 'tis thought, will in a little time be pulled down, if it is not bought by some of our dissenting brethren and converted to a more pious use, that may in part atone for the sundry transgressions occasioned by the levity which the ſtage of late has been so greatly subjeƈt to.'

Being now landed upon terra firma, we ſteered our course to Salisbury Court, where every two or three ſteps we met some old figure or another that looked as if the devil had robbed 'em of all their natural beauty, and infused his own infernal spirit into their corrupt carcases, for nothing could be read but devilism in every feature. Theft, whoredom, homicide, and blasphemy, peeped out at the very windows of their soul. Lying, perjury, fraud, impudence and misery, were the only graces of their countenance.[1]

One with slip shoes, without ſtockings, and a dirty smock (visible through a crêpe petticoat) was ſtepping from the alehouse to her lodgings, with a parcel of pipes in one hand, and a gallon pot of guzzle in the other, yet her head was dressed up to as much advantage, as if the members of her body were sacrificed to all wickedness, to keep her ill-looking face in a little finery. Another, I suppose, taken from the oyſter barrow, and set out with allurements, made a more cleanly appearance, but became her ornaments as a sow a hunting saddle. Every now and then, a fellow would bolt out and whip nimbly cross the way, being equally fearful, as I imagine, of both conſtable and serjeant, and looked as if the dread of the gallows had drawn its piƈture in his countenance.

Said I to my friend, 'What can these people be, who are so ſtigmatised in their looks that they may be known as well from the reſt of mankind as Jews from Chriſtians? They

---

[1] All this part of London was an unwholesome district where debtors and the worst criminals in London lived in security, defying the law and polluting the neighbourhood with their vices and brawling ways.

seem to be so unlike God's creatures, that I cannot but fancy them a colony of degenerate reprobates, that they admit of no comparison on this side Hell's dominions.' 'All this part,' he said, 'to the Square, is a corporation of harlots, coiners, highwaymen, pickpockets, and housebreakers, who skulk in obscure holes by daylight like bats and owls, but wander in the night in search of opportunities wherein to exercise their villainy.'

When we had taken a gentle walk through this abominable Sodom, where all the sins invented since the fall of Lucifer are daily practised, we came into Fleet Street, where the rattling of coaches loud as the cataracts of the Nile robbed me of my hearing, and put my head into as much disorder as the untunable hollows of a rural mob at a country bull-baiting.

'Now,' says my friend, 'we have a rare opportunity of re-plenishing our boxes with a pipe of fine tobacco; for the greatest retailer of that commodity in England lives in the other side of the way, and if you dare run the hazard of cross-ing the kennel, we'll take a pipe in the shop, where we are likely enough to find something worth our observation.'[1]

'Indeed,' said I, 'you may well style it a hazard, for when-ever I have occasion to go on the wrong side of the post, I find myself in dread of having my bones broke by some of these conveniences for the lame and lazy.'

However, when we had waited with patience for a seasonable minute, to perform this dangerous service, we at last ventured to shoot ourselves through a vacancy between two coaches, and so entered the smoky premises of the famous fumigator. There a parcel of ancient worshippers of the wicked weed were seated, wrapped up in Irish blankets, to defend their

[1] This was probably the shop of Benjamin Howes, at the corner of Shoe Lane, who sold 'old, mild, sweet-scented Virginia tobacco for 20d., either large cut, small cut or long cut. . . . Spanish in the roll, for 8s. a pound, and Spanish and Virginia mixed for 3s. a pound.'

withered carcases from the malicious winds that only blow upon old age and infirmity.

Their meagre jaws, shrivelled looks, and thoughtful countenances seemed to render them philosophers; their bodies seemed so very dry and light, as if they had been as hardbaked in an oven as a sea-biscuit, or cured in a chimney like a flitch of bacon, fumbling so very often at a pan of small coal, that I thought they had acquired a salamander's nature, and were seeking fire through a quill for their nourishment. They behaved themselves like such true lovers of this prevailing weed, that I dare engage custom had made their bodies incapable of supporting life by any other breath than smoke.

There was no talking amongst 'em, but puff was the period of every sentence, and what they said was as short as possible, for fear of losing the pleasure of a whiff, as 'How d'ye-do?' *Puff*. 'Thank ye.' *Puff*. 'Is the weed good?' *Puff*. 'Excellent.' *Puff*. 'It's fine weather.' *Puff*. 'G——d be thanked.' *Puff*. 'What's a clock?' *Puff*, &c.

Behind the counter stood a complaisant spark, who I observed shewed as much breeding in the sale of a pennyworth of tobacco, and the change of a shilling, as a courtier's footman when he meets his brother skip in the middle of Covent Garden; and is so very dextrous in discharge of his occupation, that he guesses from a pound of tobacco to an ounce, to the certainty of one corn; and will serve more pennyworths of tobacco in half an hour than some clumsy shopman shall be able to do in half four and twenty.

He never makes a man wait the tenth part of a minute for his change, but will so readily fling you down all sums without counting from a guinea to three pennyworth of farthings, that you would think he had it for you ready in his hand, before you asked him for it. He was very generous of his small beer to a good customer, and I am bound in justice to say thus much in his behalf, that he will show a man more civility for the taking of a penny, than many ſtiff-rump mechanics will do for the taking of a pound.

By this time the motion of our lungs had consumed our pipes, and our boxes being filled, we left the society in ſtinking miſt, parching their entrails with the drowsy fumes of the pernicious plant, which being taken so incessantly as it is by these immoderate skeletons, renders them such slaves to a beaſtly cuſtom, that they make a puff at all business, are led aſtray by following their noses, burn away their pence, and consume their time in smoke.

We soon departed hence, my friend conducting me to a place called White Friars,[1] which he told me was formerly of great service to the honeſt traders of the City, who, if they could by cant, flattery and dissimulation, procure large credit amongſt their zealous fraternity, would slip in here with their effects, take sanctuary againſt the laws, compound their debts for a small matter and oftentimes get a better eſtate by breaking than they could propose to do by trading. But now a late Act of Parliament has taken away its privilege, and since knaves can neither go broken with safety nor advantage, it is observed there are not a quarter so many shopkeepers play at bo-peep with the creditors as when they were encouraged to be rogues by such cheating conveniences.

We thus entered the debtors' garrison, where, till of late says my friend, Old Nick broached all his wicked inventions, making this place the very theatre of sin, where his moſt choice villainies were daily represented. As we passed through the gateway, I observed a ſtall of books, and the firſt that I glanced my eye upon, happened to be dignified and diſtinguished by this venerable title, *The Vanity of Chaſtity.* Bless me! thought I, sure this book was printed in Hell, and writ by the Devil, for what diabolical scribbler on earth could be the author of such unparalleled impudence? I was so surprised

---

[1] This was the famous Alsatia, a sanctuary for debtors and nesting-place for rogues of all sorts.

with the title, that I was quite thoughtless of inspecting into
the matter, but marched on until we came into the main street
of this neglected asylum, so very thin of people, the windows
broke, and the houses untenanted, as if the plague or some
like judgement from Heaven, as well as executions on earth,
had made a great slaughter amongst the poor inhabitants.

We met but very few persons within these melancholy pre-
cincts, and those by the airiness of the dresses, the forwardness
of their looks, and the affectedness of their carriage, seemed
to be some neighbouring light o' loves, who lay conveniently
to be squeezed by the young fumblers of the law; who are
apt to spend more time upon Phyllis and Chloris than upon
Coke and Littleton.

Having taken a survey of these infernal territories, where vice
and infamy were so long protected and flourished without
reproof, to the great shame and scandal of a Christian nation,
I shall therefore bestow a few lines upon this subject, which
I desire the reader to accept of:

ON WHITEFRIARS

The place where knaves their revels kept,
  And bid the Laws defiance;
Where cheats and thieves for safety crept,
Is of her filthy swarms clean swept,
Her lazy crew that skulked for debt,
  Have lost their chief reliance.

The vermin of the Law, the Bum
  Who gladly kept his distance,
Does safely now in triumph come
And if he finds the wretch at home,
He executes the fatal doom
  Without the least resistance.

Villains of ev'ry black degree,
  Were on this spot collected;
Oaths, curses, lies and blasphemy,

Passed currently from he to she,
Made virtue ſtare to hear and see
    What vices here were acted.

But now the wicked scene withdraws
    And makes an alteration;
It's purged and cleansed by wholesome laws,
And is become a sober place,
Where honeſty may show its face,
    Without disreputation.

My friend conducted me from thence through the wicket
of a great pair of gates, which brought us into a ſtately part
of that learned society, the Temple.

'This,' says my friend, 'is called the King's Bench Walk,
and here are a great many sorts of people, that are now walking to waſte their time, who are well worth your notice. We'll
therefore take two or three turns amongſt 'em and you will
find 'em the beſt living library to inſtruct mankind that ever
you met with.'

'Pray,' said I, 'what do you take that knot of gentlemen
to be, who are so merry with one another?'

'They,' replied my friend, 'are gameſters, waiting to pick
up some young bubble or other as he comes from his chamber.
They are men whose conditions are subject to more revolu-
tions than a weathercock. They are very richly dressed one
day, and perhaps out at elbows the next; they often have a
great deal of money, and are as often without a penny in their
pockets. They are Fortune's bubbles, for whatever benefits
she beſtows upon 'em with one hand she snatches away with
t'other. Their whole lives are a lottery; they read no books
but cards; all their mathematics is to truly underſtand the
odds of a bet. They very often fall out, but very seldom fight,
and the way to make 'em your friends, is to quarrel with
them. They generally begin every year with the same riches,
for the issue of their annual labours is chiefly to enrich the

pawnbroker. They are seldom in debt, because they know not where to borrow it. A pair of false dice, and a pack of marked cards sets 'em up, and an hour's unfortunate play commonly breaks 'em. They generally die inteſtate, and go as poor out of the world as they came into it.'

> As mariners with hopes their anchors weigh,
> But if cross winds, or ſtorms they meet at sea
> They damn their ſtars, and curse the low'ring day.
>
> So gameſters, when the luck of one prevails
> Above another, then the loser rails,
> Damns Fortune, and in passion bites his nails.

'You have given me a very pretty charaćter of em. But pray what sort of blades are those in antiquated wigs, whose clothes hang upon their backs as if they were not made for 'em; who walk with abundance of circumspećtion?'

'I'll tell you,' says my friend, 'they are a kind of hangers-on upon the warden of the Fleet, and the marshal of the Queen's Bench.[1] They dive into your circumſtances, and report 'em to the warden or marshal, who thus knows better how to deal with you, and screw you up to the utmoſt doit you are able to afford him. They are a kind of solicitors in this sort of business, who, whilſt they are pretending to serve you, are subtly contriving a treacherous way to pick your pocket. If any person makes his escape, they are very diligent in their enquiries after him, and if they make discovery, do secretly dispatch intelligence to the keepers aforesaid, for which they are rewarded. These are a parcel of as honeſt fellows as ever cut the throat of a friend, or robbed their own father. For a crown, they will give any bailiff help in dogging or setting even those of their acquaintance to whom they profess the greateſt friendship. They are also very serviceable agents in a bad cause. If they can say or swear anything that will do

---

[1] The two principal prisons for debtors.

your business a kindness, they will at any time, for a small fee, strain a point to your assistance. They are generally tradesmen, brought into poverty by negligence and their own profuseness, and by poverty and imprisonment have arrived to the unhappy knowledge of these shameful undertakings.

> 'Sure none like man will their own kind annoy,
> Hawks will not hawks, wolves will not wolves destroy ;
> But these inhuman sharks, worse beasts than they,
> On their own fellow-creatures basely prey;
> Surely at last such destined are to starve,
> Who can no better life than this deserve.'

' I observe,' said I, ' there are another sort of men that appear something like gentlemen, with meagre jaws and dejected countenances; each walking singly, and looking as peevish as if Fortune and he, through a mutual dislike, were frowning on each other.'

' Those, you must know,' says my friend, ' are gentlemen in distress; some coming to their estates early, before they had sense enough to preserve 'em, have been cheated by the Town parasites, taverns, women, and sharpers till reduced to misery, and made the sad examples of their own extravagance. They are now waiting with a hungry belly, to fasten upon some old acquaintance who dreads the sight of one of 'em as much as a debtor does a bailiff; but because he knew his family and him in prosperity, thinks himself obliged now and then to give him a meal, or relieve him with the gift of a shilling, which he takes with as humble an acknowledgment, as a poor parson does a dinner from his patron.

> 'How vain is Youth ? How ripe to be undone,
> When rich betimes, and made a man too soon ?
> Humour his folly, and his pride commend,
> You make him both your servant and your friend,
> But if with counsels you the wretch shall aid,
> He tells you to advise, is to upbraid,

That good your admonitions are, 'tis true,
But ſtill no more than what before he knew;
Prays you to hold your tongue, he scorns to learn of you.'

As my friend and I were walking upon the Grand Parade, I observed abundance of masked ladies with rumpled hoods and scarves, their hand charged with papers, hand-boxes, and rolls of parchment, frisk in and out of ſtaircases, like coneys in a warren, bolting from their burrows.

Said I to my friend, ' Do you think all these women that we see tripping backwards and forwards so very nimbly come hither about Law business?'

' No, no,' replied my companion, ' these are ladies that come to receive fees, inſtead of giving any. They have now extraordinary business upon their hands, with many of the young lawyers, though nothing to do with the Law; for you muſt know, these are nymphs of delight, who only carry papers in their hands for a blind. They are such considerable dealers, that they can afford to give credit for a whole vacation, and now in term-time, they are induſtrious in picking up their debts. You are now, I assure you, in one of the greateſt places of trade in Town for dealing in that sort of commodity; for moſt ladies who, for want of fortunes, despair of husbands, and are willing to give themselves up to love, without waiting for matrimony, come hither to be truly qualified for their mercenary undertaking. By the time any condescending nymph has a month's conversation with the airy blades of this honourable society, she will doubtless find herself as well fitted for the employment, as if she had had a twelvemonth's education, under the moſt experienced bawd in Chriſtendom; and if you ever chance to meet with any of the trading madams, and ask her who was her firſt lover it's ten to one but her answer will be *A Gentleman of the Temple.*'

' Pray,' said I, ' what house is this, so very different from all the reſt of the buildings?'

My friend told me 'twas the Queen's Bench Office, 'where,' says he, 'they sell broken Latin much dearer than physicians do their visits, or apothecaries their physic. Time, you know, has been always valued as a precious commodity by all men, but here they sell their minutes at an extravagant rate, as great men do their courtesies, and won't let four fingers and a thumb run once across a slip of paper, but by virtue of a custom, called the Fees of Office, they'll conjure two or three half-crowns out of your pocket, and won't put their tongues to the trouble of giving you either a Why or Wherefore for it.'

Being wonderfully pleased with the view of the Thames, the beauty of the buildings, and the airiness and spaciousness of the Court, I began to look about me with no little satisfaction; and gazing round, I espied the sundial, subscribed with this motto, *Be Gone About Your Business*.[1] 'Pray,' said I to my companion, 'what wonderful mystery lies hid in those words, for surely so learned a society would never have chosen a sentence for this purpose, unless it should be very significant, and I cannot, for my life, understand the meaning on't.'

'Truly,' said my friend, ''tis something that nobody could find out, for I never could hear it would admit of any other application or construction than what is rendered by the literal sense.'

'No,' said I, 'then I think whoever placed it here deserves to be hanged for putting such an affront upon so honourable a society.'

From thence we went towards the Hall, and turned in at a dark entry that brought us into a cloister, or piazza, where a parcel of grave blades gowned and banded, with green sacks in their hands, were busily talking alphabetically about A marrying B, and how they begat two sons, C and D, and

---

[1] This sundial was removed in 1828. It is said that the dial maker sent his lad to one of the benchers, asking him for an inscription, and the irascible old gentleman ordered the boy away with 'Begone about your business'; the lad mistook his meaning and told his master that that was to be the inscription.

how C, being the elder brother, married E, by whom he had two daughters, F and G, &c. I listened all the while with great attention, expecting I should have heard the original rise of every individual mark or letter, and how they begot one another, from A to Z throughout the alphabet, till my friend told me it was their method of stating a case, which made me blush at my ignorance. Heads, tongues, feet and hands were all moving, which occasioned me to fancy their reading so much Law French had inspired them with the Gallic grace of so much action in their talk.

We left them debating the weighty difference between John of Oaks and John of Stiles and marched forward, till we came into the Inner Temple, as my friend informed me, where we had a fine prospect of a stately hall and pleasant fountain.

Here we also found walking sundry sorts of loiterers, some I believe, through good husbandry, having chosen the broad stones for the prevention of the rough gravel wearing out of their shoe soles, others for the ease of their corns. Some were country clients, with grey coats and long staves, desired to walk there by their lawyers, I suppose, whilst their business was dispatched so that they should not spoil their chamber-floors with their hobnails. Here and there amongst 'em was a creeping old fellow, with so religious a countenance that he looked as if he had spent more pounds in law than ever he read letters in the Gospel, and had paid in his time as much money for declarations, pleas, orders and executions, sub-poenas, injunctions, bills, answers and decrees, as ever it cost him in the maintenance of his family.

' Now,' says my friend, ' I believe we are both tired with the labours of the day. Let us therefore dedicate the latter part purely to pleasure, take a coach and go and see May Fair.'

' Would you have me,' said I, ' undergo the punishment of a coach again, when you know I was so great a sufferer by the last, that it made my bones rattle in my skin, and has brought as many pains about me, as if troubled with the rheumatism ? '

'That was a country coach,' says he, 'and only fit for the road, but London coaches are hung more loose, to prevent your being jolted by the roughness of the pavement.'

This argument of my friend's prevailed upon me to venture my carcase a second time to be rocked in a Hackney cradle. So, we took leave of the Temple, turned up Temple Bar, and there took a coach for the general rendezvous aforementioned.

By the help of a great many slashes and hey-ups, and after as many jolts and jumbles, we were dragged to May Fair,[1] where the harsh sound of untunable trumpets, the catter-wauling scrapes of thrashing fiddlers, the grumbling of beaten calves-skin, and the discording toots of broken organs, set my teeth on edge, like the filing of a hand-saw, and made my hair ſtand as bolt upright as the quills of an angry porcupine.

We ordered the coach to drive through the body of the Fair, that we might have the better view of the tinsel heroes and gazing multitude, expeƈting to have seen several corporations of ſtrolling vagabonds, but there proved but one company, amongſt whom merry-andrew was very busy in coaxing the attentive crowd into a good opinion of his fraternities and his own performances; and when, with abundance of labour, sweat and nonsense, he had drawn a great cluſter of the mob on his parade, and was juſt beginning to encourage them to walk in and take their places, his unlucky opposite, whose boarded theatre entertained the public with the wonderful aƈtivity of Indian rope-dancers, brings out a couple of chatter-ing homunculuses, dressed up in scaramouch habit. Every-thing that merry-andrew and his second did on the one side,

---

[1] This was St. James's Fair, held every May in Brook Field, which is now occupied by Curzon Street, Hertford Street. It was suppressed in 1708 on account of the rowdiness and disorder that took place. Strype says, 'Young people did use to resort thither and by the temptation they met with there did commit much sin and disorder. Here they spent their time and money in drunkenness, fornication, gaming and lewdness, whereby were occasioned often-times quarrels, tumults and shedding of blood.'

was mimicked by the little flat-nosed comedians on the other, till the two diminutive buffoons, by their comical gestures had so prevailed upon the gaping throng that though merry-andrew had taken pains, with all the wit he had, to collect the straggling rabble into their proper order, yet, like an un-mannerly audience, they turned their backs upon the players, and devoted themselves wholly to the monkeys, to the great vexation of tomfool, and all the strutting train of imaginary lords and ladies.

At last out comes the figure of a careful nurse, dressed up in a country jacket, and under her arm a kitten for a nursling, and in her other hand a piece of cheese. Down sits the little matron, with a motherly countenance, and when her youngster mewed she dandled him, and rocked him in her arms, with as great signs of affection as a loving mother could well shew to a discordant infant. Then she bit a piece of the cheese, and after she had mumbled it about in her own mouth, thrust it with her tongue into the kitten's, just as I have seen some nasty old sluts feed their own grandchildren.

Beyond these were a parcel of scandalous boozing kens, where soldiers and their trulls were skipping and dancing to most lamentable music, performed upon a cracked fiddle by a blind fiddler. In another hut a parcel of Scotch pedlars were dancing a Highlander's jig to a horn-pipe. Over against 'em was the Cheshire booth, where a gentleman's man was playing tricks with his heels in a Cheshire round. These intermixed here and there with a puppet-show, where a senseless dialogue between Punchinello and the Devil was conveyed to the ears of a listening rabble through a tin squeaker, which was thought by some of 'em as great a piece of conjuration as ever was performed by Dr. Faustus.

We now began to look about us, and take a view of the spectators, but could not, amongst the many thousands, find one man that appeared above the degree of a gentleman's valet. In all the multitudes that ever I beheld, I never in my

life saw such a number of lazy rascals, and so hateful a throng
of beggarly, sluttish ſtrumpets, who were a scandal to the
Creation, mere antidotes againſt lechery, and enemies to
cleanliness.

As we were thus rambling through the fair, a coach overtook
us, wherein were a couple of girls, whose silken temptations
and more modeſt deportment gave them a juſt title to a
higher consideration than the white apron witches, who were
sitting in the crowd, could pretend to. An arch country
bumpkin having picked up a frog in some of the adjacent
ditches, peeping into the coach as he passed by, was very
much affronted that they hid their faces with their masks.
'Ads Blood,' says he, ' you look as ugly in those black vizards
as my toad here, e'en get you altogether,' and tossed it into
the coach. At this the frightened ladybirds squeaked out,
opened the coach doors, and leaped out amongſt the throng
to shed their loathsome companion.

The adjacent mob being greatly pleased at the countryman's
sport, set up a laughing as loud as an huzza, to make good
the jeſt, which occasioned the coachman to look back. Knowing nothing of the matter, and seeing his fares out of the coach,
he thought they were about to bilk him. He lighted out of
his box, and in a great fury seized one of them by the scarf,
accoſting them in these words, ' Z——ds! what, would you
bilk me? Pay me my fare, or by Gog and Magog you shall
feel the smart of my whipcord before you go a ſtep farther.'
The harlots endeavoured to satisfy their angry charioteer that
they were women of more honour than to attempt so ill an
aćtion, telling him, as well as their surprise would give them
leave, the occasion of their lighting. But this would not con-
vince the choleric driver, who refused either to quit his hold,
or suffer them to go again into his coach till they had paid
him eighteenpence, which he demanded as his fare. But they
had it not to give him, presuming to have met with some cully
in the fair that might have answered their purpose; so that

rather than stand a whipping, one of them took notice of his number, and gave him her scarf as a pledge. Notwithstanding this, he refused to carry them back for fear they might call upon some bully or other that might make him deliver up his security without any other redemption than a thrashed jacket. Thus were the unfortunate madams dismounted of their coach, and were forced to mob it on foot with the rest of their sisters.

There being nothing further that occurred, or anything to be seen worthy of notice, only a Turkey ram, with as much wool upon his tail as would load a wheelbarrow, and a couple of tigers, grown now so common they are scarce worth mentioning, I shall therefore conclude the account we give you of May Fair.

CHAPTER EIGHT

St. James's Palace and Park—Westminster Abbey and Hall—
Chancery—Whitehall—Scotland Yard

FOR want of glasses to our coach, having drawn up our tin-sashes,[1] pinked like the bottom of a cullender, that the air might pass through the holes, and defend us from stifling, we were conveyed from the Fair, through a suffocating cloud of dusty atoms, to St. James's Palace, in reverence to which we alighted and discharged our grumbling driver, who stuck very close behind us, and muttered heavily, according to their old custom, for another sixpence, till at last moving us a little beyond our patience, we gave an angry positive denial to his unreasonable importunities, and so parted with our unconscionable carrion-scourger, who we found, like the rest of his fraternity, had taken up the miserly immoral rule, Never to be satisfied.[2]

We passed through a lofty porch into the first Court, where a parcel of hobnailed loobies were gazing at a whale's rib with great amazement; being busily consulting what creature it could be that could produce a bone of such unusual magnitude. Who should come by in this juncture, but an Irishman. Seeing the country hobbies stand gaping at this puzzling rarity, he put himself among the rest to deliver his judgement of this amazing object. 'I pray you, sir,' says one

---

[1] Hackney coaches were not furnished with glass windows but had a sheet of tin, perforated with small holes, which could be drawn up in bad weather.

[2] It is curious that in all ages and in all places drivers of public vehicles have lived up to this motto.

of the countrymen to him, ' what sort of a bone do you take this to be?' To which the Dear Joy,[1] after taking a little snuff, most judiciously replied, ' By my shoul, begorroa, I believe it is the jaw bone of the ass wid which Sampson killed the Phillistians, and it ish nailed up here dat nobody should do any more mischief wid it.' ' I wonder,' said another of the plough jobbers, ' how he could use it, 'tis such a huge unwieldy weapon?' ' By my shoul,' replied Teague. ' Let Sampson look to dat his own shelf, for it ish none of my business.'

From thence we went through the Palace into the Park about the time when the Court ladies raise their extended limbs from their downy couches, and walk into the Mall to refresh their charming bodies with the cooling and salubrious breezes of the gilded evening. We could not possibly have chosen a luckier minute, to have seen the delightful park in its greatest glory and perfection, for the brightest stars of the Creation were moving here, with such an awful state and majesty, that their graceful deportment bespoke 'em Goddesses. Such merciful looks were thrown from their engaging eyes upon every admiring mortal; they were so free from pride, envy or contempt, that they seemed, contrary to experience, to be sent into the world to complete its happiness. The wonderful works of Heaven were here to be read in beauteous characters. Such elegant compositions might be observed among the female quality, that it's impossible to conceive otherwise than that such heavenly forms were perfected after the unerring image of Divine excellence.

I could have gazed for ever with inexpressible delight, finding in every lovely face and magnificent behaviour, something new to raise my admiration, with due regard to Heaven for imparting to us such shews of celestial harmony, in that most beautiful and curious creature Woman.

---

[1] Dear Joy and Teague were terms popularly applied to an Irishman in the 17th century, much as Paddy was used some centuries later.

Woman (when good) the best of Saints,
    That bright, seraphic lovely she!
Who nothing of an angel wants,
    But truth and immortality.

Whose silken limbs, and charming face,
    Keeps Nature warm with amorous fire,
Was she with wisdom arm'd and grace,
    What greater bliss could man desire ?

For troubles would our lives annoy,
    Could man on wav'ring beauty trust,
But her misguidance mars the joy,
    Thro' want of wisdom to be just.

How blessed a state would marriage be,
    Were but her temper and her love,
From lust and revolution free,
    How great a blessing would she prove ?

But pride of being great and gay,
    Tempts her to deviate by degrees,
From virtue's paths, and run astray
    For gaudy plumes and lolling ease.

Could beauty in her dressing glass,
    The charms of innocence but see,
How virtue gilds her awful face,
    She'd prize the darling rarity.

For she that's lovely, just and kind,
    Does blessings to a husband bring,
But if her honour's once resigned,
    Tho' fair, she's but a pois'nous thing.

Though I was greatly affected with the majestic deportment
of the female sex, each looking with a presence as well worthy
of Diana's bow, or Bellona's shield, as the golden apple of
Venus, yet I could by no means reconcile myself to the sheepish
humility of their cringing worshippers, who were guilty of so
much idolatry to the fair sex that I thought the laws of

Creation were greatly transgressed, and that man had dwindled from his first power and authority into pusillanimity and luxury, and had suffered deceitful women to cozen him of his prerogative. The men looked so effeminate, and shewed such cowardly tameness by their extravagant submission, as if they wanted courage to exercise that freedom which they had a just title to use.

It seemed to me as if the world was turned top-side-turvy, for the ladies looked like undaunted heroes, fit for government or battle, and the gentlemen like a parcel of fawning, flattering fops, that could bear deception with patience, make a jest of an affront, and swear themselves very faithful and humble servants to the petticoat, creeping and cringing in dishonour to themselves, to what were decreed by Heaven their inferiors.

Having thus seen what the Mall afforded, we stepped into Duke Humphrey's Walk, as my friend informed me, where he showed me an abundance of men who were walking away their leisure hours beneath the umbrage of the lime-trees and crawling about backwards and forwards, like so many straggling caterpillars in a grove of sycamores, who, for want of other food, are ready to devour the very leaves that bred them. So these looked as sharp as if they were ready to swallow their best friends for want of other subsistence.

'This walk,' says my friend, 'is a rare place for a woman who is rich enough to furnish herself with a gallant that will stick close, if she will allow him good clothes, three meals a day, and a little money for usquebaugh. If she like him when she has him, she need not fear of losing him as long as she's worth a groat, for they are very constant to anybody that has money, and he will measure out his affection by her generosity, and she will surely find (at her own cost) that nothing but her poverty will make him look out for a new mistress.

'The worthy gentlemen who chiefly frequent this sanctuary are non-commissioned officers. I mean not such who have left their commission, but such as never had any, and yet would be very angry should you refuse to honour them with the title of Captain, though they never so much as trailed a pike towards the deserving it.'

From thence we took a walk upon the Parade, which my friend told me used in a morning to be covered with the bones of red-herrings, and smelt as strong about breakfast time, as a wet-salter's shop at midsummer. 'But now,' says he, 'it's perfumed again with English breath, and the scent of Oronoko tobacco no more offends the nostrils of our squeamish ladies, who may now pass backwards and forwards free for all such nuisances; and, if with child, without the danger of being frighted at a terrible pair of Dutch whiskers.' [1]

From thence we walked up to the Canal, where ducks were striking about the water, and standing upon their heads, showing as many tricks in their liquor as a Bartholomew Fair tumbler. Said I to my friend, 'Her Majesty's ducks are wond'rous merry.' He replied, 'Well they may be, for they are always tippling.'

We then took a view of the famed figure of the Gladiator,[2] which indeed is well worthy of the place it stands in, for the exactness of its proportion, the true placing and expressing of the exterior muscles, veins and arteries, show such a perfection of art, that justly deserves our admiration. Behind this figure, upon the foot of the pedestal, my friend and I sat down to please our eyes with the prospect of the most delightful aqueduct and to see its feathered inhabitants, the ducks, divert us with their sundry pastimes. At this moment, who should come up to the front of the Gladiator but two or three merry buxom ladies, who, I suppose, by their exceptions against the statue, were women of no little experience, but very com-

[1] An allusion to the Dutch followers of William III, who used to walk in the Park.
[2] A bronze statue in the nude, which stood about where the Guards' Memorial has been erected on the Horse Guards' Parade. It is now at Windsor.

petent judges of what they undertook to censure. One of them, more forward to arraign the artist than the rest, not knowing we were behind, expressed herself with abundance of scorn and contempt, after this manner: ' Is this the fine proportioned figure I have heard my husband so often brag on? It's true, his legs and arms are strong and manly. But that's all that can be said about him.' With that my friend starts up, and like a company of merry wagtails, they ran away tittering and laughing.

We arose from thence, and walked up by the Decoy,[1] where the water glided so smoothly beneath osier canopies, that the calm surface seemed to express that nothing inhabited this watery place but peace and silence. I could have wished myself capable of living obscure from mankind in this element, like a fish, purely to have enjoyed the pleasure of so delightful a luminous labyrinth, whose intricate turnings so confound the sight that the eye is still in search of some new discovery, and never satisfied with the tempting variety so artificially ordered within so little a compass.

We turned up from thence into a long Lime walk [Birdcage Walk], where both art and nature had carefully preserved the trees in such exact proportion to each other that a man would guess by their appearance that they aspire in height, and spread in breadth to just the same dimensions, and confine their leaves and branches to an equal number beneath this regular and pleasant shade, where pensive lovers whisper their affections to their mistresses, and breathe out despairing sighs of their desired happiness. Here also were the tender off-spring of nobility taken by their fresh-looking nurses, to strengthen and refresh their feeble joints with air and exercise suitable to their childish weakness; and some were accompanied by their tutors, showing much manliness in their

---

[1] The Decoy, consisting of five or six parallel canals, connecting with the large Canal, was at the south-east corner of St. James's Park, between the Canal and Birdcage Walk. It was filled up in 1790.

presence, and such promises of virtue in their propitious looks at ten or a dozen years of age, that they seemed already fortified with grace, learning and wisdom against the world's corruptions.

The termination of this delectable walk was a knot of lofty elms by a pond side,[1] round some of which were commodious seats for the tired ambulators to refresh their weary pedestals. Here a parcel of old worn-out cavaliers were conning over the Civil Wars, and looking back into the history of their past lives, to moderate their anxiety and infirmities of age with pleasing reflections on their youthful actions.

Amongst the rest, a country curmudgeon was standing with his back against a tree, leaning forward on his oaken companion his staff, and staring towards the top of a high adjacent elm.

' Pray, friend,' said I, ' what is it you are so earnestly looking for ? ' He answered me, 'At yonder bird's nest.' I further asked him what bird's nest it was? He replied, ' What a foolish question you ask me ! Why did you ever know anything but rooks build so near the Queen's Palace ? '

This innocent return put my friend and me into laughter. I asked him if he did not think they were noble trees? ' Yes, zure,' says he, ' if the Queen's trees should not be noble, pray whose should ? ' ' I mean,' said I, ' don't they thrive and spread finely ? ' ' They have nothing else to do,' says he, ' as I know on. Everything thrives that stands upon Crown land, zure, and so does my landlord.'

Having seen chiefly what the Park afforded, we sat ourselves down beneath the pleasant umbrage of this most stately arbour, by the pond side, where I composed this following acrostic on Saint James's Park, at the reader's service.

---

[1] This was Rosamond's Pond, which was in the south-west corner of the Park opposite where is now Buckingham Gate. It was a great place of rendezvous and finds frequent mention in literature. The pond was filled up in 1770 when Buckingham House was bought by the Crown.

S ure Art and Nature, nowhere else can show
A park where trees in such true order grow.
 I n silver ſtreams the gentle Isis here
N o banks o'er flows, yet proudly swells so near,
T he pleasing cup does juſt brimful appear.

 J n Summer's longeſt days, when Phœbus takes
A pride to pierce the thickeſt shades and brakes,
M ay beauties walk beneath a verdant screen,
E xempt from duſt, and by the sun unseen.
 S o thick with leaves each plant, so green the grass,
 S ure mortal never viewed a sweeter place.

 P revailing ladies meet in lovely swarms,
A nd bless each day its umbrage with their charms.
R ev'rence the Stuarts' name for this hereafter
K ing James the Firſt clubb'd wood, his grandson Charles found
    water.

When by an hour's enjoyment we had rendered the beauty
of the Park but flat and dull to our palled appetites, we began
to think of some new objeɕt that ought to feaſt and refresh
our tired senses with pleasures yet untaſted; accordingly we
took our leave of the Park. We went through a narrow passage
that direɕted us towards Weſtminſter, in order to take a view
of that ancient and renowned ſtruɕture, the Abbey, to which
I was an utter ſtranger.

When we came in sight of this sacred edifice, I could not
behold the outside of the awful pile without reverence and
amazement. It was raised to such a ſtupendous height, and
beautified with such ornamental ſtatues that the bold ſtrokes
of excelling artiſts, whilſt the building ſtands, will always
remain visible. The whole seemed to want nothing that could
render it truly venerable. On the north side we entered the
magnificent temple with equal wonder and satisfaɕtion, which
entertained our sights with such worthy monuments and
aſtonishing antiquities that we knew not which way to direɕt
our eyes, each objeɕt was so engaging. We took a general

survey of all that's to be seen in the open parts of the church, where almost every stone gives a brief history of the memorable actions due to their pious ashes to whom the table appertaineth.

By this time the bells began to chime for afternoon prayers, and the choir was opened, into which we went, amongst many others, to pay with reverence that duty which becomes a Christian. There our souls were elevated by the divine harmony of the music, far above the common pitch of our devotions, whose heavenly accents have such an influence upon a contrite heart that it strengthens our zeal, fortifies the loose imagination against wandering thoughts, and gives a man a taste of immortal blessings upon earth, before he is thoroughly prepared for the true relish of celestial comforts. When we had given our souls the refreshment of this enlivening exercise, we made an entrance into the east end of the Abbey, which is kept locked, and payed a visit to the venerable shrines and sacred monuments of the dead nobility, where the virtues and magnanimous actions of our heroic princes are conveyed to their posterity, by the sundry inventions of our ingenious ancestors, as epitaphs, effigies, arms, emblems and hieroglyphics.

When we had satisfied ourselves with a view of these ancient curiosities, we ascended some stone steps, which brought us to a chapel that may justly claim the admiration of the whole universe, such inimitable perfections are apparent in every part of the whole building, which looks so far exceeding human excellence, that a man would think it was knit together by the fingers of angels, pursuant to the directions of Omnipotence.

From thence we were conducted by our little guide to King Charles the Second's effigy,[1] and as much as he excelled his predecessors in mercy, wisdom and liberality, so does his effigy exceed the rest in liveliness, proportion and magnificence.

[1] This was the wax figure, now exhibited in Abbot Islip's Chapel. It originally stood, protected in a case, in Henry VII's Chapel, where Charles is buried.

Having satisfied our curiosity with a sight of what was chiefly admirable, we came again into the body of the church, where my friend and I began to consider of some things which we did not think were consistent with piety, or the glory of that Power to whom the holy pile is dedicated, which are these:

1. That the Parish poor of St. Margaret's should be suffered to beg within the Abbey, even in prayer-time.

2. That those who are chosen as particular agents in the service of God [i.e. choristers] should be permitted to sing in the Play-house.

3. That the monuments should lie defaced, some with their hands off, and some with their feet off and thrown by them, without reparation.

4. That women should have Hebrew, Greek and Latin epitaphs, who never understood a word of the languages.

5. That Ben Jonson should want a tomb, and lie buried from the rest of the poets.

6. That the monument of Squire Thynne[1] whose death was so remarkable, should be without any inscription.

Having now satisfied our senses with the sight of the sundry curiosities contained within the reverend building, being Term time, we steered our course towards Westminster Hall. But just as we came out of the north portico of the Abbey, a company of Train-bands was drawn up in the yard in order to give their captain a parting volley. I could not forbear laughing to see so many greasy cooks, tun-bellied lick-spiggots, and fat wheezing butchers, sweating in their buff doublets, under the command of some fiery-faced brewer, whose belly was hooped in with a golden sash, which the clod-skulled hero

---

[1] Thomas Thynne, of Longleat, a well-known figure in London, was murdered in 1682 as he was driving his coach along Pall Mall. The murder was committed by Captain Vratz and two hired assassins, at the instigation of Count Königsmarck, who had aspired to the hand of Lady Elizabeth Percy, sole heiress of the last Earl of Northumberland, who married Thynne in 1681.

became as well as one of his dray-horses would an embroidered saddle.

When the true-blue officer (over-thoughtful of hops and grain) had by two or three mistaken words of command hustled his courageous company into close confusion, instead of order, he bid 'em make ready, which made half of them change colour, and show as much cowardice in cocking their muskets, as if half a dozen Turks had faced 'em and frighted 'em with their whiskers. Then the noble captain advancing his silver-headed cane over his head between both his hands, gave the terrible word *Fire!* popping down his noddle, like a goose under a barn door, to defend his eyesight from the flashes of gunpowder. Meanwhile, such an amazing clap of thunder was sent forth from the rusty kill-devils that it caused fear and trembling amongst all those that made it, for which the little boys gave them the honour of a great shout; then away trudged the foundered soldiers home to their wives, well satisfied.

We then marched towards the Palace Yard, which we found full of hackney coaches standing rank and file in as much order as if they had been marshalled ready for a funeral. When we had made more turnings and windings amongst the coaches, than ever were known in fair Rosamond's bower, we arrived at the Hall Gate, within which innumerable crowds of contending mortals were charming the ears of the judges with their rhetorical music. We first gave our attention at the Common Pleas, where my friend and I were much delighted, sometimes with elegant speeches from the Bench, as well as the pleasing eloquence, and powerful reasonings at the Bar.

An old yeoman happened to be a witness in one cause, and after he had sworn very heartily and knowingly in a matter of great antiquity, the counsel on the opposite side asked him how old he was. To this he answered, at first, gravely in these words, ' I am old enough to be your father, and therefore, I hope, young man, you will give that respect to my grey hairs that is due to 'em.' 'That,' replied the counsel, 'is no answer to my question. I desire to know how many years old you account yourself, for I am very apt to believe you have sworn positively to some things that are beyond your knowledge.' 'I would have you consider, Sir,' says the old gentleman, 'I am of a very great age. I am in my fourscore and seventeenth year, and yet, I thank God for it, I have memory and sense enough still left, to make a knave an answer.' With that the Court burst into a laughter which dashed the lawyer out of countenance, and made him ashamed of making any further interrogatives.

From thence we moved towards the upper end of the Hall, through such a crowd that we were shoved about like a couple of owls fallen into a company of rooks and jackdaws. As we were thus squeezing along towards the Chancery Bar, a couple of country fellows met, and greeted one another after the following manner. 'How d'ye, neighbour?' says one, 'is your suit ended yet?' 'No, trowly,' said the other, 'nor can anybody tell when it wool. To spaik the truth, neighbour, I believe my returney's a knave.' 'How shid a be otherwise,' replied the first, 'for thou seeth there are so many of 'em here, that it's impossible they shid live honestly one by another.'

We were now got to the Chancery Court, where so many smooth tongues were so vigorously contending for equity, that we found by their long harangues, and strenuous arguments, it was not to be obtained but with difficulty. Whilst we were giving our attention to that engaging harmony which flowed with such a careless fluency from their well-tuned instruments of oratory, a cause was called, wherein a tailor happened to be the chief witness. The counsel on the other side knowing his profession, took an occasion to give him this caution, 'I understand, friend, you are by trade a tailor. I would advise you to use more conscience in your depositions than you do in your bills, or else we shall none of us believe you.' ' Truly, sir,' says the tailor, ' our trade, I muſt confess, does lie under a great scandal, but if you and I were in a room together, and the Devil should come in and ask for a thief and a liar, I wonder which of us would be moſt frightened?'

We adjourned from thence to the Queen's Bench Bar, where two pleaders, very eager in dispute, were mixing their arguments with some reflections one upon another. A countryman happening to ſtand juſt by 'em seemed mightily pleased to hear 'em at such variance. At laſt, being unable to contain himself any longer, he broke out into these words: ' Well, said i'faith; this I hope will make the old Proverb good, That when knaves fall out, honeſt men will come by their right.' A little after, one of the counsel in a heat happened to say rashly, if what he had offered was not law, he'd juſtify the law to be a lottery; says the countryman, ' I wish heartily it was so, for then it would be put down by the late Act of Parliament, and I should fling away no more money at it, for I am sure it has kept me and my family as poor as Job, this fifteen years.'

From thence we walked down by the sempſtresses, who were very nicely fingering and pleating turnovers and ruffles for the young ſtudents, and coaxing them with their amorous looks, obliging cant, and inviting geſtures, to give so extravagant a price for what they buy, that they may now and then afford to fling them a night's lodging into the bargain.

We now began to take notice of the building, which seemed as noble as 'twas ancient; and looking upwards, could do no less than greatly admire the timber roof, being finely built after the Gothic order. But that which was chiefly to be observed in it, was the cleanliness thereof, it being as free from duſt and cobwebs, as if 'twas raised yeſterday.

' This,' says my friend, ' occasions some people to conjecture it is built with Irish oak, to which is ascribed this miraculous virtue, that no spiders, or any such sort of nauseous and offensive insects will ever breed or hang about it.'

' But,' said I, ' are you apt to give credit to this vulgar error, and attribute its cleanness to any quality of the wood? '

' No,' says he, ' I am apt to believe all such notions to be vain and fabulous; and that its continuing free from all such nasty vermin proceeds from another reason.'

' Pray,' said I, ' let's hear your conjecture concerning it; for I assure you, I look upon it to be very strange that a wooden roof of such antiquity should be so very free of all that filth which is most commonly collected in such old fabrics.'

' Why then,' says he, ' I'll frankly tell you my opinion, which, if it seems incongruous to your reason, I hope you will be so friendly as to excuse my weakness. You must consider,' says he, ' that the young lawyers are unhappily liable to abundance of mischances, and often require the use of mercury to repair their health, some subtle particles of which being emitted with their breath, ascend by their volatility to the top of the hall, where it condenses itself, and lies upon the beams, and so by its poisonous quality renders the roof obnoxious of all vermin. For this is certainly true, that let any person that has taken a mercurial dose, but breathe upon a spider, and it will die immediately.'

' This,' said I, ' is well enough from a surgeon, for men of your profession may take the liberty of talking like apothecaries, and not be censured for it, but I think you have fitted me with a piece of as dark philosophy as any to be found in Aristotle's masterpiece.'

Meeting with nothing further, much worth our observation, I think it may not be improper to conclude our remarks of this place, with the character of a pettifogger.

He's an amphibious monster, partaking of two natures, and those contrary; he's a great lover of peace and enmity and has no sooner set people together by the ears, but is soliciting the Law to make an end of the difference. His

learning is commonly as little as his honesty, and his conscience
much larger than his green bag. His affection for the Law
proceeds from the litigiousness of his ancestors, who brought
the family to beggary. Therefore there is nothing he abhors
more than poverty in a client. He is never more proud than
when he has a fee for a topping counsel, and would make
anybody believe Sergeant Such-a-One and he are great friends.

He gets money in Term time by sitting in a tavern, till he
has sold a quart or two at that rate, and puts the overplus
in his pocket. He seems always as busy as a merchant in
'Change time, and if ever a cause is carried that he's concerned in, he tells you it's owing to his management. Catch
him in what company soever, you will always hear him stating
of cases, or telling what notice my Lord Chancellor took of
him.

He always talks with as great assurance as if he understood
what he pretends to know. He concerns himself with no
justice but the justice of a cause, and for making an unconscionable bill, he outdoes a tailor. He is very understanding
in the business of the Old Bailey, and knows as well how to
fee a juryman as he does a barrister. He puts more faith in
the Law, than he does in the Gospel, and knows no other
religion than to get money. He has often that text of Scripture
in his mouth, The labourer is worthy of his hire, which is as
much as to say, he would not waste time to read a chapter in
the Bible without being paid for it.

Meet him wheresoever in Term time, and ask him, Whither
go you? And his answer shall be To Westminster. And indeed
you may find him in the Hall much oftener than he that has
ten times the business there, for he is one of those that loves
to hear how other people's matters go, though it does not at
all concern him. In short, he's a caterpillar upon earth, who
grows fat upon the fruits of others' labour; a mere horse-
leech in the Law, that when once he is well fastened, will
suck a poor client into a deep consumption.

Having thus taken notice of most things remarkable in the Hall, we made our exit from thence, and crossed the Palace Yard, on the east side of which lay the relics of Westminster stone clock-case, in a confused heap of ruin.[1]

'There's nothing,' says my friend, 'troubles me more than to see any piece of antiquity demolished. It always puts me in mind of the ignoble actions of the unsanctified rebels in the late domestic troubles, who made it their business to deface old images, and with sacrilegious hands threw down the urns and spoiled the monuments of the dead—a base and inglorious revenge, to gratify their choleric zeal, by robbing their own native country of its ancient beauties. It is a crime abominated by the most savage and unpolished people in the whole universe, and that Christians should be guilty of such barbarity that is held detestable among the worst of heathens, is very strange. I speak not this,' says he, 'to reflect upon the destruction of this old steeple, which was wholly useless when they had removed the clock to St. Paul's, which indeed, is far more worthy of so ponderous a bell, that affords so grave a sound.'

The common people have a notion (but of no authority as I know on) that this bell was paid for by a fine levied upon some judge, for the unlawful determination of some weighty affair in which he suffered himself to be bribed to partiality, and that it was converted to the use of a clock, with this moral intent, that whenever it struck, it might be a warning to all succeeding magistrates in the Courts at Westminster, how they do injustice. But if it were so, the judges and lawyers in this more religious age are so free from corruption that they need no other motives or memorandums to discharge their trust with unbiased honesty, than the unerring dictates of their own good conscience, so my loud-mouthed friend

[1] This was an ancient stone clock tower, in which hung the great bell of Westminster named Old Tom. In 1689 this bell was removed to St. Paul's and the old tower allowed to fall into ruin.

A Perspective View of CHARING CROSS. | Vuï de CHARING CROSS.,

A view from the west, showing (*left*) the Royal Mews, which were pulled down when Trafalgar Square was made; old Northumberland House; and (*right*) the beginning of Whitehall.

(*From an old print*)

may very well be spared to a better purpose, and hang within the hearing of all the cuckolds in the City, to call their wives twice a day to prayers, that they may ask forgiveness for the great injury they did their husbands the laſt opportunity, and also to proclaim, by the gravity of its sound, the greatness of that huge, huge, huge Cathedral, which is big enough to hold more souls than Weſtminſter Abbey, though it is not half so venerable.

From the Palace Yard we moved on progressively till we came to the tennis court, but could not for my life imagine what place that could be, hung round with such a deal of network. At laſt, thinks I, I have heard of such a place as a Plot office. I fancy this muſt be it, and those are the projeċtors' nets to catch such Jacobite fools who have no more wit than to be drawn into the design. But however, not well satisfied with my own nation, I thought it proper to enquire of my friend, before I told him my sentiments, leſt, through an innocent miſtake, I should give him juſt occasion to laugh at my ignorance.

He informed me 'twas a conveniency built for the noble game of tennis, a very delightful exercise, much used by persons of quality, and attended with these extraordinary good properties; it is very healthful to him that plays at it, and it is very profitable to him that keeps it. And rightly considered, it's a good emblem of the world. As thus, the gameſters are the great men, the racquets are the Laws, which they hold faſt in their hands, and the balls are the little mortals, which they bandy backwards and forwards from one to t'other, as their own will and pleasure direċts 'em.

We passed by this and went forward to Whitehall,[1] whose ruins we viewed with no less concern than the unhappy fate

[1] The whole of Whitehall Palace except the Banqueting Hall was burned down on April 9, 1691. The fire, says Evelyn, began 'at the apartment of the late Duchess of Portsmouth (which had been pulled down and rebuilt no less than three times to please her) and consumed other lodgings of such lewd creatures who debauched King Charles II and others and were his destruction.'

K

of such a noble structure must needs beget in each considerate
beholder, especially when they reflect upon the honour it had
to entertain the best and greatest of princes, in their highest
state and grandeur, for several preceding ages; and now at
last to be consumed by flames so near so much water. Who
can do otherwise than grieve to see that order, which the
hands of artists, at the cost of kings, had improved to such
delight and stateliness, lie dissolved in a heap of rubbish?
Those spacious rooms where majesty has sat so oft, attended
with the transcending glories of his court, the just, the wise,
the brave and beautiful, now huddled in confusion, and
nothing more than dirt and ashes; as if the misfortunes of
princes were visited upon their palaces, as well as persons, to
manifest to the world more clearly that an over-ruling power,
and not accident, always decrees their sufferings.

After we had taken a survey of the ruins, and spent some
melancholy thoughts upon the tattered object that lay in dust
before us, we walked on through several out-courts, till we
came into a place my friend told me was Scotland Yard, where
gentlemen soldiers lie basking in the sun, like so many lazy
swine upon a warm dunghill. I stood a little while ruminating
on the great unhappiness of such a life, and could not restrain
my thoughts from giving a character of that unfortunate
wretch, who in time of war, hazards his life for sixpence a
day, and that perhaps ne'er paid him, and in time of peace
has nothing to do but to mount the guard and loiter.

A foot soldier is commonly a man who for the sake of wearing a sword, and the honour of being termed a gentleman, is
coaxed from a handicraft trade, whereby he might live comfortably, to bear arms for his King and Country, whereby he
has the hopes of nothing but to live starvingly. His lodging
is as near Heaven as his quarters can raise him, and his soul
generally as near Hell as a profligate life can sink him, for
to speak without swearing he thinks a scandal to his post.
He makes many a meal upon tobacco which keeps the inside

of his carcase as naſty as his shirt. He's a champion for the Church, because he fights for religion, though he never hears prayers except they be read upon a drumhead. He can never pass by a brandy shop with twopence in his pocket, for he naturally loves ſtrong waters, as a Turk loves coffee.

No man humbles himself more upon the committing of a fault, for he bows his head to his heels, and lies bound by the hour to his good behaviour. He is a man of undaunted courage; dreading no enemy so much as he does the wooden horse,[1] which makes him hate to be mounted, and rather chooses to be a foot soldier. He makes a terrible figure in a country town, and makes the old women watch their poultry more than a gang of gipsies.

When once he has been in a battle, it's a hard matter to get him out of it, for wherever he comes he's always talking of the action, in which he was poſted in the greateſt danger, and seems to know more of the matter than the General. He's one that loves fighting no more than other men, though perhaps, a dozen of drink and an affront, will make him draw his sword, yet a pint and a good word, will make him put it up again. The beſt end he can expeƈt to make, is to die in the bed of honour, and the greateſt living marks of his bravery, to recommend him at once to the world's praise and pity, are crippled limbs, with which I shall leave him to beg a better livelihood.

> To a cobbler's awl, or butcher's knife,
>   Or a porter's knot commend me,
> But from a soldier's lazy life,
>   Good Heaven, I pray, defend me.

[1] This was an instrument of punishment consisting of a wooden horse, with a sharp edge along its back. The culprit was seated astride this, with weights tied to each foot, and then left for an hour or more.

CHAPTER NINE

The Admiralty—Man's Coffee-house—The Cobbler's Shop—The Strand—New Exchange—Covent Garden—The Hummums

AS soon as we turned out of Scotland Yard into the common road, I espied a famous edifice diametrically opposite to the gate we passed through; the freshness of the bricks and form of which building, shewed it to be of modern erection. Perpendicularly over the main door or entrance, was placed a golden anchor, which occasioned me to enquire of my friend, to what public use this noble fabric was converted.

In answer to this said he, ' This is the place where so many letters have been directed, which were put into the *Gazette* concerning abuses and irregularities committed in Her Majesty's Navy, and great encouragement was offered to the authors of those letters to appear and justify what illegal and unwarrantable practices they could charge upon any person or persons commissioned in that service under the Government!'

'And pray,' said I, ' what became of that matter at last about which there was so great a bustle?'

' You must be careful,' says he, ' how you ask questions in such affairs, and it behoves me to be as cautious how I answer them, so I'll tell you a story. A merry cobbler as he sat stitching in his stall, was singing a piece of his own composition to indulge his cheerful humour, wherein he very often repeated the following words: " The King said to the Queen, and the Queen said to the King." A passer-by was mightily desirous of knowing what it was the King and Queen said to one another, and he stood listening a considerable time, expecting the cobbler to have gone on with his ditty, wherein he should have satisfied his longing curiosity.

' But the musical translator continued to sing only the same words, till he had tired the patience of his auditor, who at laſt ſtepped up to the ſtall, and seriously asked the drolling sole-mender what it was the King said to the Queen, and the Queen to the King. The busy Crispin snatches at his ſtrap, and lays it, with all his might, across the shoulders of the impertinent queriſt, passionately expressing himself in these words, " How, now, Saucebox! It's a fine age we live in, when such coxcombs as you muſt be prying into matters of State! I'd have you to know, Sirrah, I am too loyal a subjeƈt to betray the King's secrets, so pray get ye gone, and don't interrupt me in my lawful occupation, leſt I ſtick my awl into you, and mark you for a fool that meddles with what does not concern you." The cobbler being a ſturdy old grizzle, the fellow was forced to bear both with this correƈtion and reproof, and shrugging his shoulders was glad to sneak off about his business.'

' I know,' said I, ' how to apply the moral of your ſtory, and shall therefore be very careful how I trouble you for the future, with any such queſtions that are either improper for me to ask, or inconsiſtent with your safety to answer.'

By this time we were come to the door of the moſt eminent Coffee-house[1] at this end of the town, which my friend had before proposed to give me a sight of. Accordingly we blundered through a dark entry. At the end we ascended a pair of ſtairs, which brought us into an old-fashioned tenement, where a very gaudy crowd of fellows were walking backwards and forwards with their hats in their hands, not daring to

---

[1] This was Man's or the Royal Coffee-house, situated behind Charing Cross, near Scotland Yard. It was, indeed, the most fashionable coffee-house in London, and was kept by one Alexander Man. To distinguish it from a neighbour of the same name it was sometimes called Old Man's and the other Young Man's.

convert 'em to their intended use, leſt it should put the fore-
tops of their wigs into some disorder.

We squeezed through the fluttering assembly of snufflers till
we got to the end of the room, where, at a small table, we
sat down, and observed that though there was abundance of
gueſts, there was very little to do, for it was as great a rarity
to hear anybody call for a dish of Politician's porridge [coffee],
or any other liquor, as it is to hear a sponger in a company
ask what's to pay. Their whole exercise was to charge and
discharge their noſtrils, and keep the curls of their periwigs
in their proper order. The clashing of their snuff-box lids, in
opening and shutting, made more noise than their tongues,
and sounded as terrible in my ears as the melancholy ticks of
so many Death-watches.

Bows and cringes of the neweſt mode were here exchanged
'twixt friend and friend, with wonderful exaꝰness. They made
a humming like so many hornets in a country chimney, not
with their talking, but with their whispering over their new
minuets and bories, with their hands in their pockets, if freed
from their snuff-boxes, by which you might underſtand they
had moſt of them been travellers into the seven provinces.

Amongſt them were abundance of officers, or men who by
their habit appeared to be such, though they looked as tender
as if they carried their down bed with them into the camp.
At the end of the principal room were other apartments, where,
I suppose, the Beau-politicians retired upon extraordinary occasions to talk nonsense by themselves about State affairs.

Having sat all this while looking about us, like a couple of
Minerva's birds among so many of Juno's peacocks, admiring
their gaiety, we began to be wishful of a pipe of tobacco
which we were not assured we could have the liberty of
smoking leſt we should offend those sweet-breathed gentlemen, who were always running their noses into a civet box.
But we ventured to call for some inſtruments of evaporation,
which were accordingly brought us, but with such kind of

unwillingness, as if they would much rather to have been rid of our company, for their tables were so very neat and shone with rubbing, being as nut brown in colour as the top of a country house-wife's cupboard.

The floor was as clean swept, which made us look round to see if there were no orders hung up to impose the forfeiture of mop-money upon any person that should spit out of the chimney corner. Notwithstanding we wanted an example to encourage us in our rudeness, we ordered 'em to light the wax candle, by which we lit our pipes, and blew about our whiffs with as little concern as if we had been in the company of so many carmen.

At this, several Sir Poplins that were near us, drew their faces into many peevish wrinkles. But regardless of their grimaces, by which they expressed their displeasure, we puffed on our unsavoury weed, till we had cleared one corner of the room and separated the beaus from the more sociable party, and made 'em fly to a great window next the street, where there was such shifting and snuffing that the rest of the company could scarce keep their countenances.

Just at this juncture, whilst the gaudy knot were looking into the street, who should chance to come by, on the other side of the way, but old Father Red-cap, the dumb merry-andrew, who casting up his eyes, and espying such a parcel of elegant figures standing at the window, made a full stop over against the coffee-house and began, according to his custom, to show his antic postures and buffoonery actions, dancing the soldier's dance and playing abundance of fool's antic pranks, to engage passengers to tarry and behold his apish gestures.

When he had collected a promiscuous multitude of tradesmen, and soldiers, porters, chimney-sweepers and footmen, round about him, he fronts his flaxen-wigged spectators at the coffee-house who were stroking down their straggling hairs, and began to mimic the beau, rendering himself immediately so intelligible to the rabble by his apt signs and ridiculous postures that the crowd set up a laugh, and the eyes of the whole mob were directed to our squeamish tobacco-haters. Perceiving the mob well-pleased, the poor deaf comedian persisted in his whim and buffooned with excellent humours the strut and toss of the wig, the carriage of the hat, the snuff-box, the fingering of the foretop, the hanging of the sword and to each action formed so suitable a face that the most grave spectator could not forbear laughing.

This put our sparks to blush, and made them retire from their casements, by which time our smoking had given encouragement to others to pluck out their boxes and betake themselves to the like liberty so that we smoked out the beaus till they sneaked off one by one, and left behind 'em more agreeable company. We could then discern there were some great men by the grandeur of their looks, the awfulness of their presence, and gracefulness of their deportment. There were several officers, with old English aspects, whose martial faces were adorned with weather-beaten wrinkles crossed with hacks and scars, those rugged beauty-spots of war, which they wore as true marks of their undaunted bravery.

Having by this time ended our pipes, we wound up our diversion with a fashionable mess of Turkish sobriety [coffee] and departed.

Having now squeezed back through a long dark entry full of rapscallionly skip-jacks into the open street, my friend bid me take notice of a great tavern[1] on the other side the way. In that eating-house, said he, as many fools' estates have been squandered away, as ever were swallowed up by the Royal Oak Lottery; for every fop with a small fortune who attempts to counterfeit quality and is fool enough to bestow twenty shillings' worth of sauce upon ten pennyworth

---

[1] This was Locket's Tavern, Charing Cross, on the site of Drummond's Bank. Strype describes it as ' much frequented by gentry. Where you are so nicely served that, stap my vitals! they shall compose you a dish no bigger than a saucer which shall come to fifty shillings,' says Lord Foppington in Vanbrugh's *Relapse*.

of meat, resorts to one of these ordinaries, where a man that is as rich as Crœsus may outlive Heliogabalus, and spend more open money upon a dinner than a sergeant-at-law can get in a whole term.

As we were thus talking a squadron of horse marched by in order to relieve the guard. My friend asked me my opinion of their appearance, and how I liked the sight of so many brave Englishmen on horseback, which, says he, had not been seen in these parts these many years.

' Truly,' said I, ' I think they look more like soldiers and become their post much better in their old coats, than those butter-boxes the Dutch troops did in all their finery; and indeed it's more natural for us to think they would do their own country greater service upon occasion, and would hazard their lives with more heartiness than is reasonable to expect foreigners would do for us. Dutchmen, for aught I know, may fight in defence of Holland, or a Frenchman for the security of his own nation, but whenever the necessities of England shall force upon her their assistance, she will find to her sorrow, she has but a broken reed to rely on.'

When they had passed by us we moved on till we came to the subterranean warehouse of an eminent dealer in old boots, shoes, slippers, spurs and spatter-dashes, the front of his cavern being adorned with such sorts of leathern conveniences that I could not but think he was the only human farrier appointed to shoe all the inferior quality at this end of the town.

My friend and I having proposed in a few days to ride down to Tonbridge, the well-finished palace of Coblerius Cæsar put us in mind of seizing this opportunity to fit ourselves with some accoutrements of which we were destitute. Accordingly by very steep gradations we descended into the cabin with abundance of caution, as otherwise the hillocks of dirt upon the stairs, for want of the use of a paring shovel might have endangered our necks, as the jamb above us threatened us with a broken head. But with care and gentleness we got safe to the bottom where the grizzly cobbler sat uniting of dissenting soles, who, by their stubborn disagreeableness, had broken the threads of unity and separated themselves to the maker's dishonour, from their upper leathers.

As soon as he saw us, he bid us welcome and laid by his work and asked us what we wanted. We told him boots, and he instantly furnished us with all sorts and sizes amongst which, after a little search, we pitched upon such that pleased us, and sat down upon a stool in order to try 'em on.

At this moment a ragged Irishman came down and desired him, in his Irish accent, to show him a pair of shoes. Crispin being a little busy in giving us his attendance, believing us the better customers, happened through carelessness, to hand him a couple of shoes which were not fellows. Teague drew on one and it fitted him very well, but when he tried the other he found it much too little and quite of another sort.

'By my shoul, dear Joy,' says he, ' the man's futs that wore these brogues were not fellows. Prithee let me see another pair.'

The cobbler looked upon the shoes and noticed his mistake. Casting his eye upon the fellow's feet, he discovered his stockings to be of different colours.

'I thought, master,' says he, ' you would have had your shoes as you have your stockings, one of one sort, and one of another, but however, if these won't do, I'll see further if I can fit you.' Accordingly he hands him another pair with the toe of one (as is usual) thrust into the other.

The Irishman put on his old shoes again in a great passion, and took his leave in these words:

'By Chreest and Shaint Patrick, ye are a cheating knave. Do you think I will buy a pair of brogues dat de little one ish big enough to hold de great one in its belly? How, by my shoul, can you tink dey will fit my futs, dey are both of a smallness.' And away he trips upstairs in his aged pumps, made sandals by much wearing so that they were forced to be laced on with pack-thread, and so marched off in a great fury, to relieve his pedeſtals at the next conveniency leaving us to chatter with our drolling cobbler. He fitted us with what we wanted at reasonable rates, like a man of conscience, without using half so many lies and canting reservations as a sober citizen in his shop, but gave us a hearty welcome into the bargain and so we parted.

When we had crawled up again into the ſtreet like a couple of gentleman soldiers out of a twopenny ordinary, the firſt object with which our eyes were affected, was the brazen ſtatue of that pious prince, King Charles the Firſt, on horse-back, whose righteous life, unhappy reign, unjuſt sufferings and unparalleled martyrdom shall bury monuments, outlive Time, and ſtand up with Eternity. I could not without the higheſt concern, and deepeſt reflections on his great misfortunes, behold the image of that good man, in whose effigy may be seen the piety, majeſty, mercy, patience and innocency of the matchless original, the causeless diſturbances of whose reign, and the barbarous usage of whose person, will ſtick as thorns, I hope, in the sides of Faction, till they are crushed into that anarchy from whence they had their firſt beginning.

From Charing Cross, we turned towards the Strand, at the entrance of which I observed an ancient ſtone fabric,[1] in the front of which I beheld, with satisfaction, the handiwork of our forefathers, in whose sullied antiquity I could discern much more beauty than my genius can discover in any modern building. ‘What a thousand pities,’ said I, ‘is it that so noble a palace, which appears so magnificent and venerable, should not have the old hospitality continued within, answerable to its outward grandeur.’

---

[1] Northumberland House, the palace of the Percys, had long been famous for its hospitality, but this ceased with the extinction of the family in the male line in 1674. The site of the house, demolished in 1874, is commemorated in Northumberland Avenue.

'Truly,' says my friend, 'it is a great scandal to the present age that quality should so degenerate from their ancestors that instead of imitating the liberality of their grandsires in relieving the distresses of their neighbours, supplying the wants of poor friends and relations, and (to the honour of themselves and country) giving charitable entertainment to strangers and travellers they now squander away their estates in gaming and foppery.'

We moved leisurely along the Strand, meeting nothing remarkable until we came to the New Exchange,[1] into which seraglio of fair ladies we made our entrance, to take a pleasing view of the cherubimical lasses, who, I suppose, had dressed themselves up for sale to the best advantage, as well as the fopperies and toys they dealt in. Indeed, many of them looked so very amiable, so enticing fair, that had I been happily furnished with some superfluous angels,[2] I could willingly have dealt among the charming witches for some of their commodities; but as cursed cows have short horns, I could only walk by, and lick my lips at their handsome faces, as a hungry beggar when he stares into a cook's shop, and was forced so to content myself. The chiefest customers they had, I observed, were beaus, who, I imagined, were paying a double price for linen, gloves, or sword-knots, to the prettiest of the women, that they might go from thence and boast among their brother fops what singular favours and great encouragement they had received from the fair lady that sold 'em.

[1] This stood on the south side of the Strand, opposite Bedford Street, on the site later occupied by Coutts's Bank. It was a great centre for women's shopping and was famous for its milliners and trinket-sellers. The ground-floor was a public walk, the shops being on the upper story. New Exchange was at its zenith soon after the Restoration, and it is mentioned frequently by most of the dramatists of that time. The building was demolished in 1768 when the Adam brothers built the Adelphi.

[2] An old English gold coin, worth from 6s. 8d. to 10s. They were recalled in Anne's reign.

Finding nothing else amongst 'em worth observing, I digested a little of their shop language into a song :

Fine lace or linen, sir,
Good gloves or ribbons here;
　　What is't you please to buy, sir?
Pray what d'ye ask for this?
Ten shillings is the price;
It cost me, sir, no less,
　　I scorn to tell a lie, sir.

Madam, what is't you want,
Rich fans of India paint?
　　Fine hoods or scarfs, my lady?
Silk stockings will you buy,
In grain or other dye?
Pray, madam, please your eye,
　　I've good as e'er was made ye.

My lady, feel the weight,
They're fine, and yet not slight,
　　I'd with my mother trust 'em
For goodness and for wear.
Madam I vow and swear,
I showed you this same pair,
　　In hopes to gain your custom.

Pray tell me in a word,
At what you can afford,
　　With living gain to sell 'em?
The price is one pound five,
And as I hope to live,
I do my profit give,
　　Your honour's very welcome.

Knives, penknives, combs or scissors,
Tooth-pickers, sirs, or tweezers,
　　Or walking-canes to ease ye.
Ladies, d'ye want fine toys,
For misses, or for boys?
Of all sorts I have choice,
　　And pretty things to please ye.

Having taken a satisfactory survey of this jilts' academy, where girls are admitted at nine years old, and taught by eleven to out-chatter a magpie, out-wit their parents, and by the improving instructions and example of their kind mistresses and neighbouring correspondents, are made as forward and as ripe in thought before they are out of their hanging sleeves, as a country wench is at five-and-twenty.

We then took our leave of this cloister of kind damsels, so turned up by the Half-Moon Tavern, and proceeded towards Covent Garden, where we overtook abundance of religious lady-birds, armed against the assaults of Satan with Bible and Common Prayer Book, marching with all good speed to Covent Garden Church.

' Certainly,' said I, ' the people of this parish are better Christians than ordinary, for since I came to London I never observed, upon a week-day, such a sanctified troop of females flocking to their devotions, as I see at this part of the town.'

' These,' says my friend, ' are a pious sort of creature that are much given to go to Church, and may be seen there every day at prayers, as constantly as the bell rings; and if you were to walk the other way, you might meet as many young gentlemen from the Temple and Gray's Inn, going to join with them in their devotions. We'll take a turn into the sanctuary among the rest, and you shall see how they behave themselves.'

Accordingly we stepped into the rank, amongst the lambs of grace, and entered the tabernacle with the rest of the Saints, where we found a parcel of as handsome, cleanly, well-dressed Christians of both sexes as a man would desire to communicate with, who stood ogling one another with as much zeal and sincerity as if they worshipped the Creator in the creature, and whispering to their next neighbours, as if, according to the Liturgy, they were confessing their sins to one another. This I afterwards understood by my friend, was only to make assignations, and the chief of their prayers, says he, are that Providence will favour their intrigues.

When the parson had made an end of what, with much earneſtness, but to little purpose, he had conned over to his amorous congregation, we made our exit from thence, and went through the market, where a parcel of jolly red-faced dames, in blue aprons and ſtraw hats, sat selling their garden ware, but they ſtunk so of brandy, ſtrong drink and tobacco, that the fumes o'ercame the fragrancy that arose from their sweet herbs and flowers.

'This market,' says my friend, 'and that church hides more faults of kind wives and daughters among the neighbouring inhabitants than any pretended visits either to my cousin at t'other end of the town, or some other diſtant acquaintance. For if the husband asks, "Where have you been, wife?" Or the parent, "Where have you been, daughter?" the answer, if it be after eleven in the forenoon, or between three and four in the afternoon, is "At Prayers." But if early in the morning, then their excuse is, "I took a walk in Covent Garden market, not being very well, to refresh myself with the scent of herbs and flowers." Bringing a flower or a sprig of sweet briar home in her hand suffices to confirm the matter.

'Now,' says my friend, 'we are so near, I'll carry you to see the Hummums,[1] where I have an honeſt old acquaintance, and if you will pay your club towards eight shillings, we'll go in and sweat, and you shall feel the effeƈts of this notable invention.'

'With all my heart,' said I, 'you know I am always conformable to whatever you propose.' So, accordingly, he conduƈted me to the house, through which we passed into a long gallery, where my friend's acquaintance received him with much gladness.

I had not walked above once the length of the gallery, but I began to find myself as warm as a cricket at an oven's mouth. My friend telling him we designed to sweat, the fellow introduced us from thence into a warmer climate.

[1] Hummums Bagnio or Sweating House was kept by one Mr. Small, in 1708, and was quite a fashionable resort. The rates were 5s. for a single person or 4s. each for parties of two or more.

'Pray, friend,' said I, 'what latitude do you think we are in?' 'You must consider,' says he, 'we are making a short cut to the East Indies, and are now in about twenty-three degrees and a half, that's just under one of the Tropics, but this heat is nothing to what you'll feel when you come under the Equinoctial, where I can assure you we shall find ourselves in a very little time.'

We now began to unstrip, and put ourselves in a condition of enduring an hour's baking, and when we had reduced ourselves into the original state of mankind, having nothing before us to cover our nakedness but a clout no bigger than a fig-leaf, our guide led us to the end of our journey, the next apartment, which I am sure was as hot as a pastry cook's oven so that I began immediately to melt like a piece of butter in a basting ladle, and was afraid I should have run all to oil by the time I had been in six minutes.

The bottom of the room was paved with free-stone, to defend our feet from the excessive heat of which we had got on a pair of new-fashioned brogues, with wooden soles, after the French mode, cut out of an inch deal board. As soon as the fire had tapped us all over, and we began to run at every pore like a conduit pipe, our rubber arms his right hand with a gauntlet of coarse hair camlet, and begins to curry us with as much labour as a Yorkshire groom does his master's best stone horse, till he made us as smooth as a fair lady's cheeks just washed with lemon posset, and greased over with pomatum.

At last, I grew so very faint with the expense of so much spirits, that I begged as hard for a mouthful of fresh air as Dives did for a drop of water, which our attendant let in at a sash window, no broader than a Deptford cheese-cake, but it let in a comfortable breeze that was very reviving. When I had fouled about as many calico napkins as a child does double clouts in a week, our rubber draws a cistern full of hot water, that we might go in and boil out those gross humours that could not be emitted by a gentle perspiration.

Thus almost baked to a crust, we went into the hot bath to moisten our clay, where we lay soddening ourselves, till we were almost parboiled.

Talking by accident of a pain that sometimes affected my shoulder, occasioned by a fall from my horse, my friend advised me to be cupped for it, telling me 'twas the best operation in the world for the removal of all such grievances. Being an utter stranger to this sort of phlebotomy, I was a little unwilling to undergo the experience of it, but by the persuasions of my friend, and my friend's friend, I at last consented. Upon this the operator fetched in his instruments, and fixed three glasses to my back, which, by drawing out the air, stuck to me as close as a Cantharidid plaster to the head of a lunatic till I thought they would have crept into me, and have come out t'other side.

When, by virtue of this hocus-pocus stratagem, he had conjured all the evil blood out of my body under his glass juggling cups, he plucks out an ill-favoured instrument and begins to scarify my skin, as a cook does a loin of pork to be roasted, but with such ease and dexterity that I could have suffered him to have pinked me all over full of eyelet holes had my malady required. When he had drawn away as much blood as he thought necessary for the removal of my pain, he covered the places he had carbonaded with a new skin, provided for that purpose, and healed the scarifications he had made instantly; then taking me up like a scalded swine, out of my greasy broth, after he had wiped o'er my wet buttocks with a dry clout, and telling us we had sweat enough, he relieved us of our purgatory, and carried us into the dressing room, which gave us such refreshment after we had been stewing in our own gravy, that we thought ourselves as happy as a couple of English travellers, transported in an instant by a miracle, from the torrid zone into their own country.

Our expense of spirits had weakened nature and made us drowsy, so having the conveniency of a bed, we lay down and

L

were rubbed like a couple of race-horses after a course. When we had refreshed our carcases by a plentiful dram of cordial, so full of gold that it looked as tempting as gilded ginger-bread to the eyes of a froward infant, and had taken an hour's repose, to reconcile the fermented humours of our bodies to their orderly motion, we then got up, and began to cover our indecencies with those habiliments the tailor had contrived to hide our nakedness. Our rubber gave us his assistance, during which time he also entertained us with several delightful stories, which he told us in such apt words, and with such agreeable humours, that he made us both shake with laughter. That the reader may be a partaker of our mirth, I have here made a recital of one of the short episodes in which he was the principal actor.

A gentleman of fortune, one day lying under a shrewd suspicion of debt, was dogged into our house by a bailiff, who came to the door whilst the gentleman was sweating, and asked for him. One of our rubbers, by chance opening the door, happened to know his calling, and comes into the gentleman and tells him a fellow wanted to speak with him at the door, pretendingly from such a gentleman of his acquaintance, and added that he knew him to be a bailiff. The gentleman thanked him kindly for his information, and put it into his head to get him in, and torment him a little in one of the hot rooms.

Accordingly my fellow-servant went back to the Moabite, and told him that the gentleman was within, and desired him to come to him. So he conducted the debtor-snapper, who was ready armed with his legal authority, into an ante-room of the next apartment to the gentleman, where he bid him wait a little, and the gentleman would come to him presently.

In the meanwhile my fellow-servant came to me and the stoker, to consult after what manner we should punish him. I, like a good projector of unluckiness, told him my advice was for us to put on our calico gowns with the hoods over our heads, and disguise our faces with burnt cork as frightfully as we could, and arm ourselves with fire weapons out of the kitchen and then enter upon him altogether, seize him, and carry him into the hot room, and there torment him as we should think fit.

Accordingly we put ourselves into this order, rushed in upon him, and forced him into the hot room. The fellow coming in the piazza way, was wholly ignorant what place it was, but took it to be a gentleman's house, but feeling the excessive heat, and seeing himself in the hands of so ill-looked goblins, armed with a great beef spit, tongs and a fire-fork, he began to roar out like a stuck pig, and fancied himself in Hell.

Then, in a hoarse voice, said I to my brother-infernals, 'First let us bake him, and then boil him.' To which my comrade with the spit added, 'And then I'll have him roasted,' which terrible sentences so frightened the disturber of human quiet, in this new state of damnation, that he fell into a swoon, so that we were forced to put him into a cold bath to fetch him to life again.

When he recovered, he looked as wild as a lunatic at full moon, and cried out as much against the cold as he did before against the heat. Upon this we let run the cock of hot water, till we had almost parboiled him. Then he fell into a second fit, so that we thought it proper to take him out of the bath, and carry him into the ante-room for fear he should have died. There we shaved one side of his head and beard, and fixed on a couple of cupping-horns (which we sometimes use) upon his forehead; so carried him to the back door, and turned him adrift.

He was so rejoiced to find redemption from the Devil's clutches, that away he ran as fast as a thief under a pursuit, and after him all the mob and boys in the street, crying out 'A mad cuckold! A mad cuckold!' And telling the gentleman what he had done, he returned us hearty thanks, and was mightily pleased.

CHAPTER TEN

The Wits' Coffee-house—A Poetical Letter—Bartholomew Fair

HAVING now purified our scorbutic carcases in a resemblance of Purgatory, and made our skins by sweating, bathing, rubbing and scrubbing, as smooth as an old drum-head that had been long beaten, we satisfied the demands of the house, gratified our groom for extraordinary pains in dressing our dirty hides, and then departed.

From thence we adjourned to the Wits' Coffee-house,[1] in hopes that the powerful eloquence which drops from the silver tongues of the ingenious company that frequent this noted mansion, might inspire us with such a genius as would better fit the perfection of our renovated clay. Accordingly, upstairs we went, and found much company, and but little talk; as if every one remembered the old proverb, That a close mouth makes a wise head, and so endeavoured, by his silence, to be counted a man of judgement, rather than by speaking to stand the censure of so many critics, and run the hazard of losing that character which by holding of his tongue he might be in hopes of gaining.

We shuffled through the moving crowd of philosophical mutes, to the other end of the room, where three or four wits of the upper classes were rendezvoused at a table, and were disturbing the ashes of the old poets by perverting their sense,

---

[1] This was Will's Coffee-house, which stood at the corner of Bow Street and Russell Street, and was a great resort of wits and men of letters. It was Dryden's headquarters in his old age, and he was to be seen there always; in the winter by the fireside and in the summer on the balcony overlooking the street.

and making strange allegories and allusions never dreamt or thought of by the authors. They excused some faults, which were really the slips or oversights of the poet, but made others so very gross, through prejudice and misconstruction, that none but critics of very little judgement, or very much ill-nature, could have wrested the sense of the words so much to the injury of him that writ 'em.

When they had showed their learning, as they thought, by arranging and condemning many of the old Roman muses, they condescended so low as to call some of our modern poets to stand the test of their all-judging opinions, upon whom, in brief, they conferred these characters. One was a man of great judgement, learning and fancy, but of no principle; another was one that writ well, and could write well, but would not write; a third never writ but one good thing in his life, and that he recanted; a fourth had a poetical talent, but was hid under a philosophical bushel; a fifth was a good Latin poet, but had sacrificed his muse to Bacchus, instead of dedicating her to Apollo; a sixth had got a great deal of credit by writing of plays, but lost it all by defending the stage; a seventh had got some reputation by turning of old ditties into new songs, but lost it all by turning a Spanish romance into an English stage play; an eighth had got honour by a dull poem, which his brother medico envied, and vowed he'd outdo him in verse, as he hoped also to be knighted.

Thus the carping Momuses proceeded according to the critics' custom, never to let anything escape their scrutiny, however well performed, nor any character pass their lips, though of the worthiest persons in the world, without being tagged with some calumny or other, on purpose to eclipse the brightness of these verses for which they are chiefly eminent.

At another table were seated a parcel of raw young second-rate beaus and wits, who were conceited if they had but once the honour to dip a finger and thumb into Mr. Dryden's snuff-box; it was enough to inspire 'em with a true genius of poetry, and make 'em write verse as fast as a tailor takes his stitches. These, too, were communicating to one another the newest labours of their brains, wherein were such wondrous slights, unaccountable thoughts, strange figures, hyperboles, similes, and all upon such notable subjects, that to hear 'em read their works is at any time sufficient to turn the deepest melancholy into a fit of laughter. One plucks out a panegyric upon orange-flower water; another, a satire against dirty weather; a third produces a cleanly lampoon upon nasty tobacco smokers; a fourth a poem in praise of short puff-wigs, together with the excellency of paint, powder and patches.

What I heard of their admirable flights, came too abruptly to my ears for me to make a fair recital of any part worth the reader's perusal, or else I would have gladly obliged the world with copies of some of the wild exuberance of their juvenile fancies. But one of them being, as I guessed by his garb, a young officer, happened to drop the following poem in plucking out some other papers, which my friend believing to include no great matter of moment, picked it up without notice, and taking our leave of this Wits' Sessions House, we brought it away with us. And finding something in it we thought might divert the reader, we have accordingly presented him with a copy, it being:

A LETTER FROM A LAWYER TO A NEW-MARRIED OFFICER IN THE COUNTRY

> Letters in prose, my friend are common
> As pride in priest, or love in woman,
> Our annual course of long vacation
> To business giving a cessation,
> Affords me time to thus salute-ye,
> And pay in rhyme this friendly duty.
> Not rightly knowing which is worse,
> The lawyer's or the poet's curse,
> Both silenced with an empty purse.

For now our pens, upon our words,
Are grown as useless as your swords,
We having but as little writing,
As, God be thanked, you have fighting.
You may draw sword, so we may pen,
To show our tools of war, and then
Like fools, e'en put them up again.

But what a plague is't I am doing?
Or where the Devil am I going?
Now Pegasus I've once bestridden,
Methinks I gallop like a Dryden:
Long as 'tis rhyme it's no great matter,
And bombast, whether praise or satire.
Mistake me not, and think I've writ
To show my parts, that is not it;
I'd not be envied for a wit.
For he that's rich in thought, is sure
To be in friends and pocket poor;
For wise men will not care to serve him;
And fools would all be glad to starve him.
Wit carries an edge, few can abide it,
And he that has it ought to hide it.
It is so far from being delightful
It renders him that draws it, frightful.

I only meant to let you know
I'm well, and hope that you are so;
With all the merry knaves o' th' pack
Who love the fair, the brown, the black,
And rather than submit to marry
Fly still at wench, as hawk at quarry.

Pray tell me how Lieutenant A——
Maintains his vice with half his pay
Who has, I hope, by good direction,
Repair'd his rudder of affection,
And gained his natural complexion.

But hold, what is it I am doing?
I must not here appear too knowing.

Lest you, arch wags, should turn the satire
And say I'm skilful in the matter.

But now, dear friend, I change my strain,
And grieve to think weak man so vain,
That resolutions made of late,
Against a matrimonial state,
Should not defend you from the curse
Of fools, for better or for worse.
Prithee now tell what means this riddle,
That you should be so fond and idle,
To eclipse the freedom of your life,
With that dull mournful clog, a wife?
What if she's youthful, rich and fair,
And virtuous too, she's still a care.
These are but chains to bind the faster,
And make man's plague the more his master.

But use this caution thro' thy life,
Slave not thyself to please a wife;
Lest thro' o'er fondness thou do'st prove,
A mere anatomy of love.

But since, the earthen vessel, man,
Whose life's comprised within a span,
Is by his nature weak and vain;
I must excuse your oversight,
Committed 'gainst your reason's light;
And since you're catch'd in love's decoy,
I'll wish you, like the rest, much joy.

You know, my friend, what can't be cured,
It's said of old, must be endur'd,
Since that's your case, I'll so befriend you,
As wish all happiness attend you.

May your whole lives be harmony,
Mutual your loves, from troubles free;
And dutiful your progeny.

May she so live, that all her joys
May prove her merit, not her choice,
And to complete that happiness
I truly wish you to possess,
To your fair bride may you prove true,
And good to her, as she to you.

My friend, with gladness do I hear
You find your spirits much too clear
For fens, and their gross foggy air.

That you intend, within a while,
To bless your own dear native soil,
And leave that poisonous croaking soil,
To frogs, and toads, snakes, efts and ants
Its native foul inhabitants.
But e'er you come, take care and see
You send me a retaining fee,
In cordial Nantz or some such liquor,
To move my spirits round the quicker.

For man's but heaven's water mill,
In motion kept by th' glass or gill.
And wanting liquor must stand still,
Don't thro' oblivion now neglect it,
For I assure you I expect it.

This being in rhyme my first essay,
I've jingled on a wondrous way,
Pray pardon my prolixity,
A common fault in poetry.

Excuse me, friend, in what I write t'ye,
And don't forget the Aqua-Vitae,
Is all I beg and so good by t'ye.

Having diverted ourselves with the perusal of the foregoing epistle, we steered our course into Brydges Street, with
intention to see a play; but when we came to the house, found
upon enquiry that all the wiser part of the family of tomfools

had translated themselves to Bartholomew Fair.[1] After struggling with a long see-saw between pride and profit, and having prudently considered the weighty difference between the honourable title of one of her Majesty's servants and that of a Bartholomew Fair player, a vagabond by the statute, they did at last, with much difficulty, conclude that it was equally reputable to play the fool in the fair for fifteen or twenty shillings a day as 'twas to please fools in the play-house at the same per week.

Indeed, I think there's no more distinction between a Queen's House player and a country stroller, than there is between a bulldog bred up in Clare Market and another educated in Her Majesty's Bear Garden. And as he is the most valuable dog that runs farthest and fairest, so is he the most reputable comedian that gets most money by his fooling. For he that is a mountebank, it's no matter whether he keeps his stage over against Whitehall Gate, or at Cow Cross, for if the means to live be the same, it signifies little to his credit in what place they are put in practice.

Being disappointed in what we proposed, we were obliged to defer our intended pleasures till another opportunity, and considering it would be expected we should, according to the month, take a survey of the Fair,[2] we took coach to escape the dirt and uneasiness of a crowd, and adjourned thither.

At the entrance our ears were saluted with Belfegor's Concert, the rumbling of drums, mixed with the intolerable squeakings of cat-calls and penny trumpets, made still more terrible with the shrill screeches of lottery pick-pockets, through instruments of the same metal as their faces, so that had I not been foretold by my friend of the astonishing confusions I must

[1] Drury Lane and the other theatres were usually closed during the period of Bartholomew Fair—most of the actors, as Ward says, finding it more to their advantage to perform in Smithfield.

[2] Bartholomew Fair was held in Smithfield and lasted for fourteen days from the 24th of August. It was suppressed in 1855.

expect to meet with, I should have been much frightened at this unusual piece of disorder.

We ordered the coachman to set us down at the Hospital gate, near which we went into a convenient house to smoke a pipe, and overlook the follies of the innumerable throng, whose impatient desires of seeing merry-andrew's grimaces had led them ankle deep into filth and crowded as close as a barrel of figs, or candles in a tallow-chandler's basket, sweating and melting with the heat of their own bodies. The unwholesome fumes of such a crowd mixed with the odoriferous effluvia that arose from the singeing of pigs, and burnt crackling of over-roasted pork, came so warm to our nostrils, that had it not been for the use of the fragrant weed, tobacco, we had been in danger of being suffocated.

We drank small beer bittered with Coloquintida,[1] drawn by a dirty tapster, with the impudence of a gaol-bird in his face, a bunch of keys hanging on one side of his apron-strings, to keep him in equal balance with a brush which was hugged under the contrary arm. He plagued us as constantly with his impertinent, ' Do you call, Sirs?' every two minutes, as surely as the clock strikes every hour, till at last he had so affronted us with his over-diligence, that we were forced to tell him we would kick him downstairs if he came any more till we called him.

When we were seated at the window the first object that lay within our observation, were the quality of the Fair, strutting round their balconies in their tinsel robes, and golden leather buskins, expressing such pride in their buffoonery stateliness that I could but reasonably believe they were as much elevated with the thoughts of their fortnight's pageantry, as ever Alexander was with the glories of a new conquest; looking with great contempt from their slit-deal thrones upon the admiring crowd who, in their turn, gazed at our ostentatious heroes, and their most supercilious doxies.

---

[1] This was a bitter made from colocynth, the bitter cucumber.

When they had taken a turn the length of their gallery, to show the gaping crowd how majestically they could tread, each ascended to a seat agreeable to the dignity of their dress to show the multitude how imperiously they could sit. Then entered the conjurer of the whole company, merry-andrew, I suppose as much admired by the rest for a wit, as the finest dressed jilt amongst 'em was by the mob for a beauty.

As soon as he came to the stand, where he designed to give the spectators some testimonies of his ingenuity, the first thing that he undertook to give was a singular instance of his cleanliness, by blowing his nose upon the people, who were mightily pleased, and laughed heartily at the jest. Then, after he had picked out from the whole dramatic assembly a man of most admirable acquirements in the art of tittle-tattle, and fit to confabulate with the witty and intelligible Mr. Andrew, he begins a tale of a tub which he illustrates with abundance of ugly faces, and mimical actions, for in that lay the chief of the comedy, with which the gazers seemed most to be affected.

Between these two, the clod-skulled audience were lugged by the ears for an hour; the apes blundering over such a parcel of insignificant nonsense that none but a true English unthinking mob could have laughed, or taken pleasure at any of their empty drollery.

My friend said, 'This is the dullest stuff that ever was spewed amongst the rabble since heaven made 'em fools, or ever any such coxcomb in a blue doublet undertook to prove them so.'

The epilogue of merry-andrew's farce was, 'Walk in gentlemen, and take your places, whilst you may have 'em; the candles are all lighted and we are just going to begin.' Then, screwing his body into an ill-favoured posture, agreeable to his intellect, he struts along before the glittering train of imaginary heroes, and their Water Lane beauties, leading them to play the fool within, in answer to his performances

without, whilſt some that had money went in, and those that
had none walked off equally satisfied.

The outside of the Droll booths being all garnished with the
like foolery, we found nothing further amongſt 'em worth
repeating; and being seated in a place where nothing else was
to be seen, we were forced to remove from our quarters, and
hazard our carcases amongſt the crowd, and our pockets
amongſt the nimble-fingered gentlemen of the diving myſtery,
or else we found we should see nothing worth the pains we'd
taken. Accordingly we paid our reckoning, and buttoned up
our pockets, as securely as a citizen does his shop-windows
when his family goes to church, and so launched ourselves
into the tempeſtuous multitude, amongſt whom we were
hurried along into the middle of the Fair.

Thus we swam down with the tide, till we came to the rope-
dancer's booth. There praised be our ſtars we once more got
safe footing upon terra firma, and ſtood a little to behold the
agility of the tumblers, whose pranks, when shown to a whimsical virtuoso, are enough to beget in him a new syſtem of
philosophy, and make him believe that to walk only upon our
feet with our heads uppermoſt is nothing but a ridiculous
habit we have contracted from our nurses, and that it is more
natural for mankind to run races upon their hands with their
heels upwards, if they would but practise it.

I was mightily pleased to see the women at the sport, it made
'em seem to have a due sense of the ills done by their tongues,
to degrade which, they turned 'em downwards, giving the
pre-eminence to their moſt deserving parts, for which reason
they practised to walk upside down.

' Come,' said my friend, ' let us fling away sixpence a
piece, and see within. There is something in this sort of
activity that is both diverting and amusing.'

I readily consented to his proposal, so in we went, where a
parcel of country scrapers were sawing a tune, and a mixed
multitude of lounging spectators were waiting with impatience

the beginning of the show, looking upon one another as simply as a company set down at table, that waits with an hungry appetite an hour for their dinner.

At laſt they put up a little animal, that looked as if it had not been six weeks out of a go-cart, and that began to creep along the rope, like a snail along a cabbage ſtalk, with a pole in its hand not much bigger than a large tobacco-ſtopper. This was succeeded by a couple of plump lasses, who, to ſhew their affeƈtion to the breeches, wore 'em under their petticoats, which, for decency's sake they firſt danced in. But to show the speƈtators how forward a woman once warmed is to lay aside her modeſty, they doffed their petticoats after a gentle breathing, and fell to capering as if Old Nick had been in 'em. These were followed by a negro woman and an Irish woman. As soon as the black had seated herself between the cross poles that supported one end of the rope, a country fellow sitting by me fell into such an ecſtacy of laughing that he cackled again.

'Prithee, honeſt friend,' said I, 'what doſt thou see to make thyself so wonderful merry at?'

'Maiſter,' says he, 'I have oftentimes heard of the devil upon two ſticks, but never zee it bevore in my life. Bezide, maiſter, who can forbear laughing to see the devil going to daunce?'

This was succeeded by a pragmatical brother of the same quality, who mounted the ladder next, in order to ascend the rope, who had such a Tyburn look that I was fearful of his falling, leſt his hempen pedeſtal should have catched him by the neck. He commanded the rope to be altered according to his mind, with an affeƈted lordliness, and looking ſteadfaſtly in his face, I remembered I had seen him in our town, where he had the impudence to profess himself an infallible physician. Upon this I asked my friend the meaning on't.

'Poh,' says he, 'I am sorry you are so ignorant. Why, we have dancing physicians, tumbling physicians, and fools of physicians, as well as college physicians. Nay, and some of them too, if they will, can play much stranger tricks than you are aware on. But these fellows, you must know,' says he, ' are bred up between death and remedy, that is the rope and the medicine, and as they grow up, if they happen to prove too heavy heeled for rope-dancers or tumblers, they are forced to learn first how to be fools, and once grown expert jack-puddings, the next degree they commence is doctor, and leave off a painted coat and put on a plush one.'

The person that danced against him was the German maid, as they style her in their bill, who does wonderful pretty things upon the rope, and has fine proportion in her limbs and much modesty in her countenance. She as much out-danced the rest as a greyhound will outun a hedgehog, having something of a method in her steps, and air in her carriage, moving with an observancy of time and play with her feet, as if assisted with the wings of Mercury.

Then Doctor Cozen-Bumpkin mounts the slack-rope, and after he had lain down and swung himself a quarter of an hour in his hempen hammock, he comes down, believing he had done wonderful things; then he honours the mob with a gracious nod, slips on his nightgown to prevent catching cold. Then up steps the negress to the top of the booth, and began to play at swing-swang with a rope, as if the devil were in her, hanging sometimes by a hand, sometimes by a leg, and sometimes by her toes, so that I found, let her do what she would, Providence or Destiny would by no means suffer the rope to part with her.

This scene being ended, they proceeded to the conclusion of their entertainment, the tumbling, and indeed, it was very admirable to think that use should so strengthen the springs of motion, and give that flexibility and pliableness to the joints, nerves, sinews and muscles, as to make a man capable of exerting himself after so miraculous a manner.

When we had seen all, and the master of the revels had bid us welcome, my friend asked me how I liked it? Truly, said I, as for the tumbling I am mightily pleased with it, but as for the dancing, I have seen as good in the country performed by monkeys.

The spectators being dispatched, we squeezed out of the door and instead of avoiding a crowd, we were got out of the frying-pan into the fire. Nothing was distinguishable but the shrill cries of 'Nuts' and 'Damsons.' Thinking it prudentest to take new sanctuary as soon as we could, we jostled into a booth, where was to be seen a dwarf comedy, surnamed a Droll, which most commonly proves as wonderful a monster as any's to be seen in the Fair. It was under the title of that curse of a companion, *The Devil of a Wife*,[1] which occasioned me to look round the audience, to examine whether there was the same mixture of sexes as is customary at such sort of entertainments, but found quite contrary to what may usually be observed, that there were ten men to one woman. The sex, I suppose, is so highly disgusted at the title of the farce, that they thought it greatly inconsistent with their ease and interest, to encourage such a public dishonour done to the authority of termagants, who they account are only women of spirits, who support and defend the reasonable privileges of their sex from the usurpation and encroachments of the husband.

The booth, notwithstanding, was pretty full, but of men chiefly, who had the plain-dealing looks of good sober citizens, and I believe happened most of them to be enslaved under petticoat government, and came hither to learn how to tame a shrew, and recover into their own hands the power and authority of their forefathers, which they had in vain surrendered to their wives upon the terms and conditions of peace and quietness.

By the time my friend and I had cracked a quart of filberts, and ate, each of us, two pennyworth of bergamot pears, to

[1] This was a play by Jevon, an ex-dancing master. The title was subsequently altered to *The Devil to Pay*. It was first produced at Drury Lane, in 1686

A Rowdy Christmas Scene in Cheapside.

(From a print in the Crace Collection)

keep ourselves from idleness, the minstrels scratched over a
concise piece of unintelligible discord called a Flourish and
the curtain was drawn up, and the strutting representatives
began their foolery. At their performance, I confess I was
wonderfully pleased, for every thing was done to such a perfection of uncouthness that had so many puppets made of
sticks and clouts been but qualified with speech, we could
not have laughed more heartily at their ridiculous and awkward
imitations, everyone looking, notwithstanding his dress, like
what he really was, and not like what he represented. All the
while they were playing I fancied I heard some of 'em crying
' Flag-brooms,' some ' Knives to grind,' and others ' Chimney-
sweep,' whilst their ladies were making up the concert with
' Buy my cucumbers to pickle,' and ' Here's your rare holland
socks, four pairs a shilling,' for I am certain they had accustomed their voices to some such cries, that had begot in their
speech such unalterable tones that they are not able to play
a part without giving a relish of their calling.

The whole entertainment was the strangest hodge-podge
that ever was jumbled together, and to us an excellent farce to
please an audience of such fools, who are apt to admire that
which they least understand; for I'll engage they find it a
piece of puzzle that is harder to expound than one of Partridge's[1] riddles, or Mother Shipton's prophecies. We were

---

[1] John Partridge (1644–1715) was a notorious astrologer, quack and
almanack maker, who, in 1680, began to issue almanacks under the title of
Merlinus Liberatus. These yearly publications were packed so full of absurdities
to catch the fancy of the uneducated that Swift, taking the name of Isaac Bicker-
staffe, began a series of attacks. Congreve, Steele and other writers joined in the
sport, and between them made Partridge the butt of some of their best jokes.
Matters came to a head when Swift, in the style of Partridge himself, predicted
the astrologer's death on March 29, 1709. Of this Partridge took no notice, but
on the day following that on which he was to have died, Swift brought out an
account of his death and followed it up with an elegy, concluding:

> Weep, all you customers that use
> His pills, his almanacks or shoes.

Overcome with indignation, Partridge issued all sorts of tracts and pamphlets
to show he was still alive, but the wits gravely rebuked him in a pamphlet for
his presumption in venturing to attempt to prove his own existence.

M

forced to make our patience as long as their play, being wedged in on both sides, till at last they made an end as abruptly as they began foolishly, and let down the curtain. So with the rest of the crowd, we from hence departed.

Having spent most part of the day without giving our bodies that refreshment which was requisite to enliven our spirits, and preserve health, after a short consultation we agreed to gratify our importunate appetites with a quarter of a pig, on purpose to be fools of fashion. In order to accomplish our design, with a great deal of elbow-labour and much sweating we scrambled through the throng, who came pouring into the Fair from all adjacent streets. At last, inch by inch, we gained Pie Corner,[1] where cooks stood dripping at their doors, like their roasted swines'-flesh at their fires, each setting forth with an audible voice the choice and excellency of his pig and pork, which were running as merrily round the spit as if they were striving who should be first roasted.

After we had gazed round us, to examine what cook was most likely to accommodate our stomachs with good entertainment, at last we agreed to step into a large shop where we had great expectancy of tolerable meat and cleanly usage. But no sooner had we entered this suffocating kitchen, than a swinging fat fellow, overseer of the roast to keep the pigs from blistering, who was standing by the spit in his shirt, rubbed his ears, breast, neck and arm-pits with the same wet-cloth which he applied to his pigs, which brought such a qualm over my stomach, that I had much ado to keep the stuffing of my guts from tumbling into the dripping-pan, so scouring out again through an army of flies, encamped at the door in order to attack the pig-sauce, we deferred our eating till a cleanlier opportunity.

[1] This was the Smithfield end of Giltspur Street and was famous for its cook-shops, where all who went to Bartholomew Fair resorted to eat roast pork.

CHAPTER ELEVEN

Bartholomew Fair (*continued*)—A Gaming House—The Eclipse

BEING quite surfeited with our late adventure our stomachs began to be as much averse to Bartholomew Fair, as a Court lady is to onion sauce, or a young libertine to matrimony. The eagerness of our appetites being thus assuaged without the expense of eating, we faced about to the wooden Sodom and suffered ourselves to be carried back into the body of the Fair, where, in compassion to one of the female gender, who was labouring in the crowd, like a fly in a cobweb, I laid my hands upon my friend's shoulders, and by keeping her between my arms, defended her from the rude squeezes and joftles of the careless multitude. To give me a remarkable inftance of her gratitude, she put her hand behind her and picked my pocket of a good handkerchief, in return for my civility.

When she had done her business, she shuffled into the crowd, and the next minute after I discovered my loss, which, as it was but small, begot but little concern. I could not without some shame acquaint my friend with the matter expecting he would laugh at me for my over-care of my lady, and my carelessness of myself. He ridiculed my small misfortune, and told me, smiling, you muft be as careful of women in Bartholomew Fair, as country people are of ftags in rutting time.

Having heard much of a comedian's fame, who had manfully run the hazard of losing that reputation in the Fair which he had got in the play-house, and having never seen him in his proper element, we thought the time might not be very ill-spent if we took a sight of another beſt show in the Fair (for so they all ſtyled themselves) that we might judge of his performances.

The number of kings, queens, heroes, harlots, buffoons, mimics, prieſts, profligates, and devils in the balcony, occasioned us to believe with the crowd, that there were no less varieties to be seen within than there were signs of without, for indeed we might reasonably have thought from their numerous appearance, that when they were all in the booth, there would be room for but a slender audience. So we put our pence into his worship's apron pocket, with which title the mob honoured the maſter of the booth, because they said he had been a Juſtice of the Peace, and then entered the pit where several of the top quality, of the female funétion, sat cracking nuts like so many squirrels, and looking round 'em for admirers. Their prevailing glances, I observed, soon took effeét upon some juvenile gentlemen, whose youthful opinions of the pleasures to be found in love and beauty had rendered them, like gun-powder, as liable to be inflamed with every sparkling eye, as the other is to be blown up by the casual touch of any fire it shall meet with.

The baskets of plums, walnuts, pears and peaches, began now to be handed about from the City fool to the jilt, and tittle-tattles of love were banded forwards and backwards, between the tongues and ears of those amorous frontiers of the impatient audience, who were forced to pacify themselves under their longing expeétancies with nuts and damsons. Now and then, they broke out into Bear Garden acclamations of 'Show, show, show, show,' till at laſt, in answer to their loud-mouthed importunities, the curtain was drawn up, to reveal a trunk-breeches king in a fool's cap, and a feather in it, attended by his cringing nobility, some Court jilts, and two or three flattering prieſts which I suppose the poet thought to be as true a representation of an old English Court as possibly he could think on. After these had entertained the liſtening audience a little with their fustian confabulations, they made their exeunt, and the scene was shifted into a library where Friar Bacon, by his long study, had projected a brazen head, and was to wall the kingdom with the same metal, had not the devil caught him napping, and broke his most wonderful noddle into many pieces.

The priest grown drowsy with much reading, rubbed his eyes, arose from his elbow chair, and in my opinion, seemed both by his looks and actions much too ignorant as well as too young, for such a notable undertaking. When he had raved and strutted about a little, with his magician's wand, he began, like a true priest, to make large promises to the people of wonderful things which he very well knew would never come to pass, and after he had made a short oration in praise of his brazen-head, the scene changed, and shut him up in his study to consult the devil a little farther.

Then entered the miller and his son Ralph. The father seemed to be the same thing he imitated and as for his hopeful progeny, he was the only person we were desirous of seeing. I think he kept up so true a behaviour of an idiot, that it was enough to persuade the audience that he really was by Nature what he only artfully represented. I could not but conclude the part was particularly adapted to his genius, or he could never have expressed the humour with such agreeable simplicity. But, I fancy, if he was to play the part of a wise man, it would be quite out of his way. There was nothing in the part itself but what was purely owing to his own gesture, for it was the comedian only, and not the poet, that rendered the character diverting. To be plain, they both acted and became their characters extremely well, for I cannot but acknowledge that I never saw anybody look more like a fool than the son, nor any miller look more like a cozening knave than the father.

The next part of the Droll that was diverting, was the country justice, whose weakness and indiscretion, I suppose, were designed to let the people know what ignorant magistrates have sometimes the administration of justice, and how common a thing it is for a wise man to bow a learned head to an empty noddle in authority. These were the chief of their characters, with a flying shoulder of mutton, dancing and singing devils, and such-like pieces of conjuration by the diabolical Friar Bacon, with whose magical pranks the mob were wonderfully pleased, as well as greatly astonished.

Having thus entertained us for about three-quarters of an hour, at last, with a most splendid appearance of all their lords and ladies, they concluded their Droll. Then, from the glittering assembly, one of the best-mouthed orators steps to the front of the stage and with a cringing piece of formality, promises the audience to begin again in half an hour, as if they believed people to be such fools to fling away their money so unprofitably twice in one day, when the seeing of them once is enough to tire any man of reasonable patience.

The show being thus ended, my friend asked me how I liked it?

' Truly,' said I, ' 'tis a very moral play, if the spectators have sense enough to make use of it.'

At this saying my friend burst into a laughter. ' Prithee,' says he, 'wherein lies the morality of it?'

' Why, truly,' said I, ' it will serve to let us know how familiar a priest, notwithstanding his Holy Orders, may be with the devil; how easily the clergy may impose upon the vulgar a belief in those things which never were or can be; what a blockhead may be a Justice of the Peace; how a rich cunning knave may have a fool for his son; how a woman will cheat her father to oblige her gallant; what stratagems lovers will project to accomplish their ends, and what jack-puddings men will make of themselves to get a little money.'

' On my word,' says he, ' you have made a rare use of it, indeed. But I very much question whether anybody else will be half so much the better for it, for it may be observed that

Bartholomew Fair Drolls are like State fireworks; they rarely do anybody good but those who are concerned in the show.'

From thence with much difficulty, we crossed over to the hospital gate, being jumbled about in the crowd like a couple of Tories at a Whig election. Here stood a comical figure gaping and drumming, so that his beard wagged up and down like an alderman's chin at a Lord Mayor's feast, and his eyes rolled about so that some of the ignorant spectators, that stood crowding beneath, began to cry out, ' Lord! do but see how he stares at us, and gnashes his teeth as if he could eat us for looking at him.'

On each side of him stood a wax baby which appeared so very natural that it induced us to walk in and take a sight of their whole works. Upon our first entrance of the room we were much astonished at the liveliness of the figures, who sat in such easy postures, and their hands disposed with such a becoming freedom, that life itself could not have appeared less stiff, or the whole frame more regular. The eyes were fixed with great tenderness, which I apprehended as a great difficulty, so that the most experienced of our charming ladies could not, after an hour's practice in her glass, have looked more soft and languishing.

Whilst we were thus viewing the Temple of Diana, for under that title they had distinguished their show, up comes a country carter in his boots, armed with his weapon of correction, by which he governs and chastizes his five four-legged subjects, belonging, as I suppose, to some hay-cart in the market.

As soon as the hobbady bobbody was brought to the door of the room where the figures were seated, he peeps in, and seeing, as he thought such a number of great persons steps back and doffs his hat. 'Ads-bleed,' says he, ' I waant gooe in among zo many vine voulk, not I; what dost send a man up to be made a gam on? Pray gim me my money again, for I don't come here to be laughed at.' The mistress of the show, with all the arguments she could use, had much ado to prevail upon the fellow to go in, telling him he was deceived, and that those fine people, as he thought 'em, were only waxworks, which was the sight he was to see.

At laſt the bumpkin took courage and ventured into the show-room, but could not forbear making his country honours to the ladies, till he was ready to claw the boards up with his hobnails. When he had looked round him and pretty well feaſted his eyes, he turns about to the girl that shows 'em, says he, ' They are woundy silent, I pray you, vorsooth can they speak?' At which the young damsel fell a-laughing, saying, ' You muſt speak to 'em firſt, and then, perhaps, they'll answer you.' With that the foolish ignoramus did as he was bid, crying to one of the figures, ' How d'ye forsooth? You in the black hood. Evaith I'll give ye a pot en you'n speak to a man.'

At which the whole company burſt into a laughter, which made the fellow so angry, that in a passion he thus expressed himself. 'Adsheartlywounds, why what d'ye make a gam at a body vor? A plague bran ye for a pack of zimpletons. Why, I zee some little voulk but o'er the waiy, no lighter than a flaggon; I believe they are the zons and daughters of these gentlevoulk here, and they cou'd tauk as well as I can.'

A notable pert gentlewoman ſtanding by him, says she, ' Well, countryman, what you think of that lady you spoke to for making love to?' 'Ads me loif,' says he, ' for all she looks so woundy gainly, now she's dressed, when she comes to pluck off her paint and her patches, and doff her vine clothes, she perhaps, may look as ugly as you do, forsooth.' Which clownish repartee so dashed the lady out of countenance, that her blushes shewed she had a modeſt sense of her own failings and imperfections.

Having satisfied our curiosities with art's niceſt imitation of human nature, we returned again into the multitude,

considering what folly we should commit next, that would
yield us any tolerable diversion. Upon further consideration
we at laſt agreed to spend an hour in a music-booth.

In pursuance of our design we pressed through the crowd,
till we crossed the Fair to the nor'weſt side, where music-
houses ſtood thick by another and at every door two or three
Tyburn-looking scaramouches who, rather than encourage
people to walk in, were, as I imagined, a means rather to
affright 'em from entering, for fear of having their throats
cut, or their pockets picked. But, however, hoping to fare
as well as our neighbours, we ventured into one of their
diabolical academies.

At our firſt entrance the dancing in several disguises made
it appear to me like a rendezvous of gipsies upon the eleċtion
of a new king, or like so many ſtrolling beggars making
merry in a barn. As soon as ever the curtain was put up,
and we approached the bar, a cracked bell was rung by a
weather-beaten harraden, dressed up in white, as if she had
been going to beg some rogue of a gallant from the gallows.
No sooner had the untunable alarm reached the ears of the
dispersed attendants, but a frizzle-pated drawer with a face
bloated by much tippling, and an indigo apron hanging down
to his toes followed by half a dozen of his dancing scarecrows, some in masks as ugly as the faces that were without,
bid us welcome in such hoarse voices, that their speeches
sounded to me more like the croaking of ravens, than like
the organs of human utterance. Seeing us look a degree
above common cuſtomers, I suppose, they were in hopes we
would prove the greater bubbles, and as a means to encourage
us to the utmoſt extravagancy, they conduċted us to the
further end of their fools' paradise, and placed us upon a
platform, which separate apartment was exempt from the
dishonour of inferior liquors, and nothing suffered to disgrace
your table beneath a half-crown flask.

As soon as our wine came, and we had filled a glass, the

kettle-drums and trumpets began to express their willingness
to oblige us. This was performed with such harmonious
excellence, that no sow-gelder with his horn, or cooper with
his adze and driver, could have gratified our ears with more
delightful music. This was succeeded by a concert of fiddlers,
with whose melodious diddle-daddle I was so affećted, that
it made my teeth dance in my mouth.

The next piece of harmony that laid siege to my ears, was a
moſt admirable new ballad, sung in two parts by seven voices.
I called the drawer, and bid him aſk them if they were not
singing the *Cat-Catch*. He brought me word, No, that it was
a very fine play-house song, set by the beſt composer in
England. ' Why then,' said I, ' pray tell your songſters they
deserve to be whipped at the cart's tail for attempting to sing it,
and that I had rather hear a boy beat " Roundheaded cuckolds
come Dig " upon his snappers, or an old barber ring Whitting-
ton's bells upon a citern, than hear all the music they can
make.' Which message, I suppose the fellow was afraid to
tell 'em, leſt they should crack his crown with the bass-fiddle
ſticks.

That we might have a taſte of all their varieties, the next
inſtrument they betook themselves to were hautboys, which
are undoubtedly the beſt windpipes in the world to scare a
man out of his wits, and I dare swear would raise the devil,
the father of all discord, much sooner than ever Friar Bacon
or Cornelius Agrippa[1] could by their diabolical invocations.
For my part, I declare, their disproportioned notes and
imperfećt cadences had such an effećt upon my ears that
I thought their noise would have burſt my head and put my
whole microcosm in such a disorderly trembling that had
they tooted a little longer, I believe I should have been all
disjointed, for such music is enough to make a man's bones

---

[1] A famous German scientist, of the early 16th century, who wrote *De
Occulta Philosophia* and claimed a proficiency in the Black Arts. He asserted
that he had an attendant demon who took the shape of a black dog.

dance out of their sockets, and put his whole body under a painful dislocation.

The harshness of their notes having, like a ring of bells, or a peal of cannon, boxed our ears into a deafness, they now began to treat our eyes with an entertainment, and presented us with a dance in imitation of a footpad's robbery, and he that acted the thief, I protest, did it so much like a rogue, that had he not often committed the same thing in earnest, I am very apt to believe he could never have made such a jest on't; firing his pistol, stripping the victim, and searching his pockets, with so much natural humour, seeming satisfaction and dexterity, that he showed himself an absolute master of what he pretended to. And I cannot forbear having so little charity as to fancy that his last caper will be so far off the ground, and that he will quite lose his breath before he comes down again.

The next that presented herself to the view was a bouncing beldam, who had as much flesh on her bones as a Lincoln-shire heifer, so that her hips, without the help of fardingales, looked as round as the stern of a Dutch fly-boat. The admirable qualifications of this lady were to dance with glasses full of liquor upon the backs of her hands, to which she gave variety of motions, without spilling, expressing in her exercise as much prodigality as if riches, fame and honour had been the rewards of her foolery, till at last having quite lost her spirits, she was forced to conclude her awkward steps and elephant capers and rest her unwieldy carcase on the nearest bench. There she panted like a race-horse that had won the plate, or a bear-dog after a let-go, the mob declaring their approbation and applause by clapping their hands, and knocking their heels, which was no little satisfaction to the wobbling squab, with whose unpolished salutation they were so highly delighted.

The next figure that appeared was a youthful damsel, who to render her more charming, was dressed up in her holland

smock and fringed petticoat, like a rope-dancer. Having taken
the swords of most of the gentlemen in the room she stepped
into the centre of the booth, and there began to handle them
as dexterously as a Welsh shepherdess does her knitting
needles, putting herself into a circular dance, wherein she
turned as merrily round, as the flyer of Jack, or as nimbly as
a top under the scourge of a schoolboy, shifting her swords to
all parts of her face and breast to the very great amazement
of country fools, though very little danger to her own carcase.

When, by her unalterable circumvolutions she had supplied
the defects and weaknesses of the liquor and made most of
the company drunk and giddy with observing the nimbleness
of her tail, which, according to the knife grinder's song ran
' Round, and around and around a,' she gave a stamp with her
foot which served as a period to her dance. This, according
to custom, was rewarded with a clap, being the true theatre and
music-house method of expressing our thanks or approbation.

This was succeeded by abundance of insipid stuff so very
sorrily designed and so wretchedly performed that instead of
either laughter or delight, it begot in me nothing but blushes
and contempt; for I thought it an abuse to human shape, for
anything that bore the proportions of either sex to behave
themselves so ostentatiously foolish, so odiously impudent, so
intolerably dull and void of all humour, order, or design;
there being more diversion in the accidental gestures of one
ape than in all the studied performances of the whole company
of pretending vagabonds. We therefore think it not worth
while to trouble the reader with any further particulars of their
ridiculous, poor pedantic fooleries, but shall leave 'em to
a further shameful exposing of their own ignorance and proceed to a rough draught of the company who chiefly frequent
these scandalous nurseries of all vice, vanity and villainy.

Some companions were so very oddly mixed that there was
no manner of coherence between the figure of any one person
and another. One, perhaps, would appear in a laced hat, red

stockings, puff-wig and the like, as prim as if going to the dancing-school; the next a butcher, with his blue sleeves and woollen apron, as if just come from the slaughter-house; a third, a fellow in a Yorkshire cloth-coat, with a leg laid over his oaken cudgel, the head of which was a knob as big as a turnip; another was in a soldier's habit, and looked as if he thought every fresh man that came in a constable. These mixed with women of as different appearance. One was in a straw hat and blue apron, with impudence enough in her face to dash a begging clergyman out of countenance, and he that can publicly ask alms in a parson's gown, if he has a title to wear it, one would reasonably think, has impudence enough to face anybody. Another was dressed up in hood, scarf, and top-knot, with her clothes hung on according to the Drury Lane mode; a third was in a white sarsnet hood, and had a posy in her bosom, as if she was come from the funeral of some good neighbour, and among the rest, a girl of about a dozen years of age, whom, I suppose, they were early dragging up in the wicked ways of shame and misery. These were at one table, and of one society, and though severally and singularly dressed, yet I could do no other than conjecture from their carriage and physiognomy that they were under one and the same influence, and that their unlucky stars had infused the like evil genius into every person among 'em; for the women looked like jilts; the men swore like pick-pockets, and all were as drunk as swine, and as merry as beggars.

Just beneath us on the side of the platform, sat a couple of madams over a stone bottle of ale, who, by their want of stays, the airiness of their dress, the improvement of their complexion by paint, and the multitude of patches to add a genteel air to their countenances, we could guess no other than ladies of that wretched quality, whose pride, poverty and laziness had reduced to a necessity of exposing themselves for sale at a small purchase. For in came a fellow that I have heard cry with 'Brushes and Mousetraps' about Town, and a smith along with him, that I have seen hawk about iron candlesticks, and being almost drunk they must needs, after two or three awkward scrapes and compliments, beg the ladies good company to drink a bottle of cider, which the willing damsels, without any manner of scruple, very readily complied with.

So they all removed to another table, which they thought was more commodious for their entertainment, where the old coxcombs' court to the ladies was so singular and comical that it made the whole company observe their ridiculous behaviour; but at last discovering by the people's tittering that they were become a public jest, they agreed with their mistresses, as I suppose, to remove to some private place convenient for their intrigue. But as they were leading their condescending madams out of the booth, with abundance of formal ceremony, the gallants, notwithstanding their holiday clothes, being known to some of the guests, were accosted as they made their exit with, ' Will you buy a mouse-trap, or a rat-trap? Will you buy a cloth-brush, a hat-brush, or a comb-brush?' So, they sneaked off with the doxies, as much ashamed as a perjured witness out of Westminster Hall.

At another table sat a parcel of rural sots, who were elevated to such a pitch of merriment that they began to talk like old women at a gossiping and swear as fast as a gamester curses the dice, when he meets with ill-fortune, showing as many ungainly postures over their liquor as a parcel of swine made drunk with hog-wash. These, to make their ale run down more cheerful, had got with them a female fiddler, who had charged her carcase with more than her legs were able to carry, and behaved herself in sight of the whole company with such unparalleled impudence in singing ribald songs with a hiccoughing voice, that I was afraid her nauseous behaviour, together with her odious discord, would have raised in me such an aversion to both women and music that I should never hereafter agree with the common opinion, that is, esteem 'em as the choicest of blessings on this side Heaven.

Then in came a couple of seamen in their canvas jackets, just stepped from aboard ship, to give themselves a taste of the Fair's delights, expressing in their looks such a wonderful satisfaction, that a bailiff at a prize, or a butcher at a bull-baiting, could not have showed more signs of gladness.

At last one of them ordered the music to play an old Wapping jig, and plucked out of his pocket a clean white handkerchief, which, I suppose, he borrowed of his landlady on purpose to dance with, being, as I imagined, no more able to cut a caper without that in his hand, than a fellow is able to dance the morris without his bells, or a beau court a lady without his snuff-box in his hand.

Thus equipped for the business, he stepped into the middle of the booth, and after he had made his honours with as much grace as a cow might make a curtsey, he began to caper round the room, entertaining us with so many antic steps, merry-andrew postures, and country cuts and shuffles with his feet, that no Jack Adams at Clerkenwell feast, or drunken plough-man upon my lady's birthday could have been more divert-ing. His comrade cried out every now and then, ' Gad ha' mercy, Robin! Now Kate of Dover's step! Cheer up, my lad! Ah, bravely done, boy! Now for a sea-pie and a can of flip!'

Thus he jigged it about with his greasy hat in one hand, and apron in t'other, till he was quite out of breath. Having thus put a period to his wild jig, his companion met him with a quartern of brandy and clapped him on the side for encourage-ment, as a butcher does his bulldog.

What further lay within our observation were the sundry sorts of women who sat ready, upon small consideration, to give their company to every drunken libertine. Some were very well dressed, and wore masks, who, notwithstanding their demure appearance, were as ready at your beck as a porter plying at a street corner; others were barefaced, and in mean garb, whose poverty seemed equal to their impudence, and they were so fulsome and preposterous that they were as great antidotes to debauchery as the counterfeit modest behaviour of a cunning, pretty harlot is a means to enforce desire. A third sort of strumpet were in blue aprons and straw hats, and by much loud bawling of oysters about the streets, were as hoarse as a jack-pudding at the latter end of the Fair.

Having taken notice of most of the particulars that lay within our view, by paying our reckoning we purchased our redemption from the epitome of hell, and being now almost dark, we turned round the outside of the Fair, at the back of the booths, where we found several emblems of the world's giddiness—children in flying coaches [swings], who insensibly climbed upwards, knowing not whither they were going, but being once elevated to a certain height, they came down again according to the circular motion of the sphere they move in.

' These whirligigs,' says my friend, ' may be very properly applied to the common fate of great men, for when a man is once rising, it is not very difficult for him to rise to the top, but 'tis impossible for him, as you may see by these, to continue long at the same pitch. For this world is but Fortune's well, and mankind are the buckets thereof, which are so cunningly hung, that the winding up of one must be the letting down of the other.'

From thence we moved with the stream, and passed by a couple of puppet-shows where monkeys in the balconies were imitating men, and men making themselves monkeys, to engage some of the weaker part of the multitude, as women and children, to step in and please themselves with the wonderful agility of these wooden performers. These we passed by with much contempt and squeezed on amongst the rest, till we came again to the Hospital Gate, which we entered till at last we came to the cloisters, where we met such a whispering and humming of ' G——d D——mes ; she's a cat, and t'other's a wench,' and ' That's a fine woman, t'other's a pretty creature,' that I thought the people were all mad, and that this place was a Bedlam for lovers.

A gentleman with a red face, who my friend told me was known at all gaming ordinaries, steps up to a very pert lady, who, as I suppose, was not for his turn, and claps his bare hand on her neck. ' Dear Madam,' says he, ' you are as cold as a cricket in an ice-house.' She turning short about, looked upon him, and replied, ' If you please to clap your fiery face to my back, 'twill be the ready way to warm me!' At which smart return, all that heard it fell a-laughing. The gentleman thinking it a little inconsistent with his honour to be thus put upon had a great mind to redeem his credit, by adding, ' Indeed, Madam, I find your tongue's much nimbler than the rest of your members, for your body moves like a loaded waggon up a hill.' ' Dear sir,' says she, ' you look so like a honest gentle-man, that I am bound in gratitude, to return you at least an empty cart for your loaded waggon, and as for the hill, pray, sir, let it be Holborn, and I don't question but your good life in time may direct you to the use and application of both; so, sir, your humble servant.' And away she stepped into a raffling shop, where some civil gentleman followed her, and to reward her wit, loaded her and her she-friend that was with her, with silver nick-nacks, and guarded her into a coach from the insolence of the Town cormorants, who had a wonderful mind to be snapping at so fair a bait.

This rendezvous of jilts, harlots and sharpers began now to be very full, insomuch that the foul atmosphere was so offensive that the pumping of a Derby-ale cellar could not have surprised our smell with a more intolerable nosegay. This we were forced to endure or quit the place, which we were unwilling to do till we had made a more nice inspection into the pomps and vanities of this wicked world.

To further discover these we went into one of the shops that we saw most crowded, and like poor spectators, with willing hearts and low pockets, stood in the rear peeping over the

N

shoulders of those that raffled. I observed this ridiculous vanity, that whatever the gentleman won, they presented to the fair lady that stood next though perfect strangers one to another.

'You are insensible,' says my friend, 'of the cunning that's used by sharpers, to make this kind of diversion turn to a good account. That pretty sort of a woman who receives so many presents, to my knowledge is mistress to him who is now handling the box, who has no other business but to improve such a lucky minute to his maintenance; and he seems, as you see, to be an utter stranger to that lady he's so kind to, and only makes her mistress of his winnings, purely to draw the other gentlemen on to do the like, that what presents they foolishly bestow on her to-night, may serve to furnish his pockets for the hazard table on the morrow.'

Being tired with this pastime we adjourned from thence, and crept up a pair of stairs as narrow and as steep as the stone steps of a belfry, over which was written in golden capitals THE GROOM-PORTERS[1] in two or three places, designed, as I suppose, to make fools to think it was the honester for his name being there, and that they might as fairly fling away their money here as in any place in Christendom. When, to the danger of our necks, we had climbed to the top, we stepped into a little room on the left hand, where lawyers' clerks and gentlemen footmen were mixed higgle-de-piggle-de, like knaves and fools at an East India House auction, and were wrangling over their sixpences with as much eagerness as so many mumpers at a Church door about the true division of a good Christian's charity.

Being quickly surfeited with the boyish behaviour of these callow rakes, we moved from thence into the next room, where

---

[1] The Groom-Porter was an officer in the Royal Household, whose duty it was to tend the king's apartments and see that it was supplied with cards, dice and other gambling appurtenances. At Christmas he was allowed to keep an open gaming-table. It was also part of his duty to supervise and license all gaming-houses and take action against those not conducted in an orderly fashion. Action was seldom taken, however, against ill-conducted gambling-dens, and the utmost rioting frequently took place in the Groom-Porter's own gaming-house.

a parcel of old buttered bullies, some with carbonadoed faces, and others with squashed noses, were seated close round a great table. Amongst 'em were a few declining tradesmen who, I suppose, were ready to leave for some foreign plantation, and came hither to acquire the qualifications of a libertine that their portion in this world might be a merry life and a short one.

Curses were as profusely scattered as lies among travellers, and as many eyes lifted towards the heavens in confusion of their stars, as there are on board a ship in a storm to implore safety. Money was tossed about as if a useless commodity, and several parts of the story of the Prodigal Son were acted here to a miracle. When four had the good fortune to come before seven, or ten before eight, the losers were so nettled they were unable to be easy in their seats, and could no more keep the ends of their fingers out of their mouths, than a porter, when he plucks off his hat, can forbear scratching of his head. The dice had far more influence upon 'em than the planets, for every man changed countenance according to the fortune of the cast, and some of them, I am sure, in half an hour showed all the passions incident to human nature.

He that made the most observable figure amongst 'em was a butcher in his white frock, with a head as large as a Saracen's and cheeks as plump as a trumpeter's when he proclaims his profession by his semicircular trumpet; his beard looked as frowsy and irregular as the giants' whiskers in the Guildhall, that seem so terrible to young apprentices. The hair of his head shined with the pomatum of beef and mutton, like a satin cap upon the noddle of an independent teacher. I could not but take notice, whenever he made his stake, he cried, ' Go again,' which served me to understand he was a truly Hockly-i'-th'-Hole sportsman,[1] it being the same expression they use to their dogs, after the first let-go.

[1] One of London's three bear-gardens was at Hockley-in-the-Hole, Clerkenwell. The sport of bear- or bull-baiting consisted in chaining the beast to an iron ring fixed in a stake, the chain being some 15 feet long. Butchers and others anxious to exercise their dogs stood round, each holding his dog by the ears.

I observed he was attended with great luck, enough to make us believe, according to the burlesque of Ovid's saying, that Fortune favours fat folks. Whenever he handled the dice, he had so lucky a devil in the box, or at his elbow, that he very seldom threw out under three or four hands holding in, which occasioned his peevish antagonists to view him with such sour countenances that no lover that had lost his mistress, or client that had lost his cause, could have contracted his face into a more fretful posture.

Length of time having made this diversion as dull as the rest, we left the losers to recover their losses, and the butcher to bring his hogs to a fair market; returning downstairs with as much care and caution of tumbling head foremost, as he that goes down Green Arbour Court steps[1] in the middle of winter. When we were got safe to the bottom, being quite tired with the sundry follies we had seen, and the brain-breaking noises we had heard, my friend desired my company into Charterhouse Lane, where he was obliged to make a short visit to a patient, leaving me at an ale-house hard by to divert myself in his absence with a pipe of tobacco. This I did, accordingly, and refreshed myself with a pot of excellent English liquor, which was as comfortable to my palate, after our troublesome survey, as a down bed to the haunches of a weary traveller. By the time I had lit my pipe, in came a couple of old fellows who looked as if they were the superannuated servants of some great man, who to exempt himself from the charge of keeping 'em when past their labour, and to reward the faithful service of their youth, had got 'em into a hospital. They seated themselves down in the next box, and called for a pot

At a signal one of the dogs was let loose to worry the beast—or be killed by it. Bulls and bears were never allowed to be killed in these fights, but were reserved until old age or sickness rendered them incapable of providing sport. The other bear-gardens were in Marylebone Fields (Soho Square) and Tothill Fields, Westminster.

[1] A flight of very steep and usually muddy steps that led from Green Arbour Court, in Old Bailey, down to the wharves by the Fleet River.

of warm ale, over which, after they had accommodated their
jaws with a pipe of tobacco, they began to bemoan some
great oppressions that were imposed upon 'em by the ruler
of their society, whom they charged with these following
accusations, beginning their complaint after this sorrowful
manner:

' I remember,' says one, ' two old proverbs from my youth,
which alas! I have found too true in my age. New Lords,
new Laws; when the old one's gone, seldom comes a better.
And i'faith, brother, we have found both too true to make a
jest on, for our allowance, formerly, if any of us were sick
and out of commons, was five shillings and elevenpence a
week, but now our good master, Providence reward him for
his kindness, has reduced us to four shillings and fivepence,
which, let me tell you, is a great abatement in so small a sum,
and is a very great abuse of the pious design and charitable
good will of the donor. We likewise, when we were sick, had
a bushel of coals per week allowed us, to warm our old noses,
but now we are stinted to just half the quantity, thanks to
our good master for his Christian love and kindness to us.

' Sometime since, a brother pensioner was sick with a violent
flux, from the middle of September to within ten days of
Christmas, in which time his nurse went several times to the
master, to obtain a grant of five shillings and elevenpence
per week, and a whole bushel of coals, declaring that his
short allowance was not sufficient to support him in his low
condition. But, notwithstanding all her reasonable pleas
and importunate solicitations on her patient's behalf, the
master would give no ear to her petitions, not taking into his
consideration the coldness of the weather, or the tediousness
of his sickness.

' Besides our diet is much abated of our ancient allowance,
neither is the meat so good, and notwithstanding these great
abuses and retrenchments of us poor pensioners, he has
procured his own salary to be advanced from fifty to two

hundred pounds per annum; he now keeps his coach and lives as great as the Governor of a town, instead of a master of a hospital.'

' Indeed,' replied the other, "tis a sad thing we should be so served, but since we can't help it, we must content ourselves I think, with the cold comfort of an old saying, What can't be cured must be endured; for complaint without the prospect of redress, is like a man venting his anger towards another by talking to himself.'

By this time my friend came in, to whom I communicated what I had overheard, who made light of it, as if they were such common abuses as were scarce worth listening to, saying you never knew any considerable hospital in your life, but the poor pensioners live like common seamen in an East India vessel, whose allowances are so short homeward bound that they are but just kept alive in a starving condition, whilst the officers grow fat at a plentiful table, and pinch estates in a little time, by abridging the just dues of their floating society.

Thus heartily tired with our ramble, we paid our reckoning, and posted home to bed, with as good an appetite to rest as a hungry ploughman to a plum-pudding on a Sunday, when he had walked three miles from church.

POSTSCRIPT

The wonderful eclipse which, according to the promises of astronomers, was to bring this wicked world within ambs-ace of the Day of Judgement, was invisible to us at London, by reason of a fog that arose from reeking dunghills, distillers' vats, and other nastiness, which, as the learned said, could neither be rarefied nor dispersed till the eclipse was over, by reason that the beams of the sun were intercepted by the moon's body. Letters from many credible persons in several countries, who I hope are all well as I am at this present writing, praised be —— for it, name thousands who beheld the prodigy as plain as the old woman saw the needle in the barn door, who enquired (after she pretended to see the needle) whereabouts the barn ſtood.

But to confirm our infallible planet-keepers in their unerring judgements, it was seen upon the road by many travellers, especially by ſtrolling tinkers, Scotch pedlars, gypsies, vagabonds and others, who, if you cross but their hands with a piece of silver, or clear but their eyes with a cup of humming liquor, are able to see the fairies dance, spirits walk, witches fly, prodigies in the clouds, blemishes in the sun, or the world in the moon. And since our ſtar-gazers have such good evidence to prove the matter of faċt, I think we had as good put the conteſt out of dispute, and agree with what they say, whose business it is to know moſt of the matter. But as a further proof of the eclipse, which is ſtill ridiculed amongſt some obſtinate believers, these following persons do say, or think they saw it as plain in the Town, as ever 'twas seen in the country.

A vintner behind the 'Change, being very desirous of making a clear discovery of this dangerous interposition, got a piece of clay, and beſtowed an hour's time in ſtopping up the bottom of his cullender, all but the middle hole, through which he peeped from nine to eleven, and does think he saw the moon, or a cloud between the sun and the cullender, but cannot be positive which, and therefore his evidence is of little validity.

An upholſterer in Cornhill, anxious to be as wise as the reſt of his neighbours, carried a looking-glass out of his shop into Stocks Market[1] and after he had earneſtly looked for half an hour and had observed a small glimpse of the eclipse, a porter coming by with a heavy burden, by accident ſtumbled and pitched the corner of his bundle between the upholſterer's neck and shoulders, knocked him down, and broke the looking-glass; and the porter recovering himself, marched forward

[1] This was an old market for fish and vegetables, which took its name from a pair of stocks. Its site is now occupied by the Mansion House.

with his load. Up rises the fallen gazer from the ground, with nothing but the frame and back board in his hand, and shaking his head at his misfortune, thus expressed himself to the people: 'Alas! Alas! I fear the terrible effects of this eclipse will be very fatal to poor England, for if just a glimpse of it will bring a man to this disaster, may Providence defend the whole kingdom from its malicious influence.'

Happening to be in company with a very famous astrologer, I was willing to enquire a little into what effects he thought the eclipse would have upon that part of the world to which 'twas visible, more especially England.

' Why,' says he, ' as you ask me the question modestly, I'll tell you, Master. I do understand from the authentic censures of Albumazar and Ptolemy, concerning the circumvolution of celestial bodies, which procure perpetual mutability in this lower region, that this eclipse being at the new of the moon, when she first puts on her horns, does infallibly predict as many cuckolds to be at Horn Fair[1] this year, as have been seen there this seven years. Many litigious law-lovers this year will sell their coats to contend for the value of a button, and the lawyers prate the fools into compliance by bringing them to poverty. The poor will die this year faster than the rich, because there is an hundred of the one to one of the other. The fingers of envy will pick out the eyes of many a man's reputation, and the affections of women will be as easily gained and as hardly preserved as ever. To be plain, I believe we shall have much such another world on't, as we had the last year, and so, I suppose, we shall not differ in opinion.'

[1] Horn Fair was held at Charlton, on St. Luke's Day, October the 18th, on a field adjoining the church. It was a disorderly fair of the most rowdy nature, and though antiquarians have debated upon the origin of its name, in the popular mind it was associated solely with the horns symbolical of unfortunate married men. The custom was for parties to sail down from London to Cuckold's Point, Rotherhithe, and then go in a motley procession—all wearing horns—to Charlton Church. In another book Ward gives an entertaining account of the cuckold-makers' pilgrimage thither.

CHAPTER TWELVE

A Coffee-house in Aldersgate—The wonderful piece of Beef—How it was Cooked—How it was Eaten—The Lord Mayor's Show

HAVING heard of a famed coffee-house in Aldersgate Street, where doctors of the body, who study Machiavelli much more than Hippocrates, metamorphose themselves into State politicians, we were willing to refresh our intellects with their improving discourses. Thither accordingly we steered our course, and entered the ancient fabric by antiquity made venerable, whose inside was lined with as great a number of Geneva Christians, as if they were met to sign some canting address to cheat the Government into a good opinion of their loyalty. Some were highly extolling the Dutch Government, setting forth the freedom and prosperity of all such people as flourish under the happy constitution of a commonwealth. Others commended the conduct of all affairs under the protectorship of Cromwell, and how far the felicity of the nation in those days exceeded the present happiness of the kingdom, so much boasted of by the blind lovers of kingly power and episcopacy.

At last up starts a bundle of verbosity, scarce tall enough to be a complete man, nor short enough to be a monkey. His tongue began to flutter about his mouth, spitting venom against the monarch. He has one rhetorical excellency which becomes him wonderfully, he will assert a falsity to be truth with as graceful an impudence, as ever did the Salamanca saviour of our lives and liberties,[1] when he affirmed Don John

---

[1] Titus Oates, the infamous perjurer, claimed to have taken his degree at the great university of Salamanca. This was a lie; his nearest approach to that distinction was when he studied at the Jesuit college at Valladolid, from which he was expelled, after a few months' residence, for gross misdemeanours.

of Austria to be a tall black man, though was quite opposite to this description. He is one who will never own himself to be in the wrong, and yet is never in the right; but takes as much pleasure in the justification of a lie, as if he were cut out by nature to be a plot-evidence. He has got the secret history of King Charles and King James, also *Imago Regis*,[1] and some other famed pieces of the Doctor's scurrility by heart, and has acquired from thence as rare a knack of railing against kings, justifying the martyrdom of King Charles, and blackening the race of the Stuarts, as if he was become a wasp with a natural propensity to sting and wound the memory of so unfortunate a family.

I thought it so ungrateful to any charitable ear to hear a rattle-headed prattle-box set up to reform the Church, new-model the Government, and calumniate the best of Princes, that I no longer could forbear giving him such a reproof as I thought so vain a babbler did in justice deserve. My friend and I gave him no time to cool, but still fed his passion with a supply of sharp reflections on his past talk, till we had spurred him at last to such a pitch of madness, that he boiled up into a ridiculous froth, which rendered him the laughing-stock of the whole company.

As soon as he was gone, I was desirous of knowing who this carcase full of spleen, ignorance and ill-nature could be; and to satisfy my curiosity, I enquired of a gentleman that sat next me, who showed by his talk he had some knowledge of him, and he told me, the chief of his business was to sell pictures by auction.

' Nay,' says my friend, 'if he be an auctioneer, he's the more excusable, for cozening and lying are the two most necessary talents of his profession, and I'll warrant you, he puts 'em both in practice as often as he has opportunity, because he would

---

[1] On Queen Mary's death, in 1696, Titus Oates issued a coarse libel on her father, entitled Εἰκὼν Βασιλεκή, or the *Picture of the late King James, drawn to the Life*.

not willingly lose such profitable qualifications for want of using.'

As my friend and I were reflecting between ourselves upon some of the insolent expressions of our scatter-brained rene-gado, a merry pleasant-looking gentleman stepped into the coffee-house, sat down and whilst he was filling a pipe of tobacco, entertained the company with this following intelli-gence; a remarkable breakfast would be prepared by a generous vintner, on Tuesday, the 24th, in order to treat his guests on the following Thursday morning, upon which day all customers were to be free to feast their bellies. He gave us an account of this after a comical manner, which I will endeavour to imitate, in hopes to divert the reader.

'Gentlemen,' says he, 'I have seen such a sight to-day as would make a Spaniard change his pace, and turn his stately steps into a dog-trot, to run after it, nay, make a Dutchman in surprise pluck his hands out of his pockets, and hold 'em up, like an Englishman going to be hanged, to praise the God of plenty for blessing his greedy eyes with so wonderful a feast; or put a Frenchman into as great an amazement, as the snow did the Bantam ambassador.'

'Pray, sir,' says a grave gentleman that sat by, 'would it make an Englishman do nothing?'

'Yes, sir,' answered the other, 'it would make an English-man whet his knife if it were dressed, and fall on without grace, and stuff his belly till he was as hard as a football, before he would rise from the table.'

'But, sir,' says the old gentleman, 'you'll forget, I am afraid, to tell us what it was; we want to know that, sir.'

'Why, sir,' says he, 'then I'll tell you. It was a piece of roasting beef, but of such an extraordinary size, that ten men might ride upon it without incommoding themselves in any other way than by greasing their breeches, and but turn it on its back, and it will carry as many people within side as a Gravesend wherry; it was the whole length of a huge, large, long, Lincolnshire ox,[1] fed up from a calf upon all long grass, that he might grow the longer.

'There were no scales at the Custom House big enough to weigh it, so that they were forced to drive it down to Wapping in a cart, and weigh it by an anchor-smith's steelyards, where they weigh their anchors to discover the true weight, it proving upon exact computation to be four hundred and fifteen pounds, which magnificent piece of beef, notwithstanding its ponderosity, will certainly on a day appointed, by some strong-jawed men of the law, be taken up by the teeth.'

'But, pray, sir,' says Mr. Inquisitive, 'how did they get it home to the tavern?'

The gentleman replied, 'It was killed in Butcher Hall Lane and removed from thence, by the assistance of as many butchers walking under it as there are porters under a pageant upon a Lord Mayor's day; some of the bloody fraternity walked before, with their cleavers mounted on their shoulders, like so many maces, and thus they conveyed it home in as much triumph as if it had been a City magistrate going to persecute the bakers.'

'Pray, sir,' said I, 'where is this Leviathan of beef to be devoured, that a man may view this gluttonous prodigy, before the cooks have mangled it out of all hope with their buck's-horn-handled scimitars?'

'Why, sir,' says he, 'at the King's Head Tavern near Chancery Lane End,[2] where the best wine in England is to be drank, and the stateliest piece of beef in Christendom is to be roasted.'

Our pipes being out, we determined to adjourn to the tavern where the gentleman reported this extravagant breakfast was to be eaten.

[1] A monster ox which was shown at May Fair and other London fairs in 1703. It was 19 hands high, 4 yards from forehead to rump, and the shin was 36 inches round.

[2] Ward is here blowing his own trumpet, for the King's Head Tavern in Fulwood's Rents, next door to Gray's Inn, was the house he kept for many years before his death.

Accordingly we discharged our reckoning, and made our exit, and being spurred on with the conceit of this amusing whim, as the gentleman had rendered it by his diverting account, we ſtumbled along over the pebble ſtones, as faſt as a Penny Poſtman, or a Temple ſtudent with a bill into the City to receive his quarterage, till we came to the door of this happy mansion, which, according to the report we heard, abounded with those delights that were in other taverns very difficult to be found.

But we met with such crowds in opposition, some ſtriving for entrance, and others for an exit, that we were forced to ſtruggle as hard for our admittance as a couple of belated beaus do to squeeze into the pit, when Doggett[1] is to play son Benjamin in *Love for Love*; but at laſt, with no small ſtriving, we shot the entry into a paved yard, where we waited as long for the sight of the carcase of the beaſt as a gentleman in adversity does for the sight of a great man, when his business is to beg a favour, or put him in mind of a promise he never intended to perform.

At laſt we slipped into the kitchen, where about a dozen of the moſt eminent jack-winders [cooks] in Fleet Street, some in their nightcaps and white aprons, others with their hair tied back in a black liſt garter, that it might not hang in their light, and hinder them in the performance of the difficult task they had undertaken, which was to spit this unwieldy monſter with such mathematical judgement that it should run round by the help of a turnspit with as true a poise as the sail of a windmill in a fresh gale.

In vain they wounded the back of the beef in sundry places, either an aitchbone, a shin bone, a blade bone, or a rib ſtanding in way of their massive weapon so that they puffed and

[1] Thomas Doggett's creation of Ben, in Congreve's *Love for Love*, was the sensation in the theatrical world in 1695, and it was always one of his most successful parts. He is now best known for having founded the Doggett Coat and Badge, to be rowed for on the Thames every anniversary of the accession of George I (August 1st).

blowed like so many Custom House porters lifting at a wool-pack. At last, sitting down like a jury of an inquest over a dead corpse, they began to consult how to force this stubborn piece of meat into a submission of being roasted.

At last one of the burgesses of the dripping-pan started up, and wisely made this motion to the rest of the greasy brother-hood: ' My honest friends and neighbours, since we, the pro-fessors of the noble art of cookery, are assembled together in our proper element, the kitchen, upon this solemn occasion, let us not be baffled by the backbone of an ox, but let us stir up our brains that we may see to spit this pack-saddle of beef. I therefore declare my opinion is that we forthwith send for the smith and his man and by the assistance of them and their sledges, complete our task, in as little time as a man may boil an egg, or melt a pound of butter.'

Just as the whole society of lick-fingers had with great applause very highly approved of their brother skimpot's advice, who should crowd into the cooks' territories but a carpenter, armed with a huge mallet, who undertook to do more work with one blow of his wooden weapon than all the bunglers were able to do with their united strength without him. This speech gave 'em fresh courage, so that every epicurean minion started up as nimbly to his business, as a master of anatomy at Surgeons' Hall to a dissection.

The underlings were appointed to sharpen broomstaves into skewers. When they had made a way for the spit, from the right buttock to the left shoulder there were such acclama-tions of joy that he that was the chief leader of the knights of the frying-pan, strutted about the kitchen with his arms akimbo, puffing and swelling and crying out with a majestical voice, ' 'Tis done! 'Tis done! The mighty deed is done!'

The chief operator and his assistants, who were so very joy-ful they had at last overcome the greatest of their difficulty, like prudent artificers, began now to examine the truth of their work, but they found that one side was too heavy by as many

pounds as t'other was too light, which was no way to be
remedied but by chipping and paring, till they had brought
'em to an equality, which, by the time they had cut off as
many slivers as amounted to the weight of about six stone,
was finished effectually with great gladness and applause.

Beefsteaks, we now observed, were as plenty about the house
as yolks of eggs in brewing time, which encouraged us, notwithstanding the hurry, to sit down in the kitchen, and take
share of the superfluity, and also to take notice of the divers
humours, and various sentiments of the numerous spectators,
who flocked in and out to behold the novelty.

Amongst the rest came an old gentleman, and that he might
take a more satisfactory survey of this uncommon eatable, he
at last pulls out his artificial peepers, which he mounted upon
the handle of his face, so that the wonderful object might be
rendered the more conspicuous. Round he walked with as
much circumspection as ever a prying virtuoso did round a
glass beehive, telling the ribs, measuring the length with his
crutch-headed cane, guessing at the weight, turning up the
rump and, holding up his hands at last, he broke into this
rapture: ' Look ye, d'ye see, gentlemen, on the t'other hand,
it may be we are the happiest nation in the world. For let us
but consider. D'ye hear me, what a blessing of Providence
it is, as a man may say, that such a glorious sight as this; a
glorious sight I say, is to be seen amongst us after so long
a war; that let me tell you, had it continued till now, such a
piece of beef as this, without great mercy, would have been
a much more graceful sight than the fattest alderman in
London.' Then fell a-laughing at his jest, till he brought
himself into a fit of coughing, which put a period to his
learned oration.

The next spectator that was worth our notice was a kind of
Captain Blister, who was so brimful of oaths, that he run over
like a Southwark ditch at spring-tide. ' Why a pox,' says he
to one of the drawers, ' was your master such a fool to have

the head cut off, which would have been so great a grace to your pack-saddle monster, that I'll warrant you, there's not been a wittol in town but what would have had a peep at him?' 'The reason, sir,' says the drawer, 'that my master had it cut off, was because the range is not long enough to roast it.' 'Cats nouns,' says the gentleman, 'you cooks are all blockheads, for they might have thrust it as short with the head on, as 'tis now without it.' 'How, sir?' says the master of the roast, with great indignation, 'I have been a student in the art of cookery above this twenty years, and I do affirm, sir, that what you say is impossible.' 'Then do I say,' replied the gentleman, 'that thou art a mere cod head of a cook, and I can tell thee which way it may be done if the head had been put on.' 'I'll hold you, sir,' says the cook, 'the price of the beef to a pound of kitchen stuff if the head had been on it it must have required so much the longer fire to have roasted it.' 'No, no,' says the gentleman, 'it had been but jointing the neck, and you might have brought the head round, and have stuck one of the horns through the body, as you do the bill of a woodcock; what think you of that?' 'I'faith, master,' says he, 'I did not think of that; now you have put it into my head, I don't question but I could have done it. But what should we have done with the horn that was next to the fire? For that,' says he, 'would have hung upon the range and stopped the going of the meat.' 'That,' says the gentleman, 'I should have designed for the cooks' fees.' At this the company fell into a laughter, which kindled such a fire in the cook's countenance, that his looks were almost sufficient to have scalded the company out of the kitchen.

By this time we had eaten a steak, and drunk up our flask of wine, and being quite tired with the cooks' clutter, the confusion of tongues, the hurry of the house, and other inconveniences that always attend such public novelties, we adjourned to our homes, in order to despatch some domestic business, which, together with reposing nature, took up our time till

Thursday morning, upon which day this liberal entertainment was to be in a roasted readiness to oblige the guests.

When the morning came, my friend and I, having a great desire to discover what an attractive influence such a magnificent piece of beef had upon the stomachs of the Town, resolved not to lose the opportunity of gratifying our palates, as well as feasting our eyes, and of coming in for our share of the benefit, as well as the rest of the town epicures.

When we came to the door we had more difficulty to get admittance than we had before, for as many people were crowding to see it at the fire, as there were to see the ox roasted upon the ice.[1] When we had squeezed sideways through the entry, with as much pains as a fat man takes to shove himself through a narrow turnstile, we got into the yard, where such a litter of drawers were scampering from cellar to bar, and from bar to company, that it was difficult to believe the whole house could have entertained guests sufficient to have required such a number of attendants; bells rattling; the servants all puffing and blowing like greyhounds after a course, sweating like a couple of chairmen in the dog-days who had just set down a bulky nobleman. The kitchen was now as hot as Guinea at noonday, yet we concluded we should be best attended there, being near the bar, and the least incommoded for want of room, could we but reconcile our bodies to the extraordinary heat, which we thought we could more easily endure than many other inconveniences we should have found elsewhere. Accordingly, we ventured into the kitchen, which, at first entrance, seemed hot enough to have baked a custard in the middle of it, but seating ourselves at a convenient distance from the fire, and where we drew in a little cool breath at a back door, we found ourselves well settled in a pretty moderate climate.

[1] A great frost on the Thames lasted from December, 1698, until the following 4th of February. A fair was held on the ice, a great feature of which was the roasting of an ox, whole.

o

The poor carcase of the beast was by this time so lamentably mangled by the cuts and slashes of the broiling carvers, that had Sir Courtly Nice, or my Lady Squeamish, been to have taken a view of the roasting rarity, they would scarce have longed to have been partakers of the feast; for the shoulders and the ribs were soon stripped as bare of their flesh as if the Tower lions, or the tiger, had been just at breakfast on't, and the buttock and more fleshy parts were cut and digged full of holes and furrows. Yet the poor anatomy cocked its tail, as it ran round upon the spit and the turnspit was so discoloured with sweat, soot, smoke and ashes, that both he and his cookery looked as if one devil was roasting of another, letting fall so fast his greasy tears, as if it were an emulation between both who should afford the most dripping. The cook and his attendants were so very busy about the carcase of the beast, that every round it took, it was at least two or three pound the lighter.

By this time a generous plateful of the good creature was brought as a present to my friend and I, with all the rest of the appurtenances at once, without the trouble of calling. This encouraged our appetites, and gave us a better liking to our treat which in justice I must say, according to the old English way of praising beef, was as rich, fat, young, wellfed, delicious meat, as ever was taken into the mouth, masticated between the teeth, and swallowed into the belly of a true Englishman.

By the time we had made an end of our plentiful commons, the bones of the whole carcase were pared so clean that the vintner found himself under a necessity of sending for two barons more, or half his guests would have been disappointed of their breakfast. For the Templars, whose business called them to Westminster, came roaring in crowds with such devilish stomachs, which the exercise of their lungs in the hall had made as insatiate as their consciences, that their tongues as fast as they came in, pleaded very hard in behalf of their bellies, nothing being heard but 'Beef, beef, beef,' threatening to run all to the devil presently, if the master did not entertain 'em speedily.

Having now well freighted the hold of our vessels with excellent food and delicious wine at a small expense, we scribbled these following lines with chalk upon the wall, so took our departure from thence, and steered our course to a more temperate climate.

> To speak but the truth of my honest friend Ned,
> The best of all vintners that ever God made,
> He's free of his beef, and as free of his bread,
> And washes both down with a glass of rare red,
> That tops all the town, and commands a good trade,
> Such wine as will cheer up the drooping King's Head,
> And brisk up the soul, tho' the body's half dead;
> He scorns to draw bad, as he hopes to be paid,
> But now his name's up he may e'en lie a bed,
> For he'll get an estate, there's no more to be said.

Considering coffee to be a liquor that sits most easy upon wine, and anxious to hear what news the grizzly trumpeters of fame's reports had raked up together from credulous noddies, we went into a great coffee-house[1] by the Temple Gate, where a parcel of grave men were thickening the air with the fumes of their weed. We sat ourselves down amongst the sage assembly, most of the company, we observed, being as choice of their words as a miser is of his treasure, each seemed as loth to open his mouth, as the other his cabinet, which made me think they had either something extraordinary in 'em, or else that they were a parcel of cunning fools.

At last comes in an old newshound, who enquired of the rest if any straggling news had come that way. 'News!' replied a jolly red-faced toper, 'we have news enough, I think, to

[1] Nando's Coffee-house stood near the west corner of Inner Temple Lane; above the Rainbow Tavern. It was at the back of the house and was approached from Fleet Street by a passage and stairs. It was a great resort of legal loungers.

comfort the hearts of the whole City; since the magistracy of the City is now given on the right side, the churches are everywhere full, and the assemblies of the over-righteous are grown so very thin that it is verily believed, if things succeed as they begin, the dancing masters about this town may in a little time have choice of good schools at more reasonable rate than ever, and that, I think, boys, is much better news than to see Paul's Church as empty as a Saturday's 'Change, and meeting-houses as full as Westminster Hall in term time.'

This serious speech of the old cavalier's was a key to the hearts of all the rest, who began, after one had opened, like a pack of true beagles at full cry, to hunt down the Church's enemies with all imaginable speed.

Having now wasted our time till about nine o'clock at night, we thought it a reasonable hour to take leave of the coffee-house, and repair to our own lodgings, where my business engaged me to continue close till the triumphs of the City called me to make one of the innumerable multitude of gaping spectators.

When the morning came that my Lord Mayor and his attendants were to take their amphibious journey to Westminster Hall,[1] where his Lordship, according to the custom of his ancestors, was by a kiss of calves'-leather, to make a fair promise to Her Majesty, I equipped my carcase in order to bear with little damage the hustles and affronts of the unmannerly mob, of whose wild pastimes and unlucky attacks, I had not a little apprehension. And when my friend and I had thus carefully sheltered ourselves under our ancient drabdeberries, against their dirty assaults, we ventured to move towards Cheapside, where I thought the triumphs would be most visible, and the rabble most rude, looking upon the mad frolics and whimsies of the latter to be altogether

[1] Owing to the difference of Old and New Style in the calendar, Lord Mayor's Show was held on October the 29th. The greater part of the journey to Westminster Hall, where the oaths were taken, was made by water in the State barge.

as diverting (provided a man takes care of the danger) as the solemn grandeur and the gravity of the former.

When I came to the end of Blow Bladder Street,[1] I saw such a crowd before my eyes, that I could scarce forbear thinking the very stones of the street, by the harmony of their drums and trumpets, were metamorphosed into men, women and children. The balconies were hung with old tapestry and Turkey-work tablecloths, for the cleanly leaning out of the ladies, with whom they were chiefly filled, though the mob had soon pelted them into so dirty a condition that some of them looked as nasty as the cover cloth of a horse that had travelled from St. Margaret's to London in the midst of winter. At every volley the ladies quitted their post, and retreated into dining-rooms, as safer garrisons to defend themselves from the assaults of their mischievous enemies; some fretting at their daubed scarves; others wiping their new commodes, which they had bought on purpose to honour His Lordship, each expressing anger in their looks. The windows of each house from the top to the bottom were stuffed with heads, piled one upon another like skulls in a charnel house.

Whilst my friend and I were thus staring at the spectators much more than the show, the pageants were advanced within our view, upon which such a tide of mob overflowed the place we stood in, that the women cried out for room, the children for breath, and every man, whether citizen or foreigner, strove very hard for his freedom. For my own part, I was so closely imprisoned in the multitude, that I was almost squeezed as flat as a napkin in the press, so that I heartily would have joined with the rabble to have cried, ' Liberty, liberty.'

In this pageant was a fellow riding a cock-horse upon a lion, but without either boots or spurs, as if intended, by the

---

[1] This was a small lane off Newgate Street, formerly devoted to butchers' shops.

projector, to show how the citizens ride to Epsom on a Saturday night, to bear their wives company till Monday morning.

At the base of the pedestal were seated four figures representing, according to my most rational conjecture, the four principal vices of the City, viz., Fraud, Usury, Seemingsanctity and Hypocrisy. As soon as this was past, the industrious rabble, who hate idleness, had procured a dead cat which was handed about by the babes of grace, as an innocent diversion, every now and then being tossed into the face of some gaping booby or other.

By the time this sport had gone a little about, another pageant approached us, wherein an old fellow sat in a blue gown, dressed up like a country schoolmaster, only he was armed with a scythe instead of a birch rod, by which I understood this figure represented Time, which was designed, as I suppose, to put the City in mind how apt they are to abuse the old gentleman, and not dispose of him to such good uses as the laws of God and the laws of man require, but trifle their time away in those three vanities which were represented by the three figures under the dome, viz., Falsehood, Pride and Incontinency.

When this pageant was passed, a third pageant advanced forward, which appeared to the sight much richer than the rest.

' What think you,' says my friend, ' of these emblems ? '

' I think,' said I, ' the chief figure in it represents, as I imagine, a lady of pleasure, being dressed in much costlier robes than the other female representatives, which may serve to let the City know that harlots in this wicked age wear richer apparel than honest women, and those three maids that attend her, signify the sad calamities that attend the conversation of lewd women, viz., Poverty, Shame and the Gallows.'

In every interval between pageant and pageant the mob had still a new project to put on foot. This time they had got a piece of cloth a yard or more square, which they dipped in the gutter, till they had made it fit for their purpose, then tossed it about. Expanding itself in the air, and falling on the heads of two or three at once, it made 'em look like so many bearers under a pall, every one lugging a different way to get it off his head, oftentimes falling together by the ears about plucking off their cover-slut.

By the time forty or fifty heedless spectators were made as dirty as so many scavengers, the fourth pageant was come up, which was a most stately, rich and noble chariot, made of slit deal and paste-board, and in it was sitting a woman representing, I fancy, the Whore of Babylon, drawn by two goats, signifying her lust, and upon the backs of them two figures representing Jealousy and Revenge; her attendants importing the miseries that follow her, and the kettle-drums and trumpets serve to show that wheresoe'er she comes 'tis with terror and amazement.

The rabble having changed their sport to a new scene of unluckiness, had got a bullock's horn, which they filled with drain water, and poured it down people's necks, and into their pockets, so that it ran down their legs and into their shoes, the ignorant sufferers not readily discovering from whence the wet came. When they had exercised this new invention about a quarter of an hour the fifth pageant moved forward, wherein all sorts of trades were represented; a man working at a tobacco engine, as if he were cutting of tobacco, but yet did not do so; a boy as if he were a dressing of an old woman's hat, but was not; which was designed, as I suppose, to reflect upon the frauds and failings of the City traders, and show that they often pretend to do what they do not, and to be what they are not, and will say what they think not, and will think what they say not, and that the world might see there are cheats in all trades.

> The bully cits marched after in a throng,
> Huzza'd by the mob, as drum'd and pip'd along,
> Whilst wise spectators did their pomp disdain,
> And with contempt behold the draggling train.

CHAPTER THIRTEEN

The Tower—The Lions and their Keepers—The Armoury—The Wharf—A Meeting-house

THE triumphs of the City being now passed by, they drew after them the mobility of our safe deliverance, my friend and I clinging as fast to a post as a bear to a ragged staff, to avoid being carried away by the resistless torment of the rabble; which, if we had quitted our hold, would have inevitably happened, to the further bruising of our ribs, and the great penance of our toes. But on the contrary, finding ourselves safe, we began to consider in what new adventure we should spend the remainder of the day.

At last I remembered that I had oftentimes in the country heard wonderful tales from higglers, hawkers, carriers, drovers, and such-like hobbady-bobbodies, of several four-footed barbarian kings, with many of their ravenous subjects, who had for divers years been kept close prisoners in Her Majesty's palace and prison, the Tower of London. The sundry reports of these amazing objects, together with many other enticing rarities to be visited at a small expense within the ancient battlements of this renowned citadel, had begot in me such an earnest desire of beholding these foreign monsters, and domestic engines of destruction, with crowns, sceptres and many other pompous knick-knacks, that we determined to steer our course towards this stately magazine, and to spend a little time in viewing the martial furniture of that famous garrison which statesmen dread, and common people admire.

Having so lately escaped from the punishment of a crowd, we were very cautious how we relapsed into the same condition;

for my Lord Mayor's Show being paſt, the mob began to divide their main body in diſtinct parties, a division attending each several company to their proper hall, gazing at the grave noddies, who being perplexed with either horns, corns, gout, ſtone or gravel, hobbled after their hautboys like the great old dons of the Law, when they dance the measures in an Inns of Court Hall upon the firſt day of Chriſtmas. We thought ourselves not free from danger till we got through Leadenhall Market into some of the back lanes, for the great ſtreets were the channel of the mob, who were careful, as they moved along, to improve every handful of dirt they could take up to the prejudice of somebody or other.

We found little worth our observation as we passed along, but many merchants' houses as ſtately as princes' palaces, and 'tis reported by such who have the opportunity of being judges of their inward hospitality, that their housekeeping is answerable to their outward grandeur; which if it be, it's enough to make our nobility blush, to see themselves outdone in that commendable liberality wherein the honour and splendour of a great rich man is moſt magnificently visible. There were three or four of Quality's coaches at one door, two or three chairs at another, as if the courtiers were come into the City to kiss the merchants' wives and borrow money of their husbands; an old game that has oft been played and will never be out of fashion whilſt the City's richer than the Court.

When we came upon Tower Hill, the firſt object that more particularly affected us was that emblem of deſtruction, the scaffold,[1] from whence greatness, when too late, has oft beheld the happiness and security of lower ſtations; reflecting with a deep concern on their sudden prosperity, and the reſtless ambition that had brought 'em to that fate which the contentment under a moderate fortune and a private life might have happily prevented. For he that sits too high in the

---

[1] The site of the scaffold is marked by a small, square piece of pavement at the west end of the gardens in Trinity Square.

favour of his prince is liable to be delivered up, upon public disorders, as a sacrifice to appease the fury of the people; and he that labours for a popular esteem is always looked upon by his prince to be a dangerous subject.

At a little distance from this memento mori stood a very ragged indigent prophet, delivering, with a thin pair of jaws, a tangled beard, and a devout countenance, the doctrine of Charity, with a much larger congregation round him than I have seen at church, giving as serious attention to their mendicant shepherd as if every listening member, according to his condition, designed to contribute something towards the relief of their distressed lecturer.

But before he had come to his use and application, a blind fellow, who had for many years been one of the pensioners, takes up his stand at a little distance, and out of a wallet which had as many partitions as an old country cupboard, for his silver farthings, short pipes, tobacco, and bread and cheese, etc., he pulls out a couple of little flutes, claps one to each corner of his mouth, and with his melodious roundelays drew off all the audience from Charity's poor chaplain, leaving the ubiquitarian apostle in a wonderful indignation, calling after 'em as they moved off, ' Beloved, pray, beloved, pray a little, I am just a-going to conclude. Alas! alas! what a wicked age we do live in, when men shall forsake the word of the gospel to follow a bobbling guide, and prefer the tootings of a blind piper before the delightful music of Salvation.' But away went all the people, notwithstanding his reproof, to tickle their ears with the harmony of their blind musician.

The expectancy of the pastor being quite baulked, the multitude being drawn off without throwing him one example of their charity amongst 'em, he marched mumbling away, in a great fury with his flock, saying, just as he passed by us, they were a wicked congregation that deserved to be cursed, and he would pronounce an anathema against them. And looking over his shoulder towards the people, he breathed

out this comical execration, ' I wish that you might all be
deaf, dumb, and blind, every time you stand to hear that
blind hedge-bird whistle, when you may bless your ears with
a good sermon.' And having thus expressed himself, away he
rambled.

We went into the first gate of the Tower, where a parcel
of lazy red-coats were loitering about like so many City bull-
dogs at the Poultry Compter. We were no sooner past the
first sentinel, but right before us, against the front of a house,
hung a strange sort of a picture. My friend asked me what
I thought it represented, or whether I had seen any creature
that was like it? To me it seemed the picture of some
rugged-faced man's head; and after I had compared it in
my thoughts to everybody I could recollect, and all the ideas
I could form, I thought, by its flat nose and ill-favoured
countenance, it was the likest the unborn-doctor, the seventh
son of the seventh son in Moorfields,[1] of anything that ever
I saw in my life.

My friend smiling at the oddness of my fancy, undeceived
me by telling me 'twas a lion's head, hung out as a means
to inform strangers that come to see the Tower that there is
the royal palace, where the king of beasts keeps his Court,[2]
and may every day, at a proper distance, be seen at dinner
without danger. But, like the Czar of Muscovy, if you stare
at him too near, he'll be apt to do you a mischief. ' This,'
says he, ' being the first sight, let us take it in turn, and then
you'll be better satisfied.'

Accordingly we went in, where the yard smelt as frowzily

[1] The great home of quacks and astrologers.
[2] The Royal Menagerie was on the right, at the entrance, where the ticket-
office and refreshment rooms are now placed. Various wild beasts were kept
there, but the lions were the great feature, and many superstitions were current
about them. They were named after the sovereign reigning at the time of their
first appearance in the Tower, and popular tradition said ' when a king dies the
lion of that name dies after him.' Another legend was that if a lion roared when
a pregnant woman was looking at him, her coming child would be a son. The
menagerie was moved from the Tower in 1834.

as a dove-house, or a dog-kennel. In their separate apartments were four of their stern affrighting catships, one with a whelp presented to his late Majesty; one of which the dam was as fond of as an old maid, when married, is of her first child; one couchant, another dormant, a third passant guardant, a fourth very fierce, was rampant (being a lioness), and was so angry when we spoke to her, she put out her paw to us, which was tipped with such ill-favoured sort of pruning-hooks, that rather than she should have taken me by the hand I would have chosen to have taken Old Nick by his cloven foot, and should have thought myself in less danger.

One of the keeper's servants, whilst he was showing us his unruly prisoners, entertained us with a couple of remarkable stories, which, because the tragedy of the one will render an escape in the other story the more providential, I shall proceed to give the reader. Some years since, a maidservant to the keeper, and a bold spirited wench, took pleasure, now and then, to help feed the lions, and imprudently believing the gratitude of the beasts would not suffer them to hurt her, she would venture sometimes, though with extraordinary caution, to be a little more familiar with them than she ought to be. At last, either carelessly, or presumptuously, she ventured too near their dens, and one of the lions caught hold of her arm, and tore it quite off the shoulder, after a most lamentable manner, before anybody could come to her assistance, killing her with a grip, before he would loose her from his talons, till she was made a miserable object of her own folly, the lion's fury and the world's pity.

This story was succeeded by another, wherein was shown a miraculous preservation of himself. ' 'Tis our custom,' says he, ' when we clean the lion's den, to drive 'em down over night, through a trap-door, into a lower conveniency, in order to rise early in the morning, and refresh their day-apartments, by clearing away their filth and nastiness. Having through mistake, and not forgetfulness, left one of the trap doors unbolted, which I thought I had carefully secured, I came down in the morning, before daylight, with my candle and lanthorn faſtened before me to a button, with my implements in my hands to dispatch my business, as was usual; and going carelessly into one of the dens, a lion had returned through the trap-door, and lay crouched in a corner, with his head towards me. The sudden surprise of this terrible sight brought me under such dreadful apprehensions of the danger I was in that I ſtood fixed like a ſtatue, without the power of motion, with my eyes ſteadfaſtly upon the lion. I expeſted nothing but to be torn to pieces every moment, and was fearful to attempt one ſtep back, leſt my endeavour to shun him might have made him the more eager to have haſtened my deſtruſtion.

'At laſt he roused himself, as I thought to have made a breakfaſt of me; yet, by the assiſtance of Providence, I had the presence of mind to keep ſteady in my position. He moved towards me without expressing in his countenance either greediness or anger, but on the contrary he wagged his tail, signifying nothing but friendship in his fawning be-haviour. And after he had ſtared me a little in the face, he raised himself upon his two hindmoſt feet and laying his two paws upon my shoulders without hurting me, fell to licking my face, as a further inſtance of his gratitude for my feeding him, as I afterwards conjeſtured, though then I expeſted every minute when he would have ſtripped my skin over my ears as a poulterer does a rabbit. His tongue was so very rough that with the few kisses he gave me, it made my cheeks raw, which I was very glad to take in good part, without a bit of grumbling. And when he had thus saluted me, and given me his sort of welcome to his den, he returned to his place, and laid him down, doing me no further damage; which unexpeſted deliverance hitherto occasioned me to take courage that I slunk back by degrees, till I recovered the trap-door, through which I jumped and plucked it after me; thus happily, through an especial Providence, having escaped the fury of so dangerous a creature.'

The under-keeper having thus ended his stories, we proceeded to our further view of these Beelzebub's blood-hounds. Two of them being dead and their skins stuffed, one of them having been King Charles's lion, but had no more the fierceness in his looks that he had when he was living, than the effigies of his good master as Westminster has the presence of the original. The other that was stuffed, was said to be Queen Mary's, but made such a drooping figure that it brought into my mind an old proverb, with which I could not but agree, that a living dog is better than a dead lion.

The next ill-favoured creatures that were presented to our sight were a couple of pretty looking hell-cats, called a tiger, and a cat-a-mountain, whose fierce penetrating eyes pierced through my belly to the sad griping of my guts, as if they would have killed at a distance with their looks.

In another apartment or ward, for the conveniency of drawing a penny more out of the pocket of a spectator, are placed the following animals: first a leopard, who is grown as cunning as a cross Bedlamite that loves not to be looked at.

The next creatures we observed were three hawk-nosed gentlemen called eagles, one black, another in second mourning, a third with a bald pate, as if he had been pulling a crow with his two comrades, and like unmerciful enemies they had pecked all the feathers off his crown. Next to these were a couple of outlandish owls, which besides eyes as big as the glasses of a convex-lamp, had each of them long ears that grew like horns, under which they looked as venerably grave as two aged aldermen.

The next part of the show recommended to our notice were two preternatural objects, being a dog and a cat, pupped and kittened with but two legs each; the former had a bump upon his head, which, in derision to our high-crowned ladies, they are pleased to call a top knot. 'Prithee, friend,' said I to the man that showed 'em, 'what is it that you value these imperfect vermin for? There's but little satisfaction, I should think, in the sight of such ill-favoured monsters.'

'Sir,' says the fellow, 'whether you know it or not, these vermin, as you are pleased to call 'em, are as highly prized and as well looked after as any creature in the land.'

'But pray, friend,' said I, 'for what reason are they so esteemed?'

'Why, sir,' says he, 'because they have but half their number of legs.'

To this I answered, if that be all the reason, methinks they should take as much care to feed the poor human cripples, who were born with all their legs, and have lost one half in the nation's service, and are forced to seek their bread where they can find it; I believe I saw twenty begging upon the hill as I came hither.

'Ah, sir,' said the fellow, 'but they are no rarity. Were it as uncommon a thing to see a soldier or a sailor with but one leg, as 'tis to see a dog or a cat with no more than two, no question but they would live as well and be taken as much notice of as these are.'

From thence we were removed into another division, to see that alluring creature so much talked of by the old poets, called the hyena, which, as they report, has the voice of a man, and coming near a cottage, will cry out like a traveller in some distress. By this means he decoys the shepherds out of their houses, and afterwards devours 'em; which story, whether it be truth or fiction, I could see nothing in the creature to determine.

Having thus paid homage to the kings of the quadrupeds, and the lofty monarch of the feathered kind, we moved forward to the second gate, where a parcel of bulky warders, in old-fashioned laced jackets, and velvet flat-caps, hung round with divers coloured ribbons, like a fool's hat upon a holiday, looking as fierce as a file of Artillery ale-drapers, when they are going to besiege a dunghill in Bunhill Fields, and play at soldiers one against another to please the rabble.

We had no sooner made a nimbler step than ordinary beyond the port-cullis, as cautious citizens do past the Monument, for fear it should tumble upon their heads, but one of these brawny beef-and-pudding-eating janizaries demanded whither we are going? Thought I, we are no sooner come from Her Majesty's lions but we are fallen into the clutches of some of her bears; but I dare not tell 'em so, for fear the bloody-coloured animals would have fallen into a passion with me. So instead of that, I informed 'em, like an honest tell-truth, our real business. They told us we could not be admitted to gratify our desires without we took a warder with us; which we found we were forced to consent to, or return back without the satisfaction we proposed. Upon this we ordered him to attend us, and had the honour of walking up and down the Tower, as great as a factious lord committed for suspicion of high treason.

The first thing we observed, when we were past the gate, was a great brass gun painted over of a copper colour.

Surely, thought I, this must be done in jest, to let folks who come in here see that guns, like bells, are as great turn-coats as those that command 'em, that is parsons and officers. For the one will roar, the other ring, the third preach, and the fourth fight for any power that's uppermost; and 'tis verily believed by all people who have any regard for that prevailing principle, interest, that they are all in the right on't.

The next place that fell in its turn within our notice was the Traitors' Gate,[1] where the fall of the moat-waters, or the cataracts on each side, made so terrible a noise, that it's enough to frighten a prisoner that lodges within the hearing on't out of the world before his time of execution. The passage was fortified by a parcel of iron guns, which to me, that

---

[1] The Tower moats were filled with water, stagnant and malodorous, until 1843, when they were drained and a garden laid out on the site. At low tide the water rushed through Traitors' Gate like a cataract.

A Fleet Wedding.

(From an old print)

understood 'em not, seemed as old and as rusty as the hinges of the gates of Babylon; but were, no doubt on't, in a good condition of giving a sufficient repulse to any enemy that should attempt a violent entrance.

We were from thence conducted through another gate, upon an ascent as steep as Holborn Hill, though not so often dangerous; on the right hand of which stood a stately square stone fabric, distinguished by the name of Julius Cæsar's Tower.[1] But it must needs be as dark within as a country beehive, having but one door, and never a window that I could see, only a little slit or two, and made so very close, as I conceive, to keep fire and gunpowder at their proper distance.

The next remarkable place we came to was the church, whose rugged outside appeared of great antiquity. A little beyond this holy closet of a church stood the famous armoury, now placed under a new and modish name, The Arsenal, of which I had heard such a general applause, that I was particularly desirous of seeing this martial entertainment. Accordingly we ordered our burly guide to conduct us thither. Pursuant to our request he ushered us up a stately staircase, where, at the corner of every lobby, and turning of the stairs, stood a wooden grenadier as sentinel, painted in his proper colours, cut out with as much exactness upon board as the picture of a housewife with her broom, very usually set up in great families as good examples to servant wenches, to make 'em mindful of their cleanliness.

When we came to the top of the stairs we were saluted, as I suppose, with two or three of the armourers' substitutes; one amongst the rest, who I imagine was esteemed as their principal orator, advanced before us, cap in hand, with as much ceremony as a dancing-master ushers the parents of his pupils into the school upon a ball-day; beginning to tell us at our entrance, with an audible voice, the signification of

[1] This was the ancient name for the White Tower, and commemorates the unfounded legend of the Tower having been built by Cæsar.

P

those figures which were first presented to our view; having everything as ready at his finger-ends, as the fellow that shows the tombs at Westminster, or as a Savoy vagabond has the explanation of his raree-show.

The first figure that most affected the eye, by reason of its bigness, was a long range of muskets and carbines, that runs the length of the armoury, which was distinguished by a wilderness of arms, whose locks and barrels were kept in such admirable order that they shone as bright as a good house-wife's spits and pewter in the Christmas holidays. On each side of these were pistols, bayonets, scimitars, hangers, cut-lasses, and the like, configurated into shields, triumphal arches, gates, pilasters, scallop-shells, mullets, fans, snakes, serpents, sunbeams, gorgon's-head, the waves of the ocean, stars, and garters, and in the middle of all pillars of pikes, and turned pillars of pistols; and at the end of the wilderness, fire-arms placed in the order of a great organ.

The next thing that our expositor recommended to our particular notice were Sir William Perkins' arms,[1] taken under ground at his country house, as our voucher told us, pointing more especially to Sir William's own carbine and pistols, of which he had made such a terrible story that it would have frightened a country fellow from looking at 'em; telling us they were screwed barrels, heptagonically bored.

'Why, friend,' said I, ' thou talkest as if thou understandest Greek; prithee, what is the meaning of that word hepta-gonically?'

'Oh, sir,' says he, 'it means a barrel that will mould a bullet into a slug I don't know how many times square, and will kill as many men again, and go six times as far as an ordinary barrel of bigness.'

[1] Sir William Perkins, or Parkyns, was implicated in the Assassination Plot of 1696, which had been hatched at St. Germain's. The chief plotter was Sir George Barclay. The plan was to waylay William as he rode from Kensington Palace to go hunting at Richmond and shoot him. The plot was found out overnight, many of the conspirators fled, but Perkins was caught and in due course hanged at Tyburn.

We could not forbear smiling at our interpreter's ignorance, who we expected would have told us the barrel consisted of seven sides, and answering him according to his folly, we seemed to be well satisfied with the account he gave us.

Over the top of this range of treasonable implements was placed a little brass blunderbuss, upon which he fixed his eyes, turning up the whites and shaking of his head about half a dozen times; then, plucking one of his hands out of his Dutch gloves, he pointed to it with a trembling finger, and began to open upon the subject after this manner:

' That blunderbuss,' says he, ' was designed by the bloody assassinators to have killed the king, which God of His great goodness hath most happily prevented, bringing the bloody conspirators to condign punishment, and their traitorous weapons into the power of that glorious prince whose life they so basely sought. They are here, blessed be Providence, hung up in his armoury, as the perpetual reminder of His Majesty's escape from the hands of his Popish enemies, to God's great glory, King William's safety, and England's happiness.'

Our little holder-forth having done his lecture upon the king-killing blunderbuss, we moved to another stand, where he showed us a parcel of Dutch fire-locks, with which the King landed at his first coming to England, which was carried, I suppose, by the monsters of men in bear-skins with Saracen's heads, long beards and terrible countenances; the report of which so frightened the citizens of London and their wives, that they were in as great a consternation as at the midnight cry of the coming of the cut-throat Irish.[1]

Having thus taken a short view of the most renowned armoury in Christendom, we returned downstairs with our warder, who had waited at the door to save his legs, whilst we feasted our eyes with that glittering sight which was to him no novelty. When we had descended to the bottom door

[1] See note, page 62.

a bulky frizzlepate stood in readiness to receive the customary money for that sight which had given our eyes such an extra-ordinary satisfaction.

Being now left to a further consideration of what we should see next, we took a turn to deliberate upon the matter, but were forced quickly to decide; for the Tower rooks began to flutter about us, like so many salesmen about a country fellow in Long Lane; only as the one asks whether ye may want coat, waistcoat, or breeches, will you buy any clothes; so the other, after the same manner, and in much the same dialect, whether you will see the Crown, the whole Regalia, or the King's marching train of Artillery.

My friend and I considering the marching train of Artillery consisted only in great guns, enough of which might be seen about the Tower without paying for it, agreed to pass by these, and adjourn to the Horse Armoury whither we ordered our guide to conduct us accordingly. When we were come to the door, there stood ready to receive us two or three smug-faced Vulcans, who were as amiable in complexion as if, to make themselves infernal beaus, they had powdered their frizzled locks with lamp-black and beautified their physiog-nomies with kennel water; the lines of their faces being filled with dirt from the shoulders upwards.

After our guide, who looked in his warder's robes as if he had been cut out of a tapestry-hanging, had given a caution to the smutty interpreter of this raree-show, to tell us with certitude the names of his glittering troop of superficial heroes, the spokesman introduced us among the monumental shells of our deceased princes, which only by the industry of common hands, shined bright in memory of those that wore 'em. As we gently moved along and viewed the princely scarecrows, he told us to whom each suit of armour did belong originally, adding some short memorandums out of history, to every empty iron-side; some true, some false, supplying that with invention which he wanted in memory.

He now and then endeavoured to break a jeſt to divert his
cuſtomers, but did it so like an Irishman that I had much
ado to forbear telling the fellow what a fool he was in endeavouring to be witty. In our circular progress round these
men of metal mounted on wooden horses, we came to the
armour of John of Gaunt, so famous for his ſtrength and
ſtature and, indeed, if his coat of defence was fit for his
body, I believe he was as big as any of the poetical giants that
waged war againſt heaven.

We next advanced to the armour of Will Sommers, the
jeſter, to which they had added an ill-favoured face, with
horns upon his head, and upon his nose a pair of speƈtacles,
on which our jocular commentator was pleased thus merrily
to discant.

' This figure,' says he, ' represents that drolling gentleman,
Will Sommers, who was jeſter to King Henry the Eighth.
He had the misfortune, poor gentleman, to have a very handsome wife, who loved her neighbours much better than her
husband, to which, like an honeſt well-meaning contented man,
he would never give credit, though he had often been informed
of her failings. And because he was so blind, like many a poor
fool in this age, he was presented by a nobleman who had
kissed his wife with a pair of speƈtacles to help his sight, by
which he discerned his shame. It is, therefore, ordered he
shall ſtill wear them to put in mind old men that have handsome young wives, that they may easily see they are cuckolds
by the help of their own speƈtacles.'

This being the conclusion of this war-like opera, we paid
our money, and made our exit, our ſtuttering perambulator
turning his head over his shoulder, like a fox that had ſtole
a goose, to ask us whether we would see the crowns, or no?
' Marry,' said I, ' not I. Crowns are mighty things, and ought
to be reverenced at a diſtance. I have heard many a wise man
say there's danger in coming too near 'em, if a body should
not make a leg handsomely and worship 'em as one should

do. A country clown, you know, can perform but awkwardly and they think a body stiff-necked, and take him for a disaffected person to the Government.'

'Prithee,' says my friend, 'I thought you had more wit than to be afraid of a fine thing; why, prithee, a King's crown is no living creature; it cannot bite thee.'

'I know well enough,' said I, 'it is not a living creature, no more is a King's writ, yet I have known it grip many a man to his ruin; therefore I tell you, I care as little to come near the one as I do the other should come near me. Besides, I'll warrant you, our conductor can inform us as well as if, at our expense, we had gone ourselves to see 'em.'

Upon this my friend asked old bluff-jacket what part of the Regalia, as he called it, was to be seen. He told us, there was the royal crown, and a new one made for the coronation of the late Queen Mary, and three other crowns worn by her Majesty, with distinct robes upon several occasions: also the salt-spoons, forks, and cups used at the Coronation. This account we thought as satisfactory from the mouth of our guide as if our own eyes were witnesses of the matter, and so cozened the keeper of our eighteenpence apiece, which we thought would serve much better to exhilarate our souls and feast our appetites, than to please our eyes, and satisfy our curiosity.

Having thus taken a remarkable view of most of the Tower rarities, in respect to the Governor, we gave his house the right hand as we came out; and rewarded the warder with one of her Majesty's pictures in silver, to his satisfaction; and so departed.

We now walked down from the Wharf, where, at the entrance, stood such a parcel of Greenwich water-dogs, that I thought they would have torn us in pieces, before we could have elbowed our way through 'em. At last, with much difficulty, sour looks, and negative answers, we happily cleared ourselves of these fresh-water sharks, and took a pleasant walk by the river-side, where great guns lay drawn into their proper order, ready to declare the will and pleasure of that great monarch who alone commands their voices, and gives their sound interpretation to the common people.

About the middle of the Wharf was a ſtone arch over the passage to Traitors' Gate, where ſtood a sentinel who, I observed, was very careful nobody should lean upon it, or touch it, leſt their elbows or their fingers should wear away her Majeſty's free-ſtone.

We walked round the Tower, and came again up on the Hill, where mumpers, soldiers, and ballad-singers were as busy at chuck-farthing and hussle-cap, as so many rooks at a gaming ordinary, wrangling and squabbling about their play like so many knavish pettifoggers in the King's Bench Walks, about the unfairness of their practice.

From thence we rambled into a remote part of the town, which my friend told me was as much incognito to many thousands in London, as it was to me before ever I came into't. There was as many turnings and windings in and out of every ſtreet, as I believe, could be contained in Fair Rosamond's Bower; and that which made me the more aſtonished was, we could walk by forty or fifty houses, and not see an ale-house; which was a greater sign of a sober neighbourhood, than I had observed before, since I came to London.

As we were thus wandering carelessly about, on the other side of the way we saw a door very finely painted which allured us to cross, and give our eyes the satisfaction of taking a view of what Mr. Painter, as we thought, had put up at his door to ſtand the censure of the public. But when we came over, we found, according to our apprehension, a parcel of ſtrange hieroglyphics, that would have puzzled an Egyptian magician to have told the meaning of 'em. There was a goat and a scorpion, a fish and a centaur, a ram and a crab; and many other such-like whims, at which we could not forbear laughing.

At last, reflecting more seriously upon the whim, we found it to be a representation of the Twelve Signs; from whence we presently concluded no less than an eminent conjurer, or some strange foretelling star-peeper, could be Lord of the House, whose door was so gloriously set off with such a number of constellations. As we were thus spending our conjectures upon that inhabitant's profession, out comes a figure at the door with such a malignant aspect that a beggar woman, as she asked him for a farthing, turned her head another way for fear her looking in his face might cause the child to be like him; one eye looked upwards, and the other downwards, as if he was star-gazing with one eye, and minding his way with the other. What he was, we knew not; but the house looked as if a conjurer lived in't, and the man looked as if he was bewitched.

'Pray,' says my friend, 'take notice of yonder tavern, at the sign of the Green Monster; that tavern,' says he, 'has ruined almost as many vintners as Sir Base-ill-fiery-face.[1] I have known three or four ruined by it; whether for want of trade, the knavery of the merchant or mismanagement, I know not. The first, indeed, had a very handsome wife, but very jiltish, who was supposed to be very kind to the person that set her up. But when she had once gratified his whim at a great expense, then he had cooled; so he resolved to turn his love that could not last into a revenge that should, and accordingly brought ruin upon the whole family. The husband ran away into Ireland, leaving the poor woman to shift for herself, with nothing but what God sent her; which she has since trusted into the hands of a draper, but what use he makes of it, you may easily judge.'

'Truly,' said I, 'I commend the woman for trusting what her husband left her with, in the hands of such a trader, who, when he is never so much tired with her, cannot at last,

---

[1] Sir Basil Firebrace, sheriff in 1687, was a stern magistrate who was especially strict against ale-houses.

without great dishonour to the linen-drapers' trade, leave her without a smock to her back. Which is very commonly the fate of women who unhappily enter into such illegal contracts.'

From thence, like roving pirates, we sailed about, we cared not whither, till mere accident and our own motion, without shaping any course, brought us into a street which both my friend and myself were equally strangers to, in which we espied a sumptuous tabernacle,[1] which being built so distinguishably from the House of the Lord, and contrary to the form of Solomon's Temple, we were very desirous of knowing which of the buzzing sectaries made use of it for a hive. Meeting in our way with a downright honest sort of a fellow, I asked him what he called that street? He told me Penitent Street. I asked him further, if he knew any peculiar reason why it was so christened? He answered me very roughly, because it was built, he supposed, for a parcel of deep sinners to live in, and they called it by that name, to put 'em in mind of repentance.

'Who does this meeting belong to?' said I. 'A wicked congregation,' says the fellow. 'Prithee,' said I, 'who is their teacher?' 'The Devil, sir,' says he. 'I mean,' said I, 'who is it that preaches, or holds forth here?' 'Oh, oh,' said my respondent, 'now I overstand ye; why they call him Ca-fa-fa-ca-laman-ca Doctor,[2] I think,' says he, 'or by such a kind of a hard name, which I can't remember, though I have seen him and heard him often. But for my part, he does so whine when he speaks, that I had as lief hear a capon crow, as hear him preach. As for his face, on my conscience, I think he has a chin as long as the handle of my pick-axe.'

'Honest friend,' said I, 'I thank ye, we'll trouble you no farther, for I know the man well enough by your description; good-bye to you.'

---

[1] This was a Baptist chapel where Titus Oates preached and ministered until 1701, when he was expelled as 'a disorderly person and hypocrite.'

[2] See note, page 207.

CHAPTER FOURTEEN

Christmas—A Dancing Academy—Sailors Ashore—Dancing and Jollity at Wapping—Goodman's Fields—Lotteries

THE Merry Christmas carnival was now come on, when the good housewife makes her husband eat his dinner upon a trencher to preserve her new scoured pewter plates in their shining beauty, and pinches her servants for the preceding week, that her windows might be splendidly adorned with superstitious greens, and that her minced pies and plum pudding might be richer than her neighbour's. We rambled from the reverend doctor's boarded theatre, and being quite out of our knowledge, wandered about like a couple of runaway 'prentices, uncertainty being our course, and mere accident our pilot. Every street we passed through smelled as strong of roast beef and rosemary, as Pye Corner does of pig and pork in the wicked season of St. Bartholomew. We met journeymen and 'prentices everywhere, as thick as fools in Cheapside; the former to collect their Christmas-box money and the latter to see themselves cozened out with their foolish expectancies. Every ale-house we came to was serenaded with a drum to thunder the rattle-headed customers into a good humour of spending their pence like asses.

Every now and then we came to a common Vaulting-School, where, peeping in, we saw some drunken tarpaulins and their tawdry trulls, dancing to a Scotch bagpiper or a blind fiddler. According to the prophecy, there were seven women to one man, and at least seventeen strumpets to one that had modesty enough in her looks to be thought otherwise. Sometimes we

met in the street with a boat's crew, just come on shore in
search of those land debaucheries which the sea denies 'em,
looking such wild, staring, uncouth animals, that a litter of
squab rhinoceroses, dressed up in human apparel could not
have made a more ungainly appearance. They were so
mercurial in their actions and rude in their behaviour, that
a woman could not pass by 'em but they fell to sucking their
lips like so many horse-leeches; and were ready to embrace
her in the open streets, as if they were absolute strangers to
Christian civility, and could have gone to greater length in
public, without a sense of shame, or fear of danger.

Every post they came near was in danger of having its head
broke, for everyone as he passed by, would give the senseless
block a bang with his cudgel, as if they wished it were either
the purser or the boatswain. The very dogs in the street, I
observed, shunned 'em, being so cautioned against their ill-
usage by the stripes they have formerly received, that as soon
as ever he sees a seaman, away runs the poor cur with his tail
between his legs to avoid the danger of the approaching evil.

I could not forbear reflecting on the prudence of persons
who send their unlucky children to sea to tame and reform
'em, which, I am well satisfied, is like sending a knave into
Scotland to learn honesty; a fool into Ireland to learn wit;
or a clown into Holland to learn breeding. For I am sure
they that send 'em may know that instead of mending the
ill-habits they have contracted, the first will return more wild,
the second more knavish, the third more foolish, and the
fourth a greater booby.

By the time we had made these observations and reflections
on those maritime kind of monsters, who had little more to
show they were men than that they walked upright, we had
straggled into Wapping; and being pretty well tired with our
walk, we went into a public-house to refresh ourselves with a
sneaker of punch, which was most likely to prove the best
liquor that end of the town could afford us.

The first figure that accosted us at our entrance was a female Wappineer, whose crimson countenance and double chin, contained within the borders of a white calico hood, and her fiery-face look, in my fancy, was like a round red-hot iron glowing in a silver chafing dish. The rest of her body being in proportion to her head, bore so corpulent a grace that had a bag of cotton, or wool-pack been laced into a pair of stays adorned with petticoats and put upon stilts, it would have made a figure of similitude to her person. My friend having a sword on, I observed to him she was most respectful in asking him in a voice as hoarse as a boatswain, 'What will you please to drink, noble Captain?'

After we had answered her question, she soon prepared us a little bowl of liquor, which, for want of better, we were forced to accept. Up in the chimney corner sat a great hulking fellow smoking a short pipe of stinking tobacco, looking as melancholy upon the fire as a female wretch does upon a Smithfield pile, when she is brought to be burnt for high treason. By and by in comes my landlady, and, like a true lover of industry, begins to read him a lecture against laziness, tormenting the ears of the poor dejected water-rat with a severe reprehension, after the following manner:

'Why, do you think, John, in your conscience, I am able to maintain you in this lazy life you lead? Thou knowest I have no money, God help me, but what I work as hard for as any woman in the parish. Therefore, John, it behoves thee to consider I am not able to let thee live upon me in this condition.' 'Why, what a rope ails you, mother?' replied the fellow. 'Why, would you have the conscience to turn me adrift, now I have spent all my money aboard you, before I have got me another voyage? You are as hasty with a body to turn out, as a boatswain in a storm.'

'Why, but, John,' replied the landlady, 'dost think to get a voyage by smoking in the chimney corner?' 'No,' says John, 'but how do you think a man can look out, without a penny of money in his breeches? I swear by the purser's honesty, I had as lieve step up to furl the mainsail in a gust of wind without a knife in my pocket.'

To which replied the old beldam, ' Why I would not have thee think that what I speak is out of any ill will to thee, for I hope thou think'st I am willing to do anything for thee, as far as I am able. Here, there is sixpence for thee, and prithee, John, go and look out, and don't fling it away idly. For consider these hard times, 'tis a great deal of money.'

He takes the sixpence, thanks her, and she thus continues: ' There are several ships going out bound to the West Indies, that want men, and I know thou art as able a seaman as ever walked between stem and stern of a ship, that any commander will be glad to enter thee.'

'As to that, mother,' says he, ' I can speak a proud word for myself; there is ne'er a part of a seaman, from the splicing of a cable to the cooking of the kettle, but what I know as well as the boatswain. Well, mother, wish me good luck. I'll try what I can do, as the gunner said to the cook's daughter.' She wished he might prosper in his endeavours and away he went.

I could not but reflect on the unhappy lives of these salt-water vagabonds, who are never at home but when they're at sea, and are always wandering when they're at home, and never contented but when they're on shore. They're never at ease till they've received their pay, and then never satisfied till they have spent it; and when their pockets are empty, they are just as much respected by their landladies (who cheat them of one half, if they spend the other) as a father is by his son-in-law, when he has beggared himself to give a good portion with his daughter.

Whilst we thus were busying our brains with thoughts relating to the condition of a seaman, in steps another of the tarpauling fraternity, with his hat under his arm, half full of money, which he hugged as close as a schoolboy does a bird's nest. As soon as he came into the entry, he sets up his throat like a half-drunk country bridegroom, so overjoyed at his prize as if he was hardly able to contain himself under the blessing of so much money. 'Ounds, mother,' says our marine Crœsus, 'where are you?' She hearing his tongue, thought by his lively expressing himself he had brought good news and came running with all speed to meet him, crying, 'Here I am, son Bartholomew, you're welcome ashore. I hope your Captain and ship's crew are all well.' 'By fire and gunpowder, I don't care if they be all sick. Why, we even paid off in the Downs, and I am just come up in a hoy. I hope I can have a lodging with you, mother?' 'Ah, ah! child! Dost thou think I won't find a lodging for one of my best children?' In answer to which, he returns the compliment, 'Sure never any seaman had ever such a good mother upon shore as I have. Ounds, mother, let me have a bucket full of punch, that we may swim and toss in an ocean of good liquor, like a couple of little pinks in the Bay of Biscay.' 'I always said,' said she, 'thou wert my best boy. Well, I'll go prepare thee such a bowl that every cup thou drink'st on shall make thee wish for a loving sweetheart.'

'Now you talk of that, mother, how does sister Betty?' 'She's very well,' says old suck-pocket. 'Poor girl, she'll be at home presently. I expect her every minute. I believe she has asked for you about a thousand times since you have been on board. I dare swear she would be as glad to see you as if you were her husband.'

Whilst she was mixing up a sea cordial for her adopted sea-calf, John happens to return from his enquiry after a voyage. 'Lack-a-day, John,' says his landlady, with a seeming sorrowful countenance, 'here's the saddest accident fall'n out since you went abroad, that has put me to such a puzzle, I know not how to order my affairs, unless you will let me beg one kindness of you.' 'What a pox,' says John, 'I'll warrant you now 'tis to lie upon that dirty flock bed that lies upon the boards in the garret.' ' Why, truly, John, I must needs tell thee I have one of the best friends I have in the world just come on shore; and if you don't oblige me, I shall indeed be put to a sad nonplus. Here, John, here's to thee; come drink, 'tis a cup of the best brandy, I'll assure you. Here, John, fill a long pipe of tobacco; well, son John, you say you'll let your mother's friend have your room, child, won't you?' ' I don't care, not I,' says the foolish lubber, ' he may ha't and he wool; I think I han't long to stay with you; I know now I have spent my fifty pound with you, you want to be rid of me.'

By the time the bowl was just begun between mother and son, who should step in but Sister Betty, and there was such a wonderful mess of slip-slop licked up between brother Bat and sister Bet, that no two friends, met by accident in a foreign plantation could have expressed more joy in their greeting. But as soon as ever the Whitechapel salutation was over, Mrs. Betty I found began to exact some further arguments of his kindness than just barely kissing, and asked him, what, had he brought his sister Betty no present from sea with him? ' Yes, yes,' says he, ' I have sure. I can as soon forget the points of the compass as forget my sister Betty, as good a girl as ever was kissed in a cabin. I told thee if ever I come home again I would present you with a ring, and there's money to buy it.' ' Now, now, hussy,' cries the mother, ' how dare you put your brother to this charge, you forward baggage you? Pray give it him again, you'd best, or I'll ring you, marry will I, minx.' The daughter well acquainted with her mother's hypocrisy, replied, ' I did not ask him for't, that I did not. I won't give it to him, that I won't! As long as he gave it to me I will keep it, that I will, why shouldn't I?'

By this time our punch was exhausted, and remembering we had heard of a famous amphibious house of entertainment, compounded of one half tavern and t'other music-house, it made us willing to dedicate half an hour to what diversion we might there meet with. Accordingly we left the old subtle beldam, and her young jilting daughter to empty the fool's cap of his nine months' earning, and send his hat and his pockets to sea again as empty as his noddle.

As soon as we came to the sign of the Mitre, we no sooner entered the house, but we heard fiddlers and hautboys together with a humdrum organ make such incomparable music, that had the harmonious grunting of a hog been added as a bass to a ravishing concert of caterwauling performers, in the height of their ecstasy, the unusualness of the sound could not have rendered it, to a nice ear, more engaging.

Having heard of the beauty and contrivance of the public music-room, as well as other parts of the house, very highly commended, we agreed first to take a view of that which was likely to be most remarkable. So we ascended the stairs and were ushered into a most stately apartment, dedicated purely to the lovers of music, painting, dancing, etc. No gilding, carving, colouring, or good contrivance was here wanting to illustrate the beauty of this noble academy, where a good genius may learn with safety to abominate vice; and a bad genius, with as much danger to practise it. The room, by its complete order and costly improvements, looks so far above the use it's now converted to, that the seats are more like pews than boxes and the upper end, being divided by a rail, looks more like a chancel than a music-box, so that I could not imagine it was built for a fanatic meeting-house; but they have for ever destroyed the sanctity of the place by putting an organ in it, round which hung a great many pretty whimsical pictures. There were but few companies in the room; the most remarkable person was a drunken commander, who, plucking out a handful of money, to give the music sixpence, dropped a shilling, and was so very generous that he gave an officious drawer, standing by, half a crown for stooping to pick it up again.

Finding we were much pleased with the order and beauty

of his room of state, the master was so civil as to ask us to
see his house, which kind offer we very readily embraced,
following him into several cleanly and delightful rooms, furnished for the entertainment of the best of company; and to
render 'em more diverting, they had so many whimsical
fancies painted upon the panels, that you could look no way
but you must see an antic, whose posture would provoke
laughter.

When he had showed us the most costly part of his tippling
conveniency, he brought us into the kitchen, which was railed
in with as much pomp as if nothing was to be dressed in it
but a dinner for a prince. Overhead hung an harmonious choir
of canary birds singing, and under them a parcel of seagulls
drinking. From thence he ushered us downstairs, into a subterranean sanctuary, where his Sunday friends may be protected from the insolence of the churchwardens, who every
Sunday, like good Christians, break the Sabbath themselves, to have the pleasure of punishing others for the same
fault.

Round this sots' retiring room were painted as many
maggots as ever crawled out of an old Cheshire cheese; on
one panel was a parcel of drunken women tormenting the
Devil, some plucking him by the nose like St. Dunstan, some
spitting upon his worship, others endeavouring to put his eyes
out, and many other such-like whimsies.

We then returned upstairs, where we drank a quart of good
red, thanked the master for his civility, and so departed the
house, which may be very justly styled, by such who love
good wine, and a pleasant room to sit in, the Paradise of
Wapping.

Proposing but a little more diversion at this end of the
Town, we thought it our best way to be returning home-
wards; accordingly we faced about, and to make our walk the
more pleasing, we chose a different path to what we had before
travelled, which brought us, after a little rambling, to the

Q

Danes' Church.[1] Seeming, by the outside, to be a very regular
and commodious building, I enquired of my friend, whether
he had ever seen the inside? He told me, yes, and that it was
a neat and well compact tabernacle, but the congregation to
whom it appertained were such a parcel of strange Christians,
that they were enough to scare an English parson out of the
pulpit, were he to ascend amongst 'em, and stunk so of pitch
and tar, that as soon as ever he had clapped his nose into the
church, he thought himself between decks. Their uncombed
locks, tobacco breaths, and seafaring apparel, added further
fragrancy to the former.

'Further,' says my friend, 'it is vainly and ridiculously
reported that the church is covered with one entire leaf of
copper, without joint or solder, which was cast in Denmark;
but how they stowed it on ship-board to bring it over, and
how they brought it from the waterside to the church, and
how they raised it to the roof, neither the inhabitants of the
square or anybody that reports it, could ever yet inform me.
For granting it were true, the dimensions must be so large,
and the ponderosity so great, that it would require in the
casting, as well as in the disposal, such wonderful art and
industry that would be worth discovery.'

From thence we rambled on till we came to a heathenish
part of the Town adjoining to a savoury place, which in ridicule
of fragrant fumes that arise from the musty rotten rags and
burnt old shoes, is called by the sweet name of Rosemary
Lane.[2] Here such a numberless congregation of ill-favoured
sluts were gathered together, that we thought a fleet of French
Protestants had been just arrived, and were newly come on
shore with bag and baggage, to implore the charity of English

[1] The Danish church, Wellclose Square, Whitechapel, was built in 1696 by
Christian V of Denmark, for the use of his sailor subjects frequenting London.
Caius Cibber was the architect, and he and his son Colley Cibber were both
buried there.
[2] Rag Fair, or Rosemary Lane, Whitechapel, was an old street market where
the most unsavoury of cast-off clothing was on sale.

well-disposed Christians to shelter them from the terrible persecution of rags, lice and poverty they found in their own country; but upon a true inquisition into the meaning of this tattered multitude, we were informed by a little draggle-tail flat-cap, it was Rag Fair, held every day from between two and three of the clock in the afternoon till night, where all the ragpickers in Town, and such as swop earthenware for old apparel, also the criers of old satin, taffeta or velvet, have recourse to sell their commodities. Cow Cross merchants, Long Lane sharpers, and other brokers were as busy in raking into their dunghills of old shreds and patches, and examining their wardrobes of decayed coats, breeches, gowns and petticoats, as so many cocks scraping about the filth to find out an oat worth picking.

The adjacent magistrates, we were informed, had used their utmost endeavours to suppress the meeting, but to no purpose, for their numbers bid defiance to all molestation, and their impudence and poverty are such that they fear neither gaol nor punishment.

You may here see the very scum of the kingdom in a body, consisting of more ragged regiments, than ever, I believe, was mustered together at any other rendezvous since the world's creation. It's a very healthful part of the town to cure lazy people of the Yellow Jaundice,[1] for body lice are so plenty that I dare engage that many have them without buying. It's a good market for country farmers to buy their scarecrows at, for let them but bargain with the ragwomen to dress 'em up some in imitation of themselves, and they need not fear but fright the birds out of their corn, and hogs out of their pease field.

The women that cry 'Pancakes,' and the girls that cry 'Diddle,

---

[1] There were various nostrums in favour for the cure of jaundice. 'Goose dung, gathered in the spring time, dried in the sun and finely powdered' was one specific. Live lice applied to the body, or a decoction of lice, were other remedies considered almost infallible.

diddle, dumplins ho,' were wonderful busy amongst 'em, and several little ale-houses are already crept in amongst 'em, to ease 'em of their pence as fast as they can raise 'em by the sale of their commodities. The flesh of the inhabitants, as well as the market-people, looked of dingy complexion, as if Dame Nature had mixed dirt with her clay, as bricklayers do with their mortar, to make it bind the faster, or else, as if fresh water was as scarce in their neighbourhood as 'tis in Antigua. The chief of their customers were beggars and people as ragged as themselves, who came to barter scraps for patches. I observed it was a very current swop to change food for raiment, that is, such needful repairs as a beggar's breeches may want between the legs, or his coat at armpits or elbows. Some rags I observed were parcelled out for better purposes, and would not be exposed to any but ready-money customers. Many of their stocks were so very small that I found two-pence or threepence was accounted amongst some of them as considerable takings.

Yet this observation I made, that amongst all that I beheld, as I passed through 'em, I saw not one melancholy or de-jected countenance amongst 'em; but all showing in their looks more content and cheerfulness than you shall find in an assembly of great and rich men on a public festival. From this we may conjecture that poverty is commonly attended with careless indifference that frees the mind from reflecting on its miseries; for, undoubtedly, were these despicable paupers but to let the unhappiness of their circumstances once affect their thoughts, it would have such a melancholy effect upon their spirits as would be soon legible in their looks, and discernible in their actions.

As we were thus descanting upon the ragged sons and daughters of necessity, a strange figure passed by us, in an ancient plate-buttoned suit, with an old-fashioned silver-hilted sword tucked up to the waistband of his breeches, in a long wig buckled up in small rings, as if, like an old cavalier's whiskers, every hair had been turned up with gum-water, the curls hanging all as stiff as a pig's tail, and as regular as the worm of a bottle-screw. His hat was as dusty as the top of a slut's cupboard, and his hands and face looked as rusty as an old neglected picture that had lain seven years in a garret full of rubbish. As he waddled by us in great haste, he gave my friend the civility of his hat which was by us returned, but looking after him we observed he had left the print of his fingers where he had handled his brim, as plain as a chimney-sweeper could have done if he had clapped a mealman upon the shoulders.

Taking notice of his complaisance, I asked my friend if he had any acquaintance with him. He told me, that he had seen him sometimes at the Green Dragon Tavern, but had little knowledge of him any other than that he had heard several odd stories of him from some who used the house and were better acquainted with him. He is very famous among those that know him for three slovenly neglects: he seldom washes his hands or face, very rarely brushes his hat, and never combs his wig but when he goes to church, which is not once in a twelvemonth. He is a man of extraordinary principles, but has run through a great many cunning professions without success, as merchant, brewer, lawyer, etc., and failing in all, is at last, through a natural propensity to exert his wits, turned sharper.

By this time we were got into Goodman's Fields, where passing by the Little Devil Coffee-house, my friend gave me such large encomiums both of the people and their punch, that I, like himself, was unwilling to let slip so good an opportunity of refreshing my intellects with a little of that most edifying liquor, which, if compounded of good ingredients, and prepared with true judgement, exceeds all the simple, potable products in the universe.

At our first entrance into the public room, we found a jolly company blessing one another over a plentiful bowl of this corroborating creature, whose excellencies were visible in the very looks of its lovers, the worldly air of their countenances being changed into a heavenly cheerfulness. This pleasing sight gave me a great encouragement to walk upstairs, where in a room neat enough to entertain Venus and the Graces, we were in a minute's expedition, supplied with an Indian goblet of infallible cordial, which, in half an hour, had so sublimed our thoughts that we found ourselves elated above the common pitch of human conversation.

Having the company of our landlord, and a friend or two of his, as jolly as himself, the cup passed round in a circle as an emblem of eternity, till at last I was so highly inspired by the noble virtues of our nectar, that I had much ado to forbear thinking I was in a state of immortality.

That which added much to our felicity and crowned the pleasures of our liquor, were these following advantages: My landlord was good company, my landlady good humoured, her daughters charmingly pretty, and the maid tolerably handsome. She can laugh, cry, say her prayers, sing a song, all in a breath, and can turn in a minute to all sublunary points of a female compass; yet thus much I must say in her behalf, that she's obedient to her mistress and obliging to her company, and I dare swear, as far as a man may guess by outward appearance, she'll prove an excellent wife to him that has the luck to marry her, and a kind companion to an honest friend that loves kissing in a corner.

We now turned back again to our buzzing metropolis, the City, where modesty and plain-dealing were laid aside to pursue the wonderful expectancies so many thousands had from a mixture of projectors' knavery, and their own folly. The *Gazette* and *Post* papers lay neglected, and nothing was purred over in the coffee-houses but the Ticket catalogues. No talking of the Jubilee,[1] the want of current trade with France,

---

[1] The Papal Jubilee of 1700 was much talked of in England, probably on account of the recent Catholic revival.

or the Scotch settlement at Darien; nothing buzzed about by
the purblind trumpeters of State news, but Blank and Benefit.
' My son had five pound in such a lottery,[1] but got nothing.'
' My daughter,' says another, ' had but five shillings and got
a twenty-pound prize.' People were running up and down the
streets in crowds as if one end of the town was on fire, and
the other were running to help 'em off with their goods. One
stream of coachmen, footmen, 'prentice boys and servant
wenches flowing one way, with wonderful hopes of getting an
estate for threepence; knights, squires, gentlemen and traders,
married ladies, virgin madams, jilts, chariots and coaches, were
going another way, with a pleasing expectancy of getting six
hundred a year for a crown.

Thus were all the fools in Town so busily employed in
running up and down from one lottery or another, that it was
as much as London could do to conjure together such numbers
of knaves as might cheat 'em fast enough of their money.
The unfortunate cried out, 'A cheat, a cheat, a confounded
cheat; nothing of fairness in it.' The fortunate, in opposition
to the other, crying, ' 'Tis all fair, all fair; the fairest adventure
that ever was drawn.' And thus everybody according to their
success, expressed their sentiments, though the losers who may
be said to be in the wrong of it to venture their money, were
most right in their conjectures of the project, and the gainers
who were in the right of it to hazard their money, because
they won, were most wrong in their opinion of the matter.

' Truly,' says my friend, ' I confess I cannot conceive any
extraordinary opinion of the fairness of any lottery, for I am apt
to believe that when such a number of fools fall into a knave's
hand, he will make the most of 'em, and I think Parliament
could not give the nation greater assurance of their special

---

[1] About this time there was a public madness for speculation in lotteries.
The Government lottery for £1,500,000 was opened in 1709 with 150,000
tickets of £10 each. There were 3750 bearing prizes and the rest were blanks.
This lottery was organized at the Mercers' Chapel, and the whole million and
a half was subscribed in a day or two.

regard to the welfare of the public, than by suppressing all lotteries, which only serve to buoy up the miſtaken multitude with dreams of golden showers to the expense of that little money, which with hard labour they have earned; and often to the negleċt of their business, which doubles the inconveniency. The gentry, indeed, may make it their diversion, but the common people make it a great part of their care and business, hoping thereby to relieve a necessitous life, inſtead of which, they plunge themselves further into an ocean of difficulties. What if one man in ten thousand gets five hundred pounds, what benefit is that to the reſt, who have ſtruggled hard for fools' pence to make up that sum, which, perhaps falls to one who ſtood not in need of Fortune's favours?

'Prithee,' says my friend, 'let's go to the Mercers' Chapel, and see how the crowd behave themselves there. Ten to one, we shall find something or other that may be diverting to ourselves, and worth rendering to the public.'

Accordingly we direċted ourselves thither, to which rendezvous of adventurers as well as ourselves, abundance of fools from all parts of the Town, were flocking; none shewing a despairing countenance, but all expressing as much hopes in their looks, as if every one had an assurance from a Moorfields conjurer of having the great prize. Some were thoughtful how to improve it, should it so happen; some how happily they might enjoy it; women, what fine clothes they'd wear; maids, what handsome husbands they'd have; beaus, what fine wigs they'd wear; and sots, what rare wine they'd drink; the religious, what charitable works they'd do; and young libertines, what fine wenches they'd keep.

In the porch or entry of the hall was a bookseller's shop, where the printed benefits were sold. With much ado we crowded into the hall, where young and old, rich and poor, gentle and simple, were mixed higgle-de-piggle-de, all gaping for a prize, like so many Fortune's minions waiting for a windfall from her blind lady's Golden Pippin tree, whilſt the projector and the honourable trustees sat laughing in their sleeves, to see fair play dealt out to the attentive assembly, whose avaricious hearts went pit-a-pat at the drawing of every ticket.

Every now and then, when a prize arose, some impatient novice or other crying out, ' That's mine,' bustled up to the trustees, producing his ticket to prevent that fraud, which, though he had ventured his money, he was fearful might be practised amongst 'em. It sometimes proved the adventurer had mistaken his number or the number that was drawn to the benefit, which proved such a disappointment that their silly looks would render 'em a laughing stock to the whole congregation of fortune's courtiers, every one equally big with the hopes of being a favourite.

My friend and I having no pretence or title to be ranked, by an accident, in the number of the fortunate, having ventured nothing in their plausible piece of uncertainty, thought it not worth our while to spend any further time amongst 'em, but concluded to march about our business, and leave the numerous sons and daughters of Fortune to flatter themselves with the vain hopes of their mother's kindness. So we came out and went to a neighbouring coffee-house, where we smoked a pipe and consulted of some new measures to take in our next spy.

CHAPTER FIFTEEN

Concerning Victuallers—Of Astrologers and Wise-Women—Their
Tricks

AS a fair Town Miss, of a twelve months' standing, when
she has become too common, puts on a dark foretop, blacks her eyebrows, changes the mode of her
dressing, her lodging, and her name, and sets up for a new
creature; so we, for fear of falling under the same fate, have
thought fit to vary a little from our former method, in hopes
to preserve the same liking to our design which we believe
the world has hitherto had, from the encouragement it has
given us to continue our undertaking.

Our chief alteration will be to treat more men and manners,
opening the frauds and deceits practicable in many trades,
characters of trades, and those that follow 'em; and remarks
upon all occurrences worth notice. In pursuance to which
method I shall begin with Victuallers, shewing their usual rise
and means of success, and also shall lay open their pride,
sauciness, and ingratitude, which either most men have, may,
or will find, by their own experience.

OF VICTUALLERS

In times of sobriety, when ale-houses were as scarce as
churches, with not above one in a parish; when any tradesman
was undone by the levity of his wife, the disobedience of his
children, fire or any other losses and crosses incident to a
man in this world, upon his humble application to the magistrates of the ward or precinct wherein he lived, they would
grant, or procure him to be granted, a licence to sell ale, that

he might be doing something to defend himself and his family from being burdensome to the parish. And being of peevish temper, by reflecting on his misfortunes, he was usually distinguished in his new employment with some of the following nicknames and titles, as Alderman Snarl, Captain Rusty, Sir John Tun-Belly, Squire Gruff, Doctor Grunt, or the like. Neither could his good woman, whose business it was to draw the tipple, avoid being new christened Mother Huff, Mother Damnable, the Witch of Endor, Dame Saucy, Goody Blowze, Gammer Tattle, or the like.

But now, as soon as a tradesman has got a little money by the business he was bred to, observing the lordliness of the victuallers, the laziness of their lives, the plenitude of their purses, and welfare of their families, he resolves to thrive upon his own small stock at the same rate, and pursue the hopes and prospect of growing rich with the same expedition. Accordingly he takes a house well situated for his purpose, where in a few years' time, behaving himself at first very humble, he advances himself to some petty office of the parish, with which he begins to swell and look as stiff and as wealthy as an alderman after a knighthood. From thence, in a little time, dignified with the office and title of Mr. Churchwarden, he reckons himself as great as the Pope, and measures a foot more in the waist, upon his first entrance into this parochial authority, than he did in seven years before he was chosen for it.

His wife must now be called Madam, his sons, young masters, and his daughters, misses, and he that salutes the old lickspiggot with any other title than that of Mr. Churchwarden, runs the hazard of the forfeiture of his good looks, friendship and conversation.

His own house now is not big enough to hold him. He expects great reverence from all his little neighbours, and will loll against the door and swing his bunch of little keys half a dozen times round his finger, before he will answer a poor neighbour a civil question. If he that has spent fifty pounds in his house, asks to borrow a crown of him, he says his wife made him swear not above three days ago that he would never lend sixpence again as long as he lived, or else he would have done it with all his heart.

There are three sorts of victuallers, all differing very much from each other, according to the several parts of the Town wherein they are situated. At Wapping and that way, they lord it over the people like a boatswain over a ship's company, and look as bluff upon their tarpaulin guest as a mate when first made commander. In the City he is hail-fellow-well-met with any of his customers below a Common Council man, but to all above he is forced to pay a deference, and bow as low to the deputy of a Ward, as a country innkeeper does to the sheriff of a county. At Charing Cross, you may find 'em so very humble and obliging for every twopence they take, that a gentleman foot soldier, or a lord's footman, shall have as many bows and cringes from the master and his family over the drinking of a pot, as a French dancing-master shall give the mistress of a boarding-school, when she gives him half a piece for his day's teaching. Whether it be poverty, living amongst courtiers, or being bred gentlemen's servants and so kicked and cuffed into good manners by their masters, I'll leave the reader to determine.

OF ASTROLOGERS AND WISE-WOMEN

No common errors, frauds or fallacies in the world, have so subdued the weaker, and consequently the greater part of mankind, as the jugglery and deceits practised by a parcel of pretended astrologers, who undertake to resolve all manner of lawful questions, by jumbling together those distant bodies, in whose nature or influence they have just as much know-ledge as an old country woman has of witchcraft, or a German juggler of necromancy.

In the first place, I have had an opportunity of examining several nativities calculated by those who have had the reputation of being the best artists of the age, wherein I have observed that sickness, length of days and all other fortunate and unfortunate contingencies assigned to the natives, have been as directly opposite to what has happened through the whole course of their lives, as if the tumbling star-groper had rather studied the rule of contraries, that he might always be found in the wrong on't.

In the next place, their method in deceiving people who come to enquire about stolen goods, is such a barefaced ridiculous piece of banter that I wonder any creature that bears human shape can be so stupidly ignorant as not to plainly discern the impositions that are put upon them. In the first place, he enquires about what time, and after what manner the things were lost, and what strangers they had then in the house, from whence he reasonably infers whether they have been concealed by the master or mistress on purpose to make the servants more diligent. If his conjecture be that it was taken by a common thief, he describes a swarthy black ill-looking fellow, most wisely considering that such sort of rogues are seldom without a gallows in their countenance. He says, withal, that the goods are pawned, and will scarcely be recoverable without they take the thief speedily, in order to effect which he will give them his best directions. 'Go a quarter of a mile north from your own dwelling, and then turn easterly, and walk forward till you come unto the sign of a large four-footed beast, and search within three or four doors of that sign. You will go near to take him, if you go soon enough, or hear of him. He is of a middle stature, and in poor habit.'

Away goes the fool, as well satisfied as if he had the rogue by the elbow, and if by an accident they do hear of the thief, all is ascribed to the wonderful cunning of their wizard.

But if, on the contrary, he believes it to be taken by a servant, he bids 'em go home satisfied, for they shall certainly find the spoon, etc., in three or four days' time, hid in a secret hole, in such part of the kitchen; or he'll make the devil to do with those that have it, and then force them to bring it in open shame and disgrace at dinner time, and lay it down upon the table in the sight of the whole family.

Away goes the person well satisfied with what their ptolemist has told 'em, and declares to every one in the house, how the thief was threatened, after what manner the spoon should be found within the time appointed, or else woe be to them that have it. This frightful story coming to the ears of the guilty, brings 'em under such dreadful apprehensions of the conjurer's indignation, if they do not lay what they've taken within the time, according to the direction, then the first opportunity they have, they will place it to the utmost exactness in whatever hole or corner he has appointed for the finding it.

And this is the very reason why, in such sort of cases, people so oft recover things that have been missing in their houses, according to the doctor's direction, which the ignorant looked upon to be all devilism and conjuration; or if the master or mistress had concealed anything from their servants to make 'em more careful, they are also ready to observe the dictates of the cunning man, that the servants might believe what was missing was really stolen, that they might be more watchful of things in their trust, to prevent the like mischances for the future. But as to their pretended knowledge in matters beyond the view of common reason, it is all a cheat, and I am sorry this present age should give such evidence of its weakness as to encourage such a parcel of illiterate and scandalous deceivers of the common people to flourish and live publicly great, by such base and unjustifiable means as casting figures, telling fortunes, selling charms, or sigills, or the like.

Their further frauds and practices, I shall more plainly detect in these following stories, some of which I can warrant as truths from persons of my own acquaintance.

There is now living a famous wise-woman in Whitechapel, who is a great pretendress to the gypsies' art of fortune-telling, and has acquired such wonderful credit and reputation among servant wenches and poor ignorant people, that she has forty or fifty sixpenny fools every morning to attend her. Most are women, some to know when they shall be married, some wanting to be told which was the right father of an expected child; some married women, whose husbands were at sea, or in foreign plantations, who come to know whether she can give 'em any glad tidings of their death or no; some to know whether they should be prosperous in their marriage, voyage, or business in hand, or not; others about stolen goods, and the like.

An ingenious married gentlewoman having heard much of Mother Telltroth's fame, and giving but little credit to common reports, finding it hard to believe that Providence made any of her sex so much wiser than they should be, resolved to let her own experience determine whether the woman was a witch. Accordingly she had recourse to her abode, where she thrust herself in amongst the querists, who were thronging in, like so many spectators to see a devout old woman that had hanged herself for religion. Every one took their turn, like customers at a chandler's, first come, first served, or like smiths and cobblers in a twopenny barber's, waiting for the chair.

At last it came to the gentlewoman's turn to apply herself to the oracle, and approaching near the elbow-chair of infallibility she gave a low curtsey as a type of her ignorance, as well as submission, and told her the chief of her business was to be satisfied when Providence would bless her with a husband. The most knowing prophetess, after she had ogled and examined her physiognomy with very penetrating circumspection, the lady keeping her countenance, she told her that the man was yet unknown to her whom she should certainly marry within a few weeks, by whom she should have three children, and then bury him. She should marry a second time, soon after, very much to her advantage as well as satisfaction, and should live very comfortably with him, to so great an age that she should be forced to walk with a stick.

'Sure, forsooth,' says the gentlewoman, 'you must deal with the devil, or how should you know all this?'

'Indeed, child,' replied the sorceress, 'thou art mistaken, what I tell thee is purely from my art.'

'No, no,' says the querist, 'it must certainly be from the devil, for he's the only father of lies, and I'll swear you han't told me a word of truth yet, for I have had a husband this nine years, and have had seven children by him, all living at this present, therefore your art, forsooth, has wonderfully failed you.'

'Pray,' says the old gypsy, 'let me see your hand once more.' Upon a review of it, says she, 'I find I was mistaken, for I find now thou hast a husband, but he's such a very little one, that 'tis as much as ever I can do to discern his signification in thy palm.'

In this particular she happened to guess right, for the husband was a very little man, which put the lady into such an extravagant fit of laughter, that being well pleased with the cunning of the old baggage, she went away confirmed in her opinion that there was nothing in her pretended skill, but mere guess and subtlety.

A country gentleman not long since being in Town, happened to be strangely infatuated with an opinion of astrology, and resolving to venture some money at the lottery, had recourse to a famous planet-juggler, giving him a guinea to assign him a lucky hour for his purpose aforementioned. According to their customary way of cozening people he erected a scheme, and after he had made himself half purblind by poring upon his jimcrack, and jumbling together a parcel of figures to amaze the querist, he positively prefixed a certain time wherein he should be fortunate. The gentleman pursuant to the star-groper's directions put twenty guineas into his pocket and away he went to attack the devil's treasury, where, according to his oracle's prediction, he met with such great success, that he brought off a hundred pound. He returned to his conjurer with a full assurance of breaking the lottery in a little time, and presented the old fox with ten guineas, and desired he would consider of another time wherein he might again be fortunate.

The old shark very greedily swallowed the golden bait, and made him large promises what the stars should do for him, bidding him call about two or three days hence, and he should have time to be more exact in his calculation. The gentleman goes home wonderfully pleased, and returns to his prophet according to appointment, who prefixes another night wherein he should be surely prosperous.

Away goes the gentleman a second time, flushed with an assurance of the golden fleece; but had not been long at play, but his stars, by retrogradation, brought him under a necessity of sending his man home for more money, which he was forced to replenish two or three times so that for the hundred pound he had won, he had lost two, and began to be angry with the Heavens and the stars as a young poet that had lost his mistress. Going back to his deceitful Ptolemy in a wonderful rage, he told him he and his stars were a couple of lying confederates, and for ever after he became as great an enemy to astrology as a schoolboy is to a birch rod after a sound flogging.

The third story I shall entertain you with, though it be something staler than the former, yet being applicable to my purpose, I think it may be admitted with exception. On Southwark side there lived a famous student in those two fraternal sciences, physic and astrology, who, to deceive people with more facility and assurance, had several bells placed in his study above stairs, the ropes of which hung down the wall of a dark staircase, one signifying lost sheep, another clothes

R

ſtole off the hedge, another ſtrayed or ſtolen horses, which were the chief things people had recourse to him about. So that a man who attended the door used firſt to find out what the people came about, and then ring for the doctor, and dispatch intelligence at the same inſtant.

It happened once that a butcher having loſt some sheep out of the neighbouring marshes, came to requeſt a caſt of the doctor's office, believing he could put him in a way of recovering his ſtrayed wethers. Accordingly he goes to the house, where at his firſt entrance, the servant asked him his business. Without miſtruſt, he told the fellow his mischance, who bid him not be dismayed, for the doctor, without a doubt, would do him service in the matter. ' He's a little busy,' says he, ' in his ſtudy, but however I'll venture to ring for him.' So he tinkles the sheep bell, upon which down comes the doctor, having put on his fur cap and conjuring countenance, that half frightened the poor sheep-dealer.

At his firſt appearance, ' How now, friend,' says the wise man, ' I'll warrant you you have loſt some sheep, and you want me to give you tidings of 'em.'

' Yes, noble doctor,' says the fellow.

' Come,' says the doctor, ' walk into my parlour, and I'll endeavour to give you satisfaction.'

The butcher follows the doctor, and happening to have a bulldog with him, the dog crept under one of the chairs without anybody seeing him.

According to cuſtom in such matters the servant had recourse to his wardrobe of shapes, and dressed himself up in a bull's hide ready for his maſter's conjuring homily to summons him to appear. After he had talked a little with the butcher about this business in hand, the doctor bid him be sure to sit ſtill and not be frighted at anything he saw, for nothing should hurt him; and after he had made a large circle, and mumbled over a little unintelligible jargon, he gives the devil his cue to make his terrible entrance.

The butcher's dog being of a true bear-garden breed, seeing the appearance of the bull, makes a fair run, seizes the doctor's familiar, and makes him roar like what he represented.

The conjurer rising in a great passion, ' Ounds, what d'ye mean?' says he. ' Take your dog off, you rogue; take off your dog.'

The butcher smoking the cheat, ' Not I, by my troth, doctor, I know he's as good as ever run, let 'em fight fair, doctor. If you'll venture your devil, I'll venture my dog.'

Never was poor devil so mauled by a hell-hound in this world before, and the doctor was glad to pay the fellow for his sheep to lock up his tongue from spreading abroad his detection.

A Reforming Constable

He is a man most commonly of a very scandalous necessity, who has no way left, but to live upon people's debaucheries. Every night he prays heartily that the world may grow more wicked, for one and the same interest serves him and the devil. He always walks armed with a staff of authority, sealed with the royal arms. He searches a bawdy-house as a church-warden does an ale-house, not to punish vice but to get money. He squeezes harlots as a thief catcher does highwaymen, takes from 'em the fruits of their iniquities, making them twice as wicked as they would be, by putting them upon fresh villainies to keep themselves from starving. He brings no woman to punishment for her ill-courses but for want of money. Con-stables are a sort of unlucky bird-catchers, and every naughty house their net, the wenches their decoy birds, that allure others into their trap, and are freed themselves from that danger they have brought the innocent into. They are only encouragers of what they pretend to suppress, protecting those people for bribes, which they should punish, well knowing each bawdy-house they break is a weekly stipend taken out of their own pocket.

Meet 'em when you will, you will never find one in their custody above a flat-cap or a cinder-wench, who, because her rags won't pawn for a dozen of drink, must be made an example of. She that has the prudence to carry half a crown in her pocket may sin on without danger, whilst the poor needy wagtail must be cautious how she kisses at ill hours, in ill houses, or in ill company, lest she be carried to Bridewell, where, instead of being reclaimed, she is hardened in her miserable state of wickedness.

Of all people I know, I think their employment is most like the dog-whippers of a church, whose business it is to watch the tails of hound and puppy from committing an indecency. They are wicked servants who have undertaken to insure the nation from vice, and their business is to run up and down Town, to quench vice, as the steel-cap Salamanders do extinguish fire.

CHAPTER SIXTEEN

Sailors—A Jolly Party—Quaker and Parson—Gray's Inn Walks and
the Beaus—An Irishman—A Beau—Jonathan's Coffee-house

MY companion having given me the common civility
of a London inhabitant to a country friend or
acquaintance, i.e., shewed me the tombs of Westminster, the lions in the Tower, the rogues in Newgate, the
mad people in Bedlam, and the merchants upon the 'Change,
with the rest of the Town rarities worth a country fool's
admiring, began about a month since, I suppose, to be tired
of his office. Upon which he apologized for his departure,
and so left me, saying he would wait upon me as often as the
present urgency of affairs would permit; and if anything worth
notice occurred to his knowledge, he would communicate the
same, or if he could not spare to give me his company, he
would dispatch intelligence by letter.

So being armed with good instructions and all necessary
cautions, I shifted off my rural bashfulness and began to
embolden myself in a little time so that I could call a careless
drawer, 'blockhead,' kick a saucy tapster on the breech, swear
Z——ds at a hackney coachman, or sit down amongst
aldermen in a coffee-house without plucking off my hat.

When I first left my mate, I thought myself in as disconsolate a condition as a widow for the first month after the
loss of her husband, but like the mourning dame, I found
such new diversion as quickly obliterated my old friend, and
soon made me easy without his conversation, as the good
woman is without her old bed-fellow.

Being thus left to range the Town by myself like a man

that loved no company, or like a hangman that could get none, I happened near the 'Change to step into a tavern kitchen, where seated at a corner table I found a knot of jolly, rough-hewn, rattling topers, who looked as if they'd been hammered into an uncouth shape upon Vulcan's anvil; whose iron sides, and metal-coloured faces seemed to dare all weathers, spit fire at the frigid zone, and bid death defiance. Bumpers of Canary[1] went round as fast as one could drink and his neighbour fill, so that a stander-by might have easily guessed that every glass had been a health to an emperor.

I soon found by their dialect they were masters of ships: ' Cheer up, my lads, pull away, save tide; come, boys.' Then handling the quart, being empty, ' What, is she light? You, sir, that's next, haul the bar-line, and call the cooper's mate.' The drawer being come, ' Here, you fly-blown swab, take away this damned tankard, and ballast her well. Pox take her, there's no stowage in her hold. Have you ne'er a larger vessel?'

With such sort of stuff was I diverted for a little time, till an old gentleman coming into the kitchen, whose grave and venerable head being frost-nipped with age was bleached as white as snow, his silver hairs, which should have been a fence to his weather-beaten ears, being so thin that they might be more easily numbered than his infirmities. Happening to like my side of the fire, he sat down near me, and called for his half pint of that golden-coloured cordial over which our fathers used to number up their juvenile pranks. When he had measured out a moderate dram he presents his service to me after a very courteous manner. I returned his compliment with the respect due to his gravity, but could not forbear fancying he was too complaisant to be a rich citizen, and that

---

[1] This was a still white wine produced in the Canary Islands and much drunk in England until 1853, when practically the whole of the vineyards were destroyed by phylloxera and Madeira took the place of Canary. Most Canary is made into sherry.

misfortune had taught him to be civil to a stranger; for it may be generally observed that a thrifty trader takes a pride in being surly, and seldom is burdened with more manners than a ploughman.

After he had exchanged two or three words about 'What news? What's a clock? Methinks it's cold to-day,' and the like, I observed the old gentleman, when he had discovered our neighbouring company, by their talk, to be commanders of ships, looked at 'em with as much malice as a man under suspicion of debt would a gang of officers. Every glance seemed to call 'em a pack of knaves, and at last his passion grew so high that I observed by the trembling of his lips he was fallen into soliloquy, and I believe, was the truth known, he was cursing 'em as fast within himself, as a country-hag does a farmer's hogs when he denies her a pitcher of whey, or a dish of cheese curds.

Whilst the old gentleman seemed to be under this perturbation of mind, one of Neptune's sunburnt subjects, trussed up in trousers of old sail-cloth, was ushered into the kitchen by a drawer, in order to deliver melancholy tidings, as he thought, to Father Grisle, who I understood had been drawn in to hold a fourth part of a vessel. The boatswain had been dispatched to him with all expedition from Deal, to bring this following intelligence, which, after two or three marine scrapes and *congees*, he begins after this manner:

'Ah, sir, I am beloth to let you know what I am come on purpose to tell you. I am sent as the ambassador of sad, sad news, indeed.'

'Prithee, friend,' says the gentleman, 'what is it? If my family be but safe, and my house not on fire, I thank my stars. I shall not be much frighted, let it be what it will; for I have been used to so much bad news from men of your calling that I have not received a comfortable word from that unlucky element you belong to this four year. I never see a seaman come towards me, to speak to me, but I always fancy he's as ill an omen to my family as a raven that flies over my house, and croaks three times in his passage; though now I know not what the news thou can'ſt bring me, that will trouble me. Therefore, such as it is, prithee, friend, let's hear it.'

'Ah, sir,' says the fellow, blowing his nose and wiping his eyes, ' the poor *Betty's* loſt. Coming into the Downs a ſtorm of wind sprang up at N.W. and by W. as God would have it, enough to blow the devil's head off. We made our larboard tack, and plied to windward, worked like dragons, and did all that men could do to save her, but could not weather the Goodwins, in which sand, to our great sorrow, as well as your lamentation, she lies now buried.'

' There let her lie till Doomsday,' says the old Dad. ' Here's to thee, friend, with all my heart. 'Tis the beſt news thou could'ſt have brought me, for if the old *Betty* had survived the danger of the seas much longer, I believe she and the maſter together would have brought me to the parish. I hope,' says he, ' I shall be a warning to all fools how they are drawn in by a pack of knaves, to meddle with such business as is out of their knowledge. My share coſt me two hundred pound, and three bad voyages brought her owners into debt, and now at laſt she is loſt upon the Goodwins. Good-bye t'ye, good Miſtress *Betty*, I am heartily glad to hear you're at the bottom, for 'faith, I believe if thou had'ſt not sunk, in a little time I should. No more long bills for refitting, no maſter's long accounts for repairs of damage suſtained in ſtorm. No, no, if ever they hook in the old fool again, to make ducks and drakes with his money in salt water, I'll give 'em leave to tie him to a cable to make a buoy on. I find the merchants are a pack of sharpers, maſters of ships a parcel of arrant knaves, a vessel but a doubtful confidant, and the sea a mere lottery.'

Having thus said, he paid for his nipperkin of Canary, and away he went, I ſtaying little while after him.

From thence I went to a coffee-house where I had appointed

my acquaintance to meet me at a certain hour in the day, and
there I found a letter from my friend, to request my company
to supper at a private house in the City, where a gentleman
had provided a commodious entertainment for some of his
friends that evening.

When the hour assigned for our meeting came, I accordingly went pursuant to my friend's directions, and found a
jolly company assembled whose looks sufficiently revealed
their affections to the good creature, so that I had no reason
to mistrust any obstruction of our mirth from the appearance
of parsons. Amongst 'em were two country parsons, and
a notable sharp Town Quaker, who I had reasonable foresight
would produce some good diversion, as soon as our cups, and
the season of the night, had made us fit instruments for each
other's felicity.

I shall not tire you with a bill of fare, but a plentiful supper
we had, to the as great content of the founder (it being served
up in such admirable order) as to the satisfaction of the guests.
When we had tired our hands with stopping our mouths to
assuage the fury of our appetites, and one of the parsons had
put a spiritual padlock upon the mouths of the company, and
given a holy period to our fleshy sustenance for that evening,
a magnificent bowl of punch and some bottles of right Gallic
juice were handed to the table, which received, as the glass
went round, a circular approbation. Our stomachs craving a
hearty supply of wine for the digestion of our fish, made us
at first pour down our liquor in such plentiful streams that it
soon put our engines of verbosity to work, and made us as
merry as so many schoolboys at a breaking up.

At last we came to a good-looking bottle of claret, which
at least held half a pint extraordinary; but the cork was drove
in so far, that there was no opening on't without a bottle-
screw. Several attempted to remove the stubborn obstacle with
their thumbs and fingers, but none could effect the difficult
undertaking, upon which says the donor of the feast, ' What,

is nobody amongst us so provident a toper, as to carry a bottle-screw about him?' One cried, 'No'; another, 'No, he had left his at home'; a third never carried one, and so 'twas concluded no screw was to be had. The parsons being all this time silent, at last says the lord of the banquet to his man, 'Here, take it away, though I protest,' says he, ''tis a fine bottle, and I'll warrant the wine's better than ordinary, it's so well corked; but what shall we do with it? We cannot open it. You must take it down, I think, though I vow, 'tis a great pity. But prithee, bring us up some more bottles that may not puzzle us so.'

The oldest and wisest of the parsons having observed the copious dimensions of the bottle, and well knowing by experience that sound corking is always an advantage to good liquor, 'Hold, hold, friend,' says he to the servant, who was going out with the bottle, 'I believe I may have a little engine in my pocket that may unlock the difficulty'; and fumbling in his pockets after he had plucked out a Common Prayer book, an old comb-case full of notes, and a twopenny nutmeg grater, at last he came to the matter and brings out a bottle-screw, which provoked not a little laughter through the whole company.

'Methinks, friend,' says the Quaker, 'a Common Prayer book and a corkscrew are improper companions, not fit to lodge in one pocket together. Why dost thou not make thy breeches afford 'em different apartments?' To this the parson made this answer, 'Since devotion gives comfort to the soul, and wine in moderation preserves the health of the body, why may not a book that instructs us in the one, and an instrument that makes way for the other, be allowed, just as the soul and body, for whose use they were intended, bear one another company.'

'But methinks, friend,' says the Quaker, 'a bottle-screw in a minister's pocket is like the *Practice of Piety* in the hand of a harlot; the one no more becomes his profession, than the other does hers.' To this the parson replied, 'A good book in the hand of a sinner, and an inftrument that does good to a society in the hand of a clergyman, I think are both very commendable, and I wonder why a good man should object againft either.'

'I am very glad,' says the Quaker, 'thou takeft me to be a good man; then, I hope, thou haft no reason to take anything ill that I have spoken?'

'Nay, hold,' says the parson, 'I did not design it as a compliment to thee, for to tell thee the truth, I do not think thee so good as those who, I believe, thou haft but a bad opinion of.' To which replied the Quaker, 'Thou may'ft see, the Government has a better opinion of us than it has of those people whom I imagine thou meaneft, or else they would never have made our words of equal validity with your oaths. Therefore, I think we have reason to be looked upon as the moft honeft people in the kingdom.'

In answer to this, says the parson, 'I remember a fable, which, with as much brevity as I can, I will repeat to the company in answer to thee.'

'Once upon a time, the lion found there were many divisions amongft his four-footed subjects, insomuch that he could not, without some difficulty, preserve peace in his dominions, and allay the grumblings of each disaffected party; but among all the factious beafts in the foreft, the asses were moft obftinate, and would never change their pace in obedience to those unwholesome laws provided againft their humdrum slothfulness. The lion considering they were serviceable creatures, notwithftanding their obftinacy, and would bear any burthen without complaining, let them but have their own ways, and go their own pace, thought it very necessary to make a law that every ass should have his own will, and go unshod, but with this proviso, that if they ever tripped or ftumbled, they should be soundly whipped for their fault.

'A little time after the commencement of this law, an ass

meeting with a horse, could not forbear boasting what great favourites the asses were at Court, upbraiding the horse with being iron-shod, and saying how they, by law, were made free to travel upon their own natural hoof, which is much more easy. "You are mistaken," says the horse; "shoeing makes us walk upright, and tread with more security; and pray, friend ass, remember this amidst your benefit, that you must be whipped if you stumble as well as we."'

Upon the application of this fable, the whole company burst into a laughter to the great discountenance of our merry Ananias, who had nothing left but blushes for reply. But having a great desire to be even with his antagonist, he lay so very close upon the catch, that the parson was forced to put a guard upon his tongue, lest he should give him an advantage to recover his credit. At last, in a silent interval, the glass coming two or three times quick about, made the parson neglect to take off his wine with his usual expedition, as it set down before him, which the Quaker observing, asked him what countryman he was?

The priest returned him a satisfactory answer.

'Did'st thou not lately hear of a great living that was vacant in thy county, computed to be worth about four hundred pounds a year?'

Upon this the parson began to prick up his ears, and enquired whereabouts it was, never minding his glass.

'Truly,' says the Quaker, 'I cannot tell directly where it lies, but I can tell thee 'tis in vain to enquire after it, for it is already disposed of to an eminent person of thy function, who is now in this Town, and of whom I have some knowledge. At a coffee-house which he used, I happened to hear him highly commending the hospitality and good housekeeping of the late incumbent. "It being," says he, "indeed so plentiful a benefice, that we might well afford it. And I hope," says he, "that I shall not be backward in following his example."'

The parson showed great dissatisfaction in his looks that such a living should fall, and be disposed on without so much his knowledge.

The Quaker proceeded all the while in praising the orchards, gardens, barns, stables, fine rooms, large kitchen, noble parlour, convenient buttery, etc., which set the parson so agog that he listened and gaped as if he would have catched it in his mouth. But at last, says the Quaker, ' I heard him very much complain of one great inconvenience, indeed, and that was the misplacing of his wine cellar, for which reason he would have it removed.'

' Why, where did the cellar stand?' says the parson.

' Just under the pulpit,' says the Quaker, ' and he looked upon it to be a great fault to preach over his liquor.'

The parson, who had let his glass stand charged all the time of the story, readily took the application. ' I confess,' says he, ' I very unadvisedly left a blot in my tables, and you by chance have hit it, but now you have done, it serves only to verify the old proverb, that fools have fortune.'

This unexpected retort of the parson's quite dumbfounded the Quaker, and added a great deal of pleasure to the company; our merry disposed friend took breath after this sparring blow a considerable time, sitting as silent as a young swearer before his father, endeavouring as much to hide his failings as the other does his vices.

By this time the stock of wine upon the table being exhausted, we began to apply ourselves to the punch, which upon the wine we had already drank, soon put our spirits into a fresh ferment, and made us as noisy as gamesters in a cockpit, all bawling and betting on the behalf of one side or t'other. With one impertinent question or other they had almost put the parson into a passion, during which uneasiness his Yea-and-nay adversary asked him what he thought a Quaker to be?

The parson, a little angry they had begun to tease him,

made this response. 'A Quaker,' says he, 'is some of old Nick's venom, spit in the face of God's Church, which her clergy cannot lick out with their tongues, or rub off with their lawn sleeves. Therefore the Church makes a virtue of necessity and uses them as ladies do their black patches, for foils to magnify its beauty.'

'Indeed, friend,' says the Quaker, 'thou talkest as if the liquor has disturbed thy inward man. Prithee, tell me who thou thinkest was the first Quaker, that thou talkest so profanely against so good a profession?'

'The first Quaker?' says the parson, and after a very short deliberation, answered, 'Balaam.'

'Balaam,' says the Quaker. 'How dost thou make that out?'

'It's plainly so,' says the parson, 'because he was the first that ever gave his attention to hear an ass hold forth.'

The whole company expressed by their laughter the approbation of the jest, and it was agreed on all hands, that it might reasonably pass for a good punch-bowl answer.

The potency of the liquor, and the weakness of our brains, had now drawn our mirth to the dregs, so that we were more in danger of falling into disorder than we were of recovering our almost stupefied souls to their past pitch of felicity. Several of the company had wisely submitted their distempered heads to that great physician sleep, who can alone recover the patient's giddy brains of his epidemical fever. At last down dropped the body of the Divinity, in the condition of a weaker brother, and left the Quaker one of the survivors, who, with great joy, brandished a triumphant brimmer round his head, as a trophy of the inebrious victory he had obtained over a father of the Church.

My friend and I thought it now high time to be moving off, lest Bacchus and Morpheus together should close our eyelids, as they had some others, and make us become as troublesome to the family as the rest. Accordingly, we made the gentleman a compliment for his kind and liberal entertainment, and took leave of the company, which we left in chase of their senses; some snoring and some talking, so that they made as good music as a parcel of giddy-headed sportsmen at the winding up of a venison feaſt.

My friend and I (our ways lying different) parted at the door; he retired to his own lodging, but when I got home, and in my chamber, the witty repartees, and pretty conversation of the parson so ran in my head that I could not go quietly to bed till I had communicated to paper a description of a merry Levite in his cups.

Having thus exonerated my brains of the trouble which the liquor had begot in my underſtanding, I plucked off Nature's disguise with as much expedition as a young bridegroom, leaped into bed, and gently slid into a sweet sleep, without burthening my thoughts with reflections on the cares of a wicked world, or my own paſt miscarriages. Waking at my usual hour, I made a new resurrection for the day, and slipping on my breeches over my nakedness, in imitation of our firſt parents' fig-leaves, I refitted myself for a walk, in as little time as a beau spends in powdering his periwig.

When I had washed and combed me, and put myself into a cleanly condition of appearing abroad, I determined to give myself an hour or two's breathing in Gray's Inn Walks, in order to carry off the dregs of yeſterday's debauchery. Accordingly I ſteered my course to the lawyers' garden of contemplation, where I found (it being early in the morning) none but a parcel of superannuated debauchees huddled up in cloaks, frieze coats and wadded gowns, to preserve their old carcases from the searching sharpness of Hampſtead air.[1] They were creeping up and down in pairs, no faſter than the hand of a dial, or a country convict walking to execution; some talking of law, some of religion, and some of politics, arguing the matter in hand with so warm a zeal in defence of

[1] There was unbroken country between Gray's Inn and Hampstead.

their opinions that I thought every now and then some of the feeble peripatetics would have made a combat of skeletons, and have rattled their old bones together, in order to decide with their hands what their tongues could not determine.

After I had taken two or three turns round, I sat myself down in the Upper Walk, where just before me, upon a stone pedestal, was fixed an old rusty horizontal dial, with the gnomon broke short off. A bullet-headed Irishman coming up into the same walk, entered the bow or half moon where I sat, and after he had spent near a quarter of an hour looking at the dial, ' Be my fait,' said he, ' I did never see such a ting id my lifesh. I pray ye, dear Joy, Egra, vat ish de ush of it ? '

I could not forbear smiling at his ignorance, and told him 'twas a sundial to shew the hour of the day. ' I pray,' said he, ' will you tell me vat it ish a clock den ? '

It being a cloudy morning and the sun quite obscured, I replied I could not shew the hour unless the sun shone out. ' Ub bob bou,' says he, ' erra be Chreesht den it ish not half so gude as a vatch, for dat vill show me de hour without sunshine.' And away he shuffled upon an Irish trot, seeming to be as much conceited with his expression as if he had spoke like a Ben Jonson.

The ignorance of the common Irish hath rendered them a jest in all nations, though amongst the gentry there are many brave and well qualified persons, who have given sufficient testimonies, both of their courage and their learning. Therefore, as the foregoing story will opportunely introduce a character of an illiterate silly Irish peasant, the following piece of Micro-Cosmography is only intended upon the most ignorant of 'em, and quite apart from all such of the same country as have had the advantage of a better education.

The Character of an Irishman

He is commonly a huge fellow, with a little soul, as strong as a horse, and as silly as an ass; very poor and very proud.

The Stocks Market, Poultry, and Statue of Charles II.
Upon the site of this market was built the present Mansion House.

(From a print in the Crace Collection)

Lusty and yet lazy; foolish yet knavish; impudent but yet cowardly; superstitiously devout yet infamously wicked; very loose in his morals; a loyal subject to his prince, and as humble servant to his master, for he thinks 'tis his duty to make a rogue of himself at any time to serve the one, and a fool of himself at any time to serve the other; that is, to back a plot, or make a bull, he is the fittest calf in Christendom. He has a natural propensity to be a bully, and at his first coming into England most certainly lists himself into a harlot's service and has so much a day out of her earnings to be her Guard du Corps, to protect her in her vices.

His next degree of ascension is to a bailiff's follower, so that by catching strumpets and debtors, he makes a decent shift to sing 'hall-la-loo' over usquebaugh, and thinks himself as great as an Indian emperor over a bottle of rum. He has as little kindness for his native country, as a Scotchman, when once he's come out of it, and seldom cares for returning. He's much of the nature of pumpkins, thrives best within filthy places; he loves most base means to live, and honesty's a soil that won't agree with him. To conclude, he's a coward in his own country, a graceful footman in France, a good soldier in Flanders, and a valuable slave in our western plantations, where they are distinguished by the ignominious epithet of White Negroes.

By the time I had digested this character in my thoughts, as I sat musing by the dial, I found by the sundry Turkish and Arabian scaramouche figures, who were gracing the walk with their most glittering appearances, that the beaus began to rise and come forth in their morning plumes, in order to attract the eyes of some mercenary Bellsa's. The sundry sorts of unusual figures I beheld transported my thoughts beyond the Equinoctial, and made me fancy I was travelling in some distant territories, where unpolished men show the rudeness of their natures by the uncouthness of their garbs, some having covered their tender skulls with caps in the fashion of

s

a Turkish turban, and had gaudy figures wove into their gowns so that they looked as if they had been frightened out of their beds by fire, and not having time to dress, had wrapped themselves up in tapestry hangings and Turkey-work tablecloths, as the readiest shift they could make to cover their nakedness; others had thrust their calves' heads, some in bags like pudding-pokes, and some in caps fashioned like an extinguisher, which hung down half-way their backs. Others masqueraded in morning gowns of such diversity of flickering colours, that their dazzling garments seemed like so many rainbows, wove into a Scotch plaid.

The Character of a Beau

He is a Narcissus that is fallen in love with himself and his own shadow. Within doors he's a great friend to a great glass; without doors he adores the sun like a Persian, and walks always in his rays. His body's but a poor stuffing of a rich case, like bran to a lady's pin-cushion, that when the outside is stripped off, there remains nothing that's valuable. His head is a fool's egg which lies hid in a nest of hair. His brains are the yolk, which conceit has addled.

He's a strolling assistant to drapers and tailors, shewing every other day a new pattern and a new fashion. He's a very troublesome guest in a tavern, and must have good wine changed three or four times, till they bring him the worst in the cellar, before he'll like it. He's a bubble to all he deals with, from his wench to his periwig-maker, and hates the sordid rascal that won't flatter him. He scorns to condescend so low as to speak to any person beneath the dignity of a noble-man: the Duke of such a place, and my Lord such a one, are his common cronies, from whom he knows all the secrets of the Court, but dares not impart 'em to his best friends, because the Duke enjoined him to secrecy.

He is always furnished with new jests from the last new play, which he most commonly spoils in repeating. Though

his parents have given him an expensive education, he's as
dumb to rhetoric as a fool to reason; as blind to philosophy as
an owl in the sunshine; and as deaf to underſtanding as a
prieſt to charity. He's a coward among brave men, and a brave
fellow among cowards; a fool amongſt wise men, and a wit in
fools' company.

By the time I had finished the piċture of my beau, the
wenches in their morning gowns and wadded waiſtcoats,
without ſtays, began to flow faſt into the walks. I was mightily
pleased at the various diverting scenes with which I was
entertained.

From thence I took a turn into the City, where people were
running about with as much concern in their countenances,
as if they had received news of the French landing, or that
an army of Irish Papiſts had taken possession of Stock Markets,
in order to massacre the Proteſtants, and plunder the City.

At laſt I went to Jonathan's Coffee-house[1] by the 'Change,
to enquire into the meaning of this ſtrange disorder. There
I saw a parcel of men at one table, consulting together,
with as much malice, horror, anger and despair in their looks,
as if a new peſtilence had sprung up in their families and their
wives had run away with their journeymen to avoid infeċtion.
At another table was a parcel of merry hawk-looking blades,
laughing and pointing at the reſt, as if, with abundance of
satisfaċtion, they triumphed over the others' affliċtions.

At laſt, upon a little enquiry into the matter, I found the
honeſt brotherhood of the Stock Jobbers were in a lamentable
confusion, and had divided themselves in two parts, fools and
knaves. A few of the latter had drawn in a few fools, some
three, some four or five hundred pounds deep, to the ruin of
many, and the great disadvantage of more; who having been
under the reputation of knaves all their lives' time, have at
laſt, by the unexpeċted ill-success of an unlucky projeċt,

---

[1] This was in Exchange Alley, and was a great resort of stock jobbers and
others of a like business.

undeceived the world at once, and proved themselves the arrantest fools in the whole City.

A Stock Jobber

He is a compound of knave, fool, shop-keeper, merchant and gentleman. His whole business is tricking. When he cheats another, he's a knave; when he suffers himself to be out-witted, he's a fool. He's as great a lover of uncertainty as some fools are of the Royal Oak Lottery, and would not give a farthing for an estate got without a great deal of hazard. To-day he laughs, and to-morrow he grins; the third day he's mad, and always labours under those twin passions, hope and fear, rising one day, and falling the next, like mercury in a weather glass, and cannot arrive to that pitch of wisdom as to know one day what he shall be the next. He spins out his life between Faith and Hope, but has nothing to do with Charity, because there's little to be got by't. He's a man whose great ambition is to ride over others, in order to which, he resolves to win the horse, or lose the saddle.

CHAPTER SEVENTEEN

Dealers in Money and their Tricks—Bankers—A Christening—
Dryden's Funeral—Scene in Chancery Lane

HAVING received a note from my friend to meet
him at the sign of the Dolphin in Lombard Street
(which fish, by mistake of the painter, is rendered
more like a crooked billet than the creature it's designed to
represent), I accordingly went at the time appointed where
my friend over a penny nipperkin of rum sat ready to receive
me. When an accustomary salutation had passed between us,
we began to consult about our dinner, being posted in a very
convenient house for that purpose. At last we agreed to
placate our bodies with a slice of beef, fit food for either saint,
soldier or sailor, the king of meats, and the most delicious of
all dainties.

When we had suppressed our hunger, the most powerful
of all appetites, and tired our jaws with tedious mastication,
we began to fall into talk about our neighbouring scavengers,
whose houses are the stalls of that filthy dross which defiles
the virgin, corrupts the priest, contaminates the fingers of the
judge, is the cause of every ill, and the very seed of human
misery; the mistaken happiness of mankind, which brings
with it, wheresoe'er it comes, a thousand curses worse than
poverty.

'Prithee,' says my friend, 'don't rail so against money;
it's talk that becomes nobody but a mendicant, who is always
endeavouring to put other people that have it out of conceit
with it, so that they may the more willingly part with it to
those that want it. There's a great deal to be said on behalf

of money, and if you were but to hear a rich parson preach upon it, according to his real sentiments, he would teach you, perhaps, to have as good an opinion of it as e'er an alderman of the City. To despise riches when they are out of your power, savours more of envy than philosophy, but to seem not to value wealth when you have it in possession is an argument of generosity.'

I thanked him for his opinion and then began to enquire of him what method those great dealers in money chiefly take for the improvement of such mighty sums which were trusted in their power.

In answer, my friend gave me the following information. ' The best of their harvest,' says he, ' is now over. Since the alteration of the coin[1] has put a period to the project of diminution, their trade has been in a declining condition, but they have, most of them, so feathered their nests, that they have no occasion to fear the greatest disadvantages the difficulties of the times can bring them under.

'As an argument of their dealings in that profitable affair, I will give you a convincing instance of my own knowledge in the very heat of these mysterious times. I had a bill upon an eminent banker, not far off, to receive twenty-five pounds. Waiting in the shop till he had despatched his business with some other persons, in comes a spark in a good camlet cloak, lined with red, a sword, long wig and beaver hat, and gave the banker a bag of money, desiring him to lay it by for him, and he would call for it on the morrow morning. He took it from him, and laid it down upon a seat on the other side of the counter. The person that brought it becoming his habiliments but awkwardly, occasioned me to take more than

---

[1] Under the Stuarts the coinage had become very debased by clipping, etc. William III appointed a commission to reform it, and, not without much opposition, a Bill was passed in 1696 withdrawing debased coin from circulation. The change incurred an expense of £1,200,000 to the Government, which was raised by a Window Tax.

ordinary notice of his face, which I had often seen, but could not, till he was gone, recollect where. At last I fully satisfied myself that about a twelvemonth before he was a cobbler at Westminster, who had mended many a pair of shoes, and run many an errand for me, I then lodging within three or four doors off where he kept his stall.

' When the banker had told several sums, and satisfied the demands of the first comers, I accosted him, and showed him my authority for another sum, which he was ready to pay on sight of the bill, as if he were never better pleased than when he was getting rid of his money. And taking up the bag my old acquaintance had left, he attempted to pay me in scrupulous and diminutive pieces that I thought nothing but a knave would offer to pay, or a fool be willing to receive. I refused to take it. He urged the money was passable, telling me that a gentleman left it with him just before, which he thought, I suppose, I had not observed. Pray, said I, what was that gentleman? He answered me, an Essex gentleman of six or seven hundred pounds a year. Said I, I saw the person that left it, and if he be worth such an estate as you speak of, he has got it in a very little time, for within three months he has soled me a pair of shoes for sixteenpence, and I am sure he had not land enough then to raise a bunch of carrots in, or money enough to spare to buy the seed, therefore I fancy you are mistaken in the man. " O dear! sir," says he, " your eyes are strangely deceived; he's a very worthy honest gentleman. I have had money of his in my hands, at times, this seven years. But, however, sir, if you don't like this money, I'll see if I can look you better." With that he goes and finds me out good market money, which I suppose, I should have had some difficulty to have got, had it not been for my accidental discovery.'

' Well,' said I, ' but this golden age is past, and what methods do they take now to improve their cash? '

' The chief advantage,' says he, ' that they now make, is by supplying the necessities of the ſtraitened merchants and great dealers to pay the duty of goods imported, or by assiſting 'em in the purchase of great bargains, or the like, for which they make 'em pay such unreasonable extortion, that they devour more of the merchant's profits than snails, worms, or magpies do of the farmer's crops, or the gardener's induſtry.

' In relation to this I'll inform you of a pretty disappointment that lately happened to one of these unconscionable usurers, who insiſted upon a very extravagant gratuity for the loan of a very considerable sum to a very eminent merchant.

'A person of quality having made a banker in Lombard Street his cashier, and having occasion to talk with him about some pecuniary affairs, ordered his coachman to drive him to his shop, where he found the banker talking very busily with a merchant. The banker, out of regard for his quality, came immediately to his coach side, to know the gentleman's pleasure, who desired him firſt to dispatch his business with the person he was before talking to, and he would tarry in his coach till he had done, for he was in no great haſte. Upon this the banker retiring into the shop they proceeded again to the matter in hand, which was about lending the merchant a sum of money, who was very unwilling to come up to the banker's unreasonable demands for the use of it, which the merchant required but for one month.

' The banker being well acquainted with the necessity of the merchant for money, though a very rich man and a great dealer, ſtuck close to his firſt proposals, and would abate nothing of the extortion he required, which occasioned 'em at laſt to talk so warmly, that the gentleman overheard their discourse, and calling his footman, whispered him, and bid him dog the gentleman till he had fixed him, and bring an account of where he left him to Lloyd's Coffee-house.

' The merchant being very unwilling to comply with the

banker's avaricious terms, went out of the shop in a huff, and told him he would see what he could do elsewhere, before he would submit to so inhuman an exaction. As soon as he was gone, the footman observed the commands of his master, who, after he had talked a little with the banker, bid his coach wait till he walked over to Lloyd's. In a little time his footman brought him intelligence that the gentleman was gone into a great house in Mincing Lane, which he believed was his own habitation, because, when the door was opened to him, he went readily in, without asking the servant any questions.

' Upon this the gentleman orders his footman to direct the coach to the house, where the gentleman orders his man to knock, and ask the servant that should come to the door, whether their master was within, who answered, Yes, but that he was just sat down to dinner. The gentleman bid the servant not disturb him, but desired to walk into a room, and he would stay till he had dined. Upon which they showed him into a parlour where he waited but a little time before the merchant, upon his servant's information, came to him. The gentleman finding it to be the same person, asked him if about an hour since, he was not treating with such a banker about such an affair. He told him, Yes, he was, and seemed to be surprised that the gentleman should know anything of the matter. To make the merchant easy he related by what means he became acquainted with what had passed between him and the banker, expressing himself to the merchant, after this manner:

' " I have," says he, " in the hands of the banker you were talking to between three and four thousand pounds, and if he can think it safe to trust part of my money in your hands for the sake of an unreasonable advantage, I don't know why I may not trust you as well myself upon more reasonable terms. He pays me no interest. Therefore, since he was so hard with you, if you will let me know what sum your occasions require, I will give you my note upon the same person to pay you the money, which you shall use for any reasonable time without a penny interest or gratuity."

' The merchant, amazed at so generous an offer from a stranger, expressed himself in all the thankful acknowledgments imaginable, and gladly accepted of his kindness, telling him six hundred pounds would do his business, for that three or four ships were come in, on board of which he had considerable effects, and that the money was to help pay the customs.

' The gentleman accordingly, as the merchant's straits required, draws him a bill upon the banker for six hundred pounds, and afterwards found such agreeable honesty from the merchant that he drew all his money out of the banker's hands, and put it into the merchant's, by which means he is become one of the richest men and greatest merchants in the City; and the banker lost a friend, to his great injury, as a just reward of his covetousness.'

I had a relation in town, who, about twelve months since had the courage to suffer a parson to rob him of his native liberty, and bind him fast, with fetters of matrimony, to man's misery, a wife. The first fruits of their marriage having lately crept into this world of affliction, the joyful father very closely solicited me to do the penance of a godfather, that the little epitome of the lad might be craftily cleansed from the sin of his birth. I submitted to his request, and engaged myself, for once, to stand as a Tom-Doodle for an hour or two, to be bantered by a tittle-tattle assembly of female gossips.

The time appointed for the solemnization of this ancient piece of formality being come, after I had put on a clean band, and bestowed two pennyworth of razoridge on the most fertile part of my face, whose weekly crop required mowing, away I trotted towards the joyful habitation of my friend and kinsman, but with as aching a heart as a wise man goes to be married, or a broken merchant comes near the Compter. At last I came to the door, which I passed three or four times, as a bashful lover does by his mistress's lodgings, before I had courage enough to enter, fancying every time I went up to the door, that I heard a confusion of women's tongues come through the keyhole.

At last I plucked up my spirit and gave a rap at the door, which brought Nurse Busybody to give me admittance. She introduced me into a back parlour, and called her master, of whom I enquired after the welfare of the mother. I told my kinsman I dreaded the fatigue I was bound to run through, who heartily pitied my condition, and advised me to put on the best assurance I could, telling me he was equally obliged to be partner in my sufferings, for that he expected to be tongue-teased by the time the wine had gone a little about. The women, Heaven be praised! were ushered upstairs, so that I was in no great danger of having my ears stretched upon the rack of verbosity, till the sacerdotal administration of the sacrament was over.

By this time in came my brother nominator, who was to stand the bears with me, and after we had made ourselves a little acquainted, by enquiring of each other ' What news? ' and the like, we began to look forward, and consider of the difficulties we were to run through.

' Poh,' says he, ' never fear, I warrant you; we'll deal with 'em well enough, let me alone to bring you off, I have been used to't. This is sport,' says he, ' that I have been at so often, that I believe half the children in the parish call me godfather. I am as well known to all the gossips hereabouts, as St. Austin is to the parson, or Amen to the clerk. Do but take my method amongst 'em, and you will gain their hearts for ever, and be accounted as pretty a man by 'em as ever came into a woman's company. Be sure you highly praise the fair sex, and speak very honourably of the state of matrimony, rail soundly against all those jealous-pated coxcombs that abuse their wives, though with good reason, and declare every man that thinks himself deceived, deserves to be so, and that it is always men's own faults that they are so. Be sure to remember a woman's freedom is an argument of her honesty, and that the still sow eats all the draught; that a woman ought to have a cup as well as a man; and that she may go into a tavern with another without her husband, and may be very honest for all that; and that she may like another man's company for his good humour, merry jests, and witty conversation, without doing an ill thing, or abusing her husband. If you hear a woman rail against her husband before you, second her, and say he's a very morose man to use so good a woman after so ill a manner; be sure you preach up female authority, that a husband ought to mind nothing but his trade, and let the wife alone to govern the family. Say that no woman who has no children by her husband, ought to be blamed if she raises seed with discretion by another, since it takes off from her the reproach of being barren, not forgetting the old saying, " There's no harm done when a good child's got." Follow but these instructions, and lard your talk now and then with a little waggery, wrapped up in clean linen, and you need not doubt but you will find yourself an acceptable man amongst 'em.'

I thanked him kindly for his serviceable advice, and was mightily satisfied I had so experienced a partner to assist me at the solemnity, not fearing but so good an example would be a means of carrying me cleverly through the whole ceremony without baulk or discountenance. By this time in came the parochial sprinkler with the clerk at his heels, who were ushered upstairs among the assembly of helpmates.

Now, thought I, the curtain's to be drawn, and the show is ready to begin presently. Whilst I was thus thinking, down came the nurse to desire us to walk up. She had so adorned her withered countenance with tape-laced headclothes that her weasel face looked as disproportioned to her commode, as a tom-tit's egg put into an owl's nest, having a scallop-laced handkerchief round her neck, that looked as old-fashioned as if Eve had spun the thread and made the lace with the same needle she sewed her fig-leaf apron with.

As soon as we came into the room, and had bowed our backs to the old cluster of harridans and they in return had bent their knees to us, I sneaked up to the parson's elbow and my partner after me, and there I stood as demurely as if I had just turned Jew, and was circumcised before all the company. The parson began in solemn wise the preface to the business in hand, whilst old Mother Grope stood rocking of the bantling in her arms, wrapped up in as rich a mantle as if both Indies had clubbed their utmost riches to furnish a noble covering for my little kinsman, who came as callow into the world as a bird out of an egg-shell.

At last the babe was put into my hands to deliver, though not as my act and deed, to the parson, who having consecrated some New River water for his purpose, washed away original sin from my new nephew, and brought him amongst us Christians into a state of salvation. But when my forward godson felt the cold water in his face, he threatened the priest with such a parcel of angry looks that if he had been strong enough I dare swear he would have served him the same sauce, and if under the same ignorance would have returned him but little thanks for his labour.

After we had joined together in a petition for the good of the infant Christian, the religious part was concluded, and now kissing, feasting and jocularity were to follow in their proper places. I left it to my partner to be the leading man, resolving to be a true copy of his impudence to the utmost of my capacity.

The first example he set me was to kiss the godmother, who had a very passable face and tolerable mien, and as for her age, I believe she was near upon the meridian. I followed his directions to a tittle, and kissed her so very close, that I am confident the inside of her lips could do no less than take off an impression of her teeth, as deep as a child leaves when he bites a mouthful of bread and butter.

As soon as ever the parson had refreshed his spirits with a bumper of Canary, dedicated to the mother, and the clerk had said 'Amen' to his master's good wishes after the like manner, each of 'em accepted a paper of sweetmeats for his wife or his children, and away they went, leaving the rest of the company behind, to make a rehearsal of the good old custom, always practicable at those neighbourly sort of meetings.

The next piece of lip exercise my partner set me, was to make a regular service of kisses round the room, keeping such exact time in the discharge of this ceremony, not daring to stay too long in a place for fear the rest should have taken it ill, that if he had but smacked as he kissed, he would have kept much the same measure, have made much the same music as a church clock that clicks every quarter of a minute.

By the time he had ended his first ceremonious essay to please the ladies, and had sucked a vermilion colour to the lips of the young ones, I began to succeed him in the drudgery of osculation, which I went about with as ill a will as a security pays a debt he never drank for, though there were two or three as tolerable temptations as a man would desire to meet with. Yet the public formality of the matter so took off the pleasure of lip service, that instead of a satisfaction, I thought it but a very troublesome ridiculous piece of ancient superstition. One old woman having the palsy in her head, happened, by a sudden resolution of the sinews which govern the under jaw, to snap my under lip between her gums, that had it not been for shame, I had cried out; but as Providence would have it she had ne'er a tooth, or else I believe she would have spoiled my kissing for a fortnight. This accident begot in me ever since such aversion to the kissing of old women, that I sincerely protest I had rather kiss twenty young ones, twenty times a piece, than run the like hazard of having my lips disfigured.

Having very orderly proceeded this far without a baulk, the greateſt uneasiness that remained now was only a little tittle-tattle, which I did not doubt but the wine would inspire me with courage enough to cope with. When this was over, the next piece of folly that my kinsman was guilty on, in sub-mission to his wife's vanity, was to usher the assembly into the next room, where was a very good hot supper ready upon the table, and two or three dozen of several sorts of wine to entertain their ladyships. But before they sat down, the gossips pitched upon me to bless the good creatures, and being at a nonplus for a grace, and thinking it a scandal to acknowledge it, I was forced to blunder out one extempore:

> Bless the good ladies and good food,
> That Heaven has set before us;
> And may we men prove all so good
> The women may adore us.
> God save the Queen, and send quiet through the realm
> Men may obey and women rule the helm.

This lucky thought so obliged them that scarce a woman in the company could forbear clapping me, and the good wives falling to, were all so ready to help me with a choice bit, that I had a plate piled up in half a minute, enough to have feaſted a whole family of French Proteſtants juſt landed.

As soon as the edges of our hungry appetites were taken off, and our mouths were a little at leisure to employ the glass, and give way for our tongues to express our sentiments, the women were presently so wonderful busy in drinking the chaplain's health that they had like to have forgot the mother and her offspring, if it had not been for the midwife who put 'em in mind of it. By that time three or four glasses had washed away their counterfeit or acquired modeſty so we had as great a jargon of confused talk arise amongſt us, as ever you heard amongst a crowd of female neighbours gathered at a woman's door that had just hanged herself. They talked as much of the ill qualities of their servants, and good humours of their children, as a parcel of country gentlemen over a tub of double ale do of their dogs and horses. The failings of their husbands also, was a great subject of their discourse, with now and then a whisper, which, I suppose, was touching some secret disabilities or neglects, which were not proper or consistent, though with the most free and unrestrained modesty, to speak in public.

At last a great talk arose about a certain woman who had been married two years and lately made an elopement from her husband with a courtier who had got her close in his lodgings at Kensington, even to the distraction of the poor husband, who offers to take her again, but she won't live with him.

'Fie upon her,' says old Mother Tumble-Tuzzy, 'for a naughty woman; if she had taken my advice, I am sure it had been better for her; if things were as she told me, I am sure she had no great reason to complain; but in short, I don't believe she loved her husband, for if she did, she would never have done so by him. I'll swear I pity the man with all my heart; I look upon him to be as honest a man as any dwells in the parish, and indeed, I believe he loved his wife very well. Ay, indeed, neighbour, much better than such a minx deserved.'

'Why so, madam,' says a third, 'why do you rail against the poor woman behind her back? She might have reason enough to do what she did for ought you know.'

'Reason! Marry hang her,' says a fourth, 'what reason could she have to bring herself under this scandal, and her husband, poor man, under all this shame and sorrow? If she wanted a lover there are journeymen and 'prentices enough in the house, that she need not have been such a slut to have run away from him.'

'Oh fie,' says another, 'why sure you would not have her disgrace herself with so mean a thing as a servant, would you?'

'Servant!' replied the former. 'Marry, come up! How little you make of servants! You see the Court ladies have wit enough to be content with their own coachmen and foot-men, and not come into the City to expose themselves.'

'Nay, truly, neighbour,' says the other, 'I must confess there is something of reason in what you say, but indeed, I think 'tis a burning shame that such a man should be so foolish as to marry a woman, and bring her to these hardships, for they ought to consider that we are flesh and blood as well as they.'

In this sort of hopeful tittle-tattle, they tired their lungs and wasted their time, till they were most of them got as merry as so many bumpkins at a wake, or tippling loyalists upon the King's birthday. Then they began to call upon me, their chaplain, to give them a discharge which put me to a second nonplus, believing they had drank themselves at supper past all grace; but I found myself mistaken. I made shift to blunder a ceremonious piece of thanksgiving:

> Our hearty thanks we humbly pay
> For the blessings we have tasted,
> Lord send such christenings every day
> That we may thus be feasted.
> Bless all good women in their married state,
> Make their days easy and their pleasures great.

This so obliged the assembly of fruitful matrons, that I dare swear I might have picked and chose as the Turk does in his seraglio. I was now esteemed as the prettiest, wittiest and best humoured gentleman that ever they were in company with in their lives; and what a thousand pities it was I should be a bachelor, everyone offered to help me to a wife, so that I began to be afraid they would have made a priest of the

T

midwife and married me in spite of my teeth before I could get out of their company.

Even this generous entertainment was not sufficient to plague my poor kinsman enough, but after all this, the extravagancy muſt be summed up with a service of sweet-meats which every gossip carried away in her handkerchief. Then were my brother-witness and I forced to conclude all with a final repetition of old Judas's ceremony and to send 'em packing home to their own dear spouses, to tease their ears with a rehearsal of their welfare.

What now remained for me to do was to go upſtairs to bid my bedridden relation much joy of her new Chriſtian, and to receive thanks for the trouble she had put me to. I kissed the good woman with good enough will, but having no great kindness for a creature so newly calved as my little kinsman, I could not salute him, but with as indifferent an appetite as I did the old woman.

Having now ſtruggled through every difficult part of these accuſtomary formalities, I had nothing to do but to thank them for their liberal entertainment, wish the woman well again, and both much happiness in their male offspring, and so take my leave, which I did accordingly, and was as greatly overjoyed when I got out of the house as ever conviƈt was that had broke gaol, or deteƈted pick-pocket that had escaped a horse pond.

A deeper concern hath scarce been known to affeƈt in general the minds of grateful and ingenious minds, than the melancholy surprise of the worthy Mr. Dryden's death[1] has occasioned through the whole Town, as well as in all other parts of the kingdom, where persons of wit and learning have taken up their residence. Wheresoever his incomparable writings have been scattered by the hands of the travellers into foreign nations, the loss of so great a man muſt needs

---

[1] At his house in Gerrard Street, 1 May, 1700.

be lamented amongst their bards and rabbis, and 'tis reasonable to believe the commendable industry of translators has been such as to render several of his most accurate performances into their own language, so that their native country might receive the benefit, and themselves the reputation of so laudable an undertaking.

Those who were his enemies while he was living (for no man lives without) cannot but in justice give him this character, that he was one of the greatest scholars, the most correct dramatic poet, and the best writer of heroic verse that any age has produced in England. And yet, notwithstanding his merits had justly entitled his corpse to the most magnificent and solemn interment, yet 'tis credibly reported that they had like to have let him pass in private to his grave, had it not been for that true British worthy who, meeting with the venerable remains of the neglected bard passing silently in a coach, unregarded to his last home, ordered the corpse, by the consent of his few friends that attended him, to be respited from so obscure an interment; and most generously undertook, at his own expense, to revive his worth in the minds of a forgetful people, by bestowing on his peaceful dust a solemn funeral answerable to his merit. This memorable action alone will eternalize his fame with the greatest heroes, and add that lustre to his nobility, which time can never tarnish; but will shine with equal glory in all ages, and in the very teeth of envy bid defiance to oblivion. The management of the funeral was left to Mr. Russell, pursuant to the directions of that honourable great man, the Lord Jeffreys,[1] concerned chiefly in the pious undertaking.

The first honour done to his deserving relics was lodging 'em in Physicians' College, from whence they were appointed to take their last remove. The constituted day for the celebration of that office was Monday, the 13th of May, in the afternoon, at which time, according to the notice given, most

---

[1] Son of the famous Lord Chancellor.

of the nobility and gentry now in Town, assembled themselves together at the noble edifice aforesaid, in order to honour the corpse with their personal attendance.

When the company were met, a performance of grave music was communicated to the ears of the company by the bands of the best masters in England. When this part of the solemnity was ended, the famous Doctor Garth [1] ascended the pulpit where the physicians make their lectures, and delivered, according to the Roman custom, a funeral oration in Latin on his deceased friend; which he performed to the great approbation and applause of all such gentlemen that heard him, and were true judges of the matter. When these rites were over in the college, the corpse was handed into the hearse drawn by six stately Flanders horses and adorned with plumes of black feathers, and the sides hung round with the escutcheon of his ancestors, mixed with that of his lady's. All things being put in due order for their movement they began their solemn procession towards Westminster.

The two beadles of the College marched first with the heads of their staffs wrapped in black crape scarfs; next to these moved a concert of hautboys and trumpets, playing and sounding together a melancholy funeral march; after these the undertaker with his hat off, dancing through the dirt, like a bear after a bagpipe (I beg the reader's pardon for foisting in a jest in so improper a place, but as he walked by himself within a parenthesis, so I have here placed him, and hope none will be offended). Then came the hearse most honourably attended with abundance of quality in their coaches and six horses. In this order the nobility and gentry attended the hearse to Westminster Abbey, where the last funeral rites being performed by one of the prebends, he was honourably interred between Chaucer and Cowley, where, according to

---

[1] Sir Samuel Garth, the poet-physician, was really responsible for the fitting interment of Dryden. He had the body taken to Physicians' Hall and embalmed, and started a public subscription to defray the cost.

report, will be erected a very stately monument, at the expense
of some of the nobility, in order to recommend his worth, and
to preserve his memory, to all succeeding ages.[1]

The cause of his death being very remarkable, it will not
be improper in this place to take notice of it, as a means to
put the world in mind of what slender accidents are sufficient
to change the state of man, and hurry him into the darkness
of Eternity. The occasion of his sickness was a lameness in
one of his feet, springing from so trivial a cause as the flesh
growing over one of his toe-nails, which being neglected begot
a soreness, and brought an inflammation of his toe; and being
a man of gross body, a flux of humours falling into the part
made it very troublesome, so that he was forced to put himself into the hands of an able surgeon,[2] who foreseeing the
danger of mortification advised him to part with the toe
affected, as the best means to prevent the ill-consequence
likely to ensue. This he refused to consent to, believing a
cure might be effected by less severe means than the loss of
a member, till at last his whole leg gangrened; this was
followed by a mortification, so that nothing remained to prevent death but an amputation of the member thus putrefied.
He refused to consent to this, saying that he was an old
man and had not long to live by course of nature, and did
not care to part with one limb, at such an age, to preserve an

[1] A monument was erected twenty years later, at the cost of the Duke of
Buckinghamshire. Farquhar describes Dryden's funeral as being incongruous
and burlesque, 'fitter for Hudibras than him.' Shortly after his burial some
would-be wag laid on the grave a paper with the following lines :—

> John Dryden had enemies three,
> Sir Dick, Old Nick, and Jeremy.
> The fustian knight was forced to yield,
> The other two maintained the field.
> But had the poet's life been holier
> He had o'ercome the Devil and Collier.

Sir Dick, 'the fustian knight,' was Sir Richard Blackmore, the poetical
doctor; Jeremy Collier was a divine who launched a fierce—and partially
successful—attack against the immorality of the stage.

[2] This was Hobbs.

uncomfortable life in the rest, and therefore chose rather to
submit to death. A little time after, according to the foresight
of his surgeons and physicians, this did unhappily happen.

I shall now return to the end of Chancery Lane, where I
stood to see the funeral pass by, observing there some passages
between hackney coachmen and the mob worth delivering to
the reader. The great number of qualities' coaches that
attended the hearse so put the hackney drivers out of their
bias that against the King's Head Tavern,[1] there happened
a great stop, occasioned by a train of mourning coaches which
had blocked up the narrow end of the lane and obstructed
a number of hackney coaches.

One impudent driver had run his pole against the back
leather of the coach in front to the great damage of a beau's
reins, who peeping out of the coach door, with at least a fifty-
ounce wig on, swore, ' Damn him! if he came out, he would
make as great a slaughter amongst hackney rogues with his
sword, as ever Samson did amongst the Philistines with the
jaw bone of an ass.'

Whilst he was thus cursing and swearing like an old sinner
in a fit of gout, his own coachman flinging back the thong
of his whip in striking of the horses, gave him such a cut
over the nose that he jerked in his head as if he had been
shot, not knowing from whence the blow came, and sat raving
within his leathern territories, like a madman chained down
to his seat, not daring to look out, for fear he should a second
time pay for his peeping.

The coachmen, all the while were saluting one another
with such diabolical titles, and confounding one another with
bitter execrations, as if everyone were striving which should
go to the devil first. At last by sundry stratagems, painful
industry, and the great expense of whip-cord, they gave
one another way, and then with their ' hey-ups,' they began

---

[1] This was Ward's own tavern.

clattering over the ſtones and making such a noise that my head was like to have come off with the din.

No sooner had they dispersed themselves toward the several places they were bound to by their fares, than one of the prize-fighting gladiators from Dorset Gardens Theatre,[1] where he had been exercising the several weapons of defence with his bold challenger, upon a clear ſtage without favour, was conducted by in triumph, with a couple of drums to proclaim his victory. He was attended by a parcel of ruffians, whose faces seemed to be as full of cuts as a ploughed field is of furrows, some of their countenances being chopped into the form of a Good Friday bun with cuts across one another, as if they were marked out for Chriſtian champions. These were hemmed in with a cluſter of journeymen shoemakers, weavers and tailors, with whom the victorious combatant came off with flying (yet 'twas with bloody) colours; for by the report of the mob, like a true cock, he won the day after he had loſt an eye in the battle.

[1] It had been turned into a boxing booth.

INDEX

The Mayflower Press, Plymouth. William Brendon & Son, Ltd.
F30.127

THE LONDON SPY